Pueblo Artists

Pueblo Artists

Portraits

Photographs by Toba Pato Tucker

With contributions by
Alfred L. Bush, Rina Swentzell, and Lonnie Vigil

Museum of New Mexico Press
Santa Fe

For my Daughter, Dena

Manufactured in Italy

Project Editor: Mary Wachs
Design and Production: David Skolkin
Set in Granjon text and display

10 9 8 7 6 5 4 3 2 1

Library of Congress Cataloging-in-Publication Data Available

MUSEUM OF NEW MEXICO PRESS
Post Office Box 2087
Santa Fe, New Mexico 87504

Contents

Acknowledgments

I wish to thank the Pueblo people of New Mexico and Arizona for joining me in creating this memorable document, the result of my aspiration to photograph the individuals and families who are the artists and artisans of the pueblos. To all those who allowed me to photograph them and whose portraits appear in this book, as well as the many who do not, I am very grateful.

I acknowledge with gratitude the Horace W. Goldsmith Foundation for generously supporting and sustaining this project, and with special appreciation to Robert Menschel for his enduring faith in my work throughout the years.

I am grateful for additional funding from the Daniele Agostino Foundation and Flavia Robinson Derossi for her warm friendship, generosity, and endless kindness; the Thanks Be to Grandmother Winifred Foundation and Deborah A. Light for her continued interest in my photography; and the Friends of Historic Onondaga Lake for their long-standing support.

In Santa Fe, New Mexico, I am particularly pleased to acknowledge and express my appreciation to Bruce Bernstein, Ph.D., former director of the Museum of Indian Arts and Culture/Laboratory of Anthropology, for his invaluable guidance and advice. I also wish to thank Jonathan Batkin, Ph.D., director of the Wheelwright Museum of the American Indian; Robb Lucas, director of the Case Trading Post; and Southwestern Association for Indian Arts (SWAIA) and Director Paul Rainbird for their referrals and generous assistance.

I am very grateful to family, friends, and professional associates who added to my achievements as a photographer. I particularly wish to thank Helen A. Harrison for her continuing assistance in editing my efforts to write about my work; Robert Giard, my good friend and fellow portrait photographer, for his moral support and sharing his insights and experiences; and my daughter, Dena, who is a photographer and who inspired me to become a photographer. My appreciation to Gary Hood for his initial encouragement for this project and to Sheryl Hartley of SWAIA for her recommendations; and special thanks to Alissa Marquis for expertly printing my photographs.

I extend my appreciation to the esteemed authors who join me in creating this portrait of the Pueblo people: Rina Swentzell, architectural historian and a member of Santa Clara Pueblo; Alfred L. Bush, curator, Princeton Collections of Western Americana; and Lonnie Vigil, Tewa micaceous potter, Nambé Pueblo.

And to Mary Wachs, my editor at the Museum of New Mexico Press, sincere gratitude for her intelligent guidance and insight in the preparation of this book; and to David Skolkin, who designed this book, special appreciation for his elegant interpretation of my photographs for this format.

Meeting and photographing the Pueblo people of the Southwest has been an especially rewarding and pleasurable experience, and I thank them for honoring me with their trust.

Foreword

LONNIE VIGIL
TEWA MICACEOUS POTTER, NAMBÉ PUEBLO

Many families and individuals are represented throughout this photo-anthology of Pueblo artists of the Southwest. Families are a very strong and important part of the creative process, and so although pieces may be signed by one individual they are group efforts of family, friends, and community. How does this happen? It may not be through the direct involvement of family members, but the support, kindness, encouragement, and appreciation of those individuals become a part of the creative process nurtured by the closeness of the family and community life. In other situations a family member, relative, or friend may be directly involved in the creative process of an individual piece or many pieces. Help may come from parents, children, brothers and sisters, and extended family. So therefore, the creative process is blessed and enhanced by the participation of family and community.

It is very difficult to judge one creative work from another when every effort made is significant and valuable. The judging process becomes nonexistent when these efforts are seen from a place of appreciation for the effort made and given in the creation of each particular piece. The love and care that is given in the creative process cannot be judged but is appreciated by those who are drawn to it. We each have an individual way of being attracted to and moved by a piece of pottery, jewelry, or painting. That attraction is to the love and attention that was given to the creation of the physical and moving beauty of the admired piece.

Because of this relationship of family, of community, and of environment, too, the creative process is a way of interpreting and expressing one's life as we understand it.

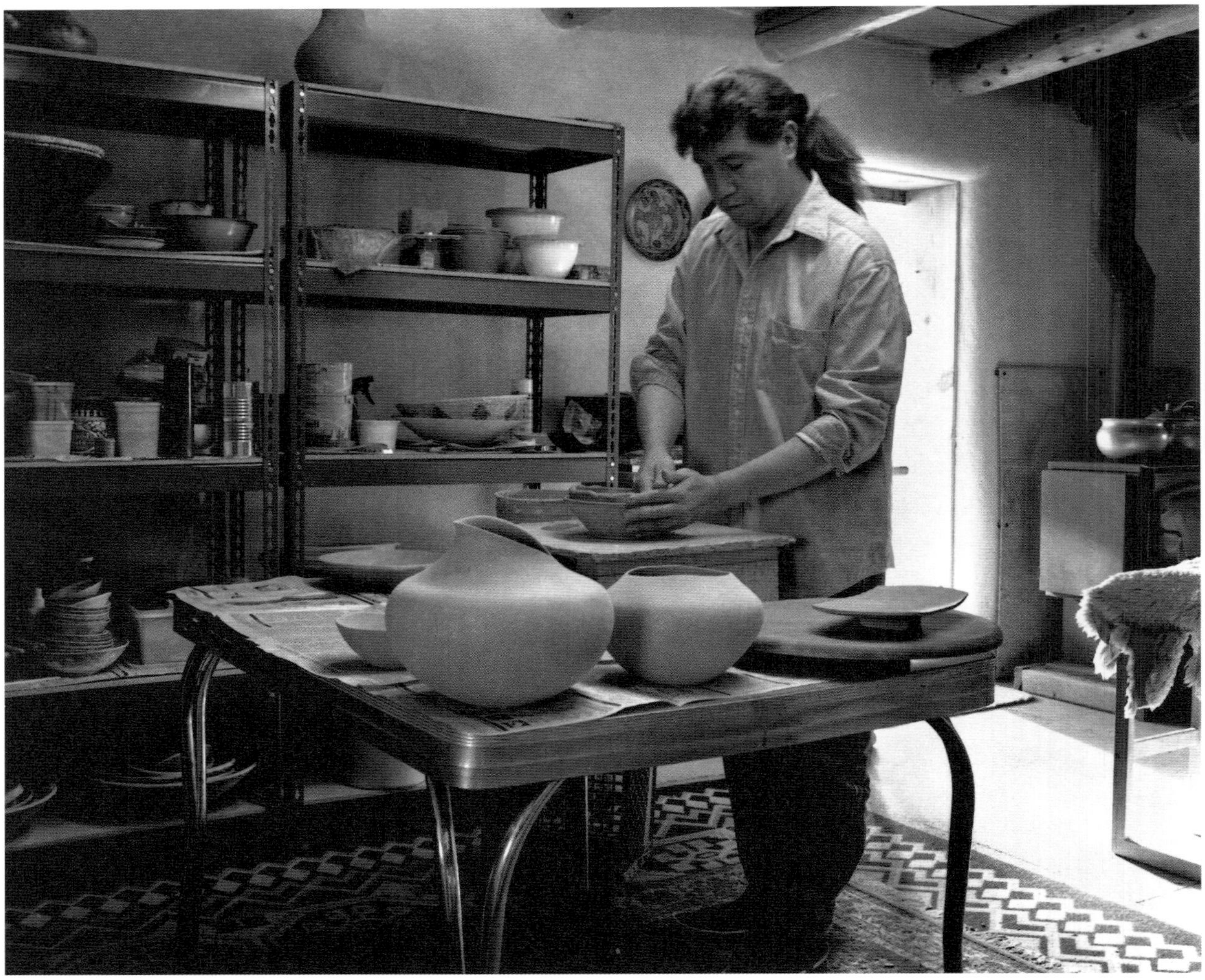

LONNIE VIGIL
coiling pot in studio

And because of this life and through this life we give the love and beauty that in turn gives presence, beauty, appreciation, and shared love to these creative life-giving works.

Each creative effort made with love and caring is like every effort made with similar feelings. There is a corresponding appreciation for each and every effort that is made in a loving and caring way in the creative process. How can we judge one better than another? Everyone counts, everyone is important, and everyone has feelings.

Introduction

TOBA PATO TUCKER

My first experience driving through the awe-inspiring landscape of the Southwest was in 1980, when I made portraits of the Navajo people living in the Joint Use Area of Arizona. That was the beginning of my quest to photograph Native Americans. Since then I have photographed the Shinnecock and Montauk Indians of eastern Long Island; the Onondaga Nation, one of the Six Nations of the Iroquois Confederacy in upstate New York; and recently, for this volume, the artists and artisans of the ancient pueblos of the Southwest.

People often ask me why I am drawn to photograph Native Americans, and I have struggled to find words that explain the purpose behind my images. Several years ago I made a statement about my work that still holds true: Collectively, Native Americans are an ancient people striving to retain their traditional way of life and integrity while confronting modern society and the dominant culture, and I want to record them for history and art at the end of the twentieth century. As individuals, they emanate an air of quiet wisdom and are a compellingly handsome people, with strength and inner dignity written on their faces. I believe that this dignity is inherent in all people, but Native Americans seem to epitomize it and give it a visible presence that I try to present in my portraits. And, remarkably—in spite of their usual reluctance to be photographed because they know Native Americans have been exploited by the camera throughout history—they give me permission to photograph them. It is by our collaboration—I with my camera, they with their cooperation—that we create the essential images by which their future generations, and the outside world, will remember them.

My projects begin with a premise, an idea that pulls me visually to a particular community of people. It is only when I begin photographing, as I work and observe the people and listen to them, that the true essence of the project and its goals reveal themselves. This shows me a path, and I am led from one person to another, from one portrait to the next, and their story unfolds for me visually.

In the spring of 1995 I came to New Mexico to begin a new project. I was interested in photographing Pueblo families of artists and artisans who make both traditional and contemporary pottery, jewelry, weavings, drums and kachinas, and also paintings and sculpture. I wanted to make portraits of individuals and family groups in order to record the remarkable and prevalent incidence where several generations in one family work together creatively, passing their traditions from one to the next, from the old to the young, creating a link from the past to the present. There are many books showing the traditions of Pueblo arts but none that portray in a singular way those who make the work. I set out to photograph the Pueblo people who make things—but more importantly, I wanted to portray them as the unique individuals they are—and to honor them.

While making these portraits I lived in Santa Fe. A significant part of my time was spent driving to where the people I photographed lived and worked in each of the twenty pueblos, most of them located close to the Rio Grande. Taos is the pueblo farthest north, then along a somewhat southerly route is Picurís, San Juan, Santa Clara, San Ildefonso, Pojoaque, Nambé, and Tesuque. Next is Santa Fe, and traveling further south, Cochiti, Jémez, Santo Domingo, Zia, San Felipe, Santa Ana, Sandia, and Isleta. Turning west near Albuquerque one reaches Laguna, Acoma, and Zuni, and further west into Arizona are the Pueblo villages at Hopi.

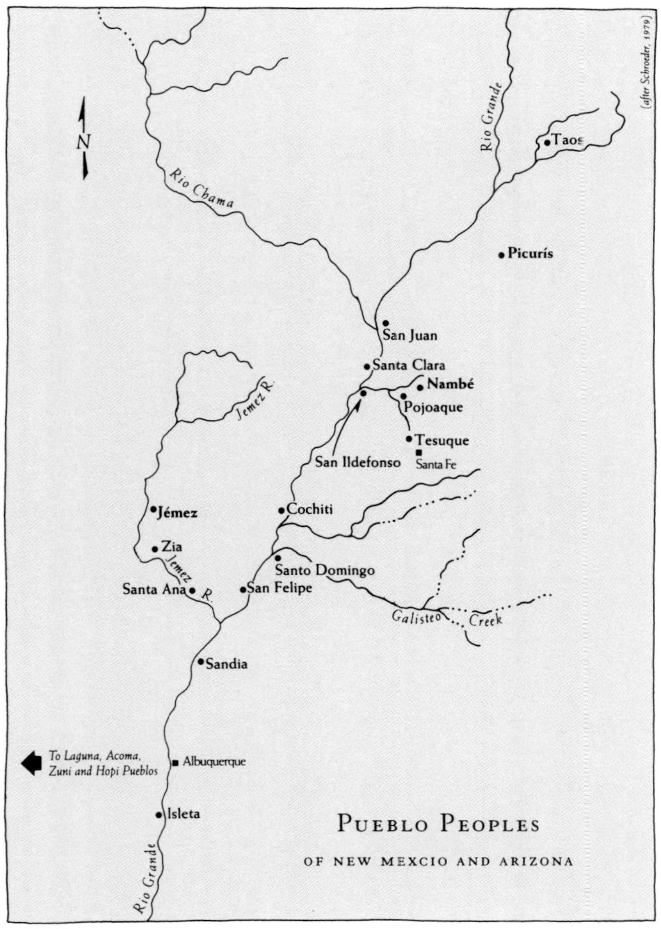

Pueblo Peoples
of New Mexcio and Arizona

Driving south from Santa Fe, I would see a distinctive and spectacular landscape—the rich, red earth of the mesas, canyons, and sandy arroyos. Driving north, something entirely different unfolds. Santa Fe's high-desert plateau broadens into a panorama of distant, magnificent white rock mesas near Santa Clara and San Ildefonso pueblos that appear pale pink in the morning light. Encountering this particular vista at the start of my day's journey was always inspiring. Continuing northward, the landscape near Picurís and Taos pueblos features forested mountains and some of the area's oldest Hispanic villages. To reach the relatively secluded Picurís Pueblo necessitates driving on a steep and curving road through mountains that seem to contain ancient secrets.

I was fascinated and enthralled by the landscape but also understood that this vast and mysterious land held more meaning to the Pueblo people than I could begin to comprehend. The pueblos are the oldest continously inhabited dwellings in North America, and their people have lived here since about A.D. 1300, encompassing some thirty generations of traditions, of spiritual and ceremonial life inexorably connected to the earth and the clay, the rocks and mesas and canyons.

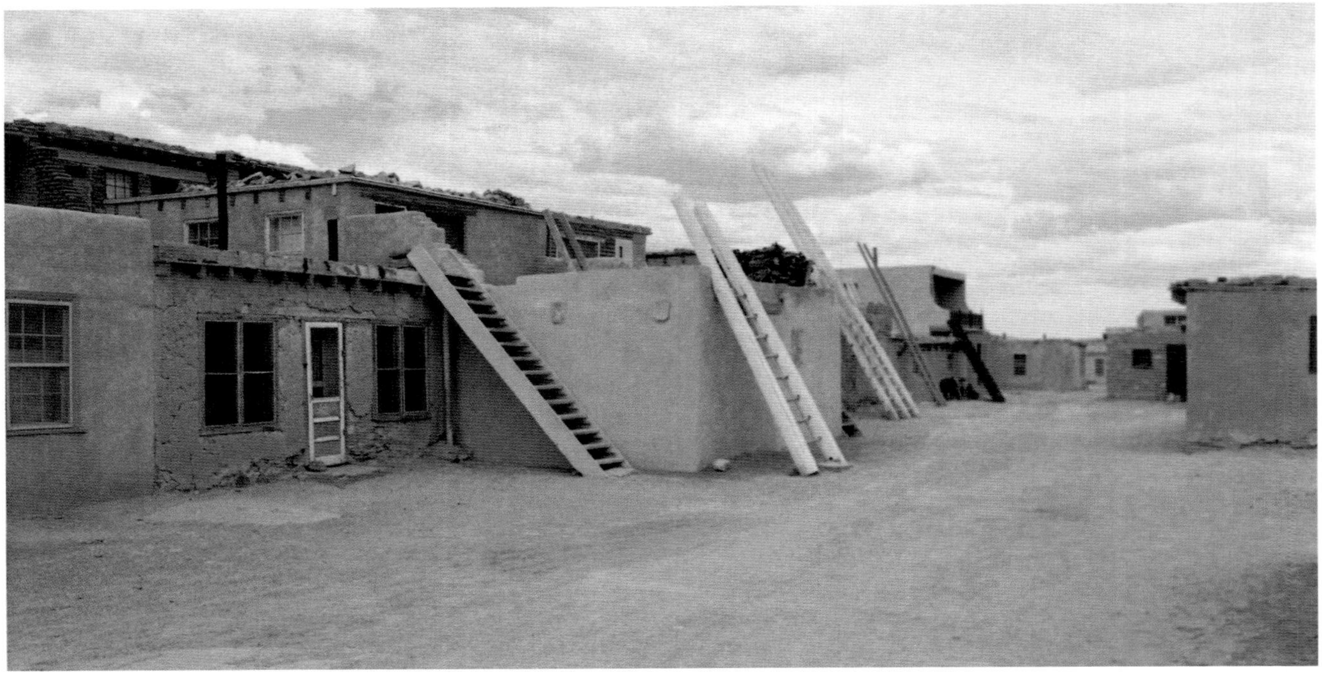

ACOMA PUEBLO

My familiarity with the landscape goes beyond experiencing it by car. I have walked countless miles among ruins and through the pueblos in the hot sun to attend various events, and have trudged in sandy arroyos and hiked through the canyons and up into the mountains.

Above all I enjoyed the Pueblo feast days, when I often made contact with the people I wanted to photograph. These were opportunities to witness aspects of the public ritual life that the people often spoke about and to see for myself the symbols used in creating the designs and motifs of their artwork. A feast day is a ceremonial event with religious and social significance involving traditional song, dance, and dress in intricate and profound expressions. It is also a social occasion for the Pueblo people.

During most feast days the streets surrounding the plaza are lined with vendors' booths and food stalls arranged along the dusty, irregular streets. The vendors' stalls are where the Pueblo artists and artisans sell their works to the spectators and visitors. The booths are small, usually containing chairs and tables covered with cloth on which pottery, silver and turquoise jewelry, moccasins, drums, and artworks are modestly displayed. The creators of these beautiful wares sit behind the tables, many times with family members who do similiar work, while babies sleep in the shade of the protective overhang. The work of children and young people, often showing remarkable creative abilities, is displayed and sold. I was always touched by the sight of three or four generations of Pueblo women and girls sitting serenely together under an umbrella behind the small table displaying the pottery each had made.

In spite of the crowded, bazaarlike atmosphere the scene is fairly quiet, except for the sound of the dancers, chanting, and the drum playing coming from the plaza area. The stalls selling food typically are clustered at one end of the pueblo, and the odor of the home-cooked food is tempting—Indian fry bread and honey, Indian tacos, mutton stew, stews made with hot chiles, posole, and tamales wrapped and tied in corn husks—all made by the Pueblo women.

The Pueblo people are hospitable, and on feast days I was sometimes asked by several families to come to their homes for a meal, which I considered a privilege as well as a wonderful experience. Since all the invitations were for the same time of day, I customarily was expected to eat some food in each of the houses I visited. Inside the adobes, to accommodate the large number of guests and family members, there are benches placed on either side of long tables holding serving bowls of fragrant foods prepared and served by several generations of women who have been cooking together since early morning. Guests sit down and eat when there is a seat available as people come and go without formality. Occasionally, I met new people here to join my growing collection of portraits.

I started out early on the days I was to photograph, happily packing the Jeep with my camera box and tripod, food and water, the two sizes of black background paper and the portable poles already in their permanent place in the car. Because the pueblos do not have any road signs I also had with me the complicated directions down washboard roads. A typical instruction would be, "Turn east at the fork and go about three miles, then go south along the wash at the two cottonwoods . . . ," which made it necessary to install a compass on my dashboard.

Photographing brought me into the adobe homes at the pueblos, occasionally to modern dwellings in Santa Fe or Albuquerque, and many times to homes of people I hadn't met in person but only had spoken to on the telephone. I always came with a portfolio of my photographs to show before I brought in my camera. A portrait is a collaboration between the photographer and the sitter; viewing my photographs gave the person an idea of what we would be striving for together and resulted in an unspoken trust between us.

Before unpacking my equipment I instinctively assessed the available light and its source, usually near a window or opened door, and decided where I would set up my black background paper and where, and on what, my subject would sit. Since I don't use artificial light, finding enough natural light is always a challenge for me, especially in some of the small, low-ceiling adobe houses.

Usually the people to be photographed were already dressed for the portrait, either in traditional dress and accessories or in everyday attire, depending upon how they chose to present themselves. It was not unusual for family members to observe the sesssion since a formal photograph is considered a special occasion; sometimes I included them in the photograph. In order to photograph some of the elders it was necessary to contact their children or grandchildren first to get permission because

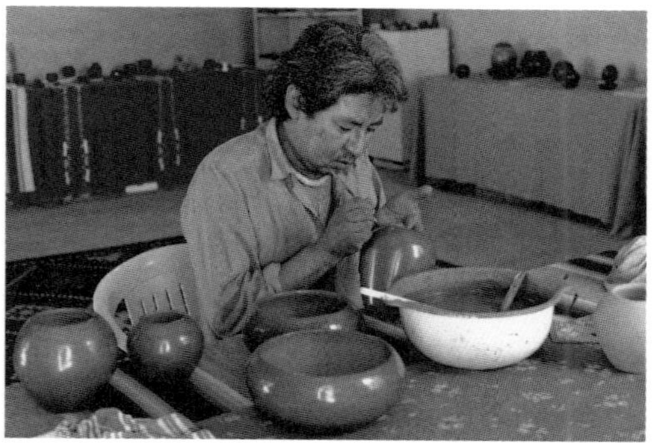

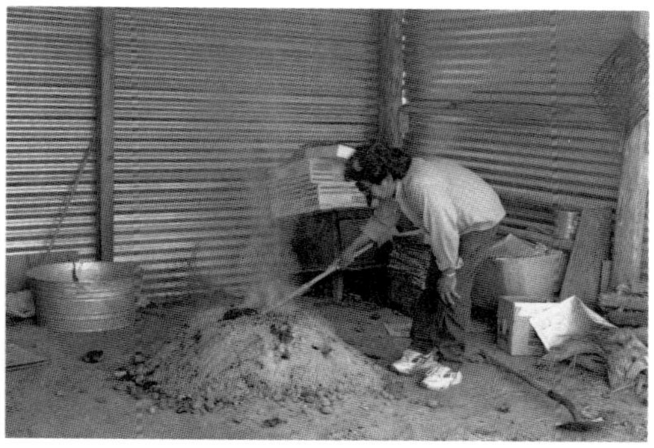

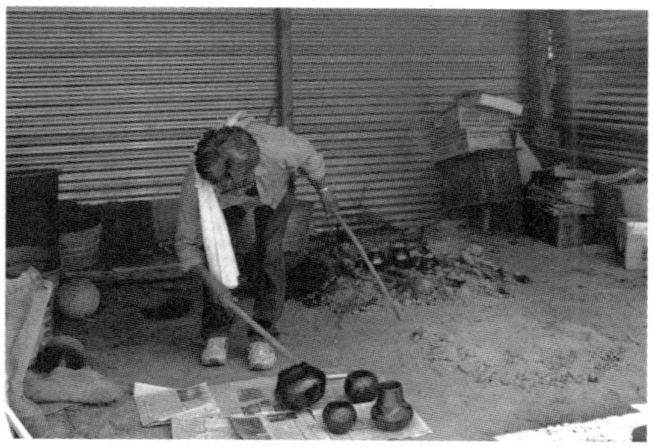

JUAN TAFOYA
firing pottery
San Ildefonso Pueblo

they themselves no longer dealt with people from outside the pueblo. Although some were ninety years old and more, they still lived in their own homes, surrounded and cared for by their extended families. When I arrived, these dignified elders would be freshly groomed and dressed, ready to be photographed, but a family member was always on hand to straighten a collar or smooth a strand of hair while I was photographing them. This was very moving to observe.

No matter how shy or reticent initially, while sitting in front of the camera people became visibly confident, presenting themselves proudly—and this was the moment I released the shutter.

Many of my photographs include the work made by the artisans, and some portray the artisits while working. I was always invited into work areas and shown how the pots, jewelry, or drums were made, and there was a willingness to share with me recollections of how they learned their craft. For instance, I was told stories of potters being taught traditional pottery-making from parents, grandparents, and other family elders, and how cherished stones used for polishing pots are passed from one generation to the next. The pots were usually made on the kitchen table, and in many cases are still made there, no matter how finely rendered. This is where the children are first given the clay and where the love of shaping it begins. In the homes I visited, shelves of pots standing side by side, representing the work of several generations, were proudly pointed out to me. Many artists re-create pots using traditional motifs passed down in their families, their execution and design virtually unchanged for generations, while others have created works that reflect new and rich influences. Pueblo creativity involves both tradition and innovation—two inseparable cultural forces.

At the end of the day, when the landscape is bathed in the changing colors and shifting light of the setting sun, I would drive home, tired but with a sense of accomplishment, feeling inspired by the people I had just met and photographed.

Photographing some three hundred Pueblo people has left an indelible impression coupled with vivid recollections. The families and individuals I met during my two-and-a-half-year project affected me with their quiet dignity, confidence, devotion to their families, and gracious hospitality to a stranger with a camera. I feel forever enriched for having been invited into their world, if only briefly, and in return, I offer them this volume of their portraits.

Pueblo Cosmos

RINA SWENTZELL
SANTA CLARA PUEBLO

> The sun was moving in and out of autumn rainclouds. When it broke through the clouds, the dried grass of the mesa turned golden and the dark, almost black, shadows returned. There were raindrops hanging off the low bushes and piñon trees. Khuun-Tsaweh walked through the wetness of the morning and felt a sense of well-being. She paused with uplifted head to lick a raindrop from an overhanging piñon branch. She shifted her body to adjust the rolled deerskin and string of dried meat as she looked south through the nearby trees toward Puje Mesa. Her eyes followed the back side of the mesa to the east and across the lower plateau until the land dropped into the valley where the river, the Posongeh, flowed. The valley lay in a mist that morning. The mountains beyond the valley were cloaked in a soft cloud blanket above which snow-covered peaks showed themselves (Swentzell, n.d.).

It is out of such settings that the modern-day Native peoples of the Southwest emerged. A keen awareness of clouds, rain, mountains made our ancestors sensitive to the spirit within the clay, wood, and rocks that were modeled into ceremonial and functional items of everyday use. In those days, sensitivity was expected not only of special people, or people called "artists." Every person was expected to be sensitive to his or her physical, emotional, and spiritual context. Therefore, every person was a

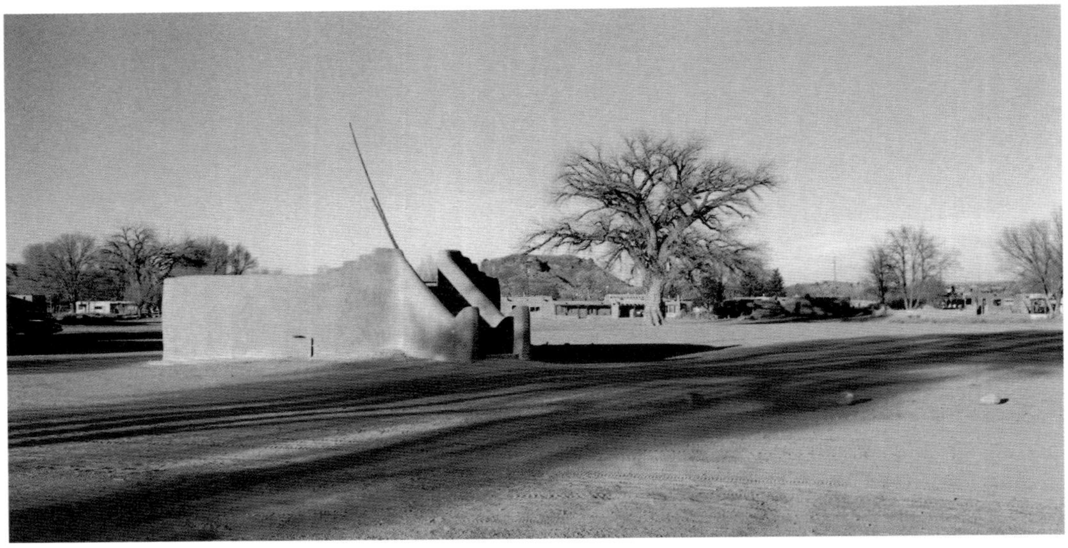

Kiva
SAN ILDEFONSO PUEBLO

creator, a reshaper, who had the capability to bring unassociated elements into some definable whole or form. These forms—pots, moccasins, drums—that these traditional people created were known to have breath and were treated as alive beings because the essence of life flowed through their parts as well as through the created whole. These created items shared in the world because they interacted with their makers in daily activities. Their connectedness to life was undeniable. Moreover, pots, baskets, drums, and humans were believed to have distinctive qualities and personalities because they were part of, and flowed from, the breath of the cosmos.

Because there was no disdain for the earth, or the mother, human creativity was an extension of the breath that flowed through her and consequently through the entirety of existence. All of existence, as humans knew it, was created by the coming together of the sky and the earth, the male and the female. Therefore, all parts of place between the earth and sky were known to be interconnected. Human separation from nature, from the trees, rocks, birds, had not yet happened in those times before European/Christian contact. Our ancestors remained an intimate part of the life forces of the earth and did not view themselves as separate and above other creatures since both humans and nonhumans were acknowledged children of sky and earth. Respect by humans for all of life, including nonhuman entities, was part of the acknowledgment that the entire world is a sacred place and that no part is more special than any other.

Here, in this work, we see photographic images of present-day native peoples of the Southwest. Although these people are called "artists," they are representative of the larger grouping of the Pueblo peoples of New Mexico and Arizona. Their personalities, lives, and works reflect the complicated life issues of different cultures living in the common physical, ecconomic, and political reality of the present-day southwestern United States where the separation of humans from nature and the superiority of human life over all of creation are the basis for daily life.

The psychological space of living within rather than separate from nature immediately attributes different life meanings and, hence, art expressions. For the most part, traditional Pueblo creativity is more confirming and consoling rather than exploratory and self-expressive because its primary purpose is to restate the culturally accepted precepts of relationships at all levels, including that between the human and nonhuman realms. In other words, traditional native arts tend to focus on relational qualities that restate and confirm the human place within the natural world. In that world, there is no such thing as an independent action. Individual focus is shunned because everything and everyone are tied to everything and everyone else. Any motion and action by an individual affects the whole because, as noted earlier, all parts of the whole are interrelated. In traditional pottery making the essential oneness of people and clay is known and clearly illustrated in the story of Water-Jar-Boy:

> Water-Jar-Boy was born as a clay water jar. He grew up with all the other children of the pueblo and wanted to do whatever they did. One day his grandfather was going rabbit hunting. Water-Jar-Boy begged his grandfather to take him. But Grandfather said, "You have no arms or legs. You cannot hunt." Water-Jar-Boy told his grandfather that he could roll. Grandfather agreed to take him. When they came to a low hill he placed Water-Jar-Boy on his side and gave him a gentle shove. Water-Jar-Boy rolled and rolled until he crashed into a big rock. He broke into many pieces, but in the pieces sat a young boy! Water-Jar-Boy ran and hid behind a small pinon tree. When Grandfather reached the bottom of the hill, he could not find his grandson. Then he heard Water-Jar-Boy calling, "Grandfather, Grandfather, here I am." Grandfather saw a young boy coming out from behind a tree and he was surprised. The boy was smiling. When Water-Jar-Boy explained who he was, Grandfather was very happy. Hand in hand they hurried back to the pueblo to show everybody that Water-Jar-Boy was now a boy with arms and legs (translation by Rina Swentzell).

We see, however, in these modern photographs of contemporary artists glimmers of the rift occuring within the traditional Pueblo world as the people move away from the old belief of oneness with the natural world. The European/American tendency to embrace human superiority over all of life is challenging and transforming the tradi-

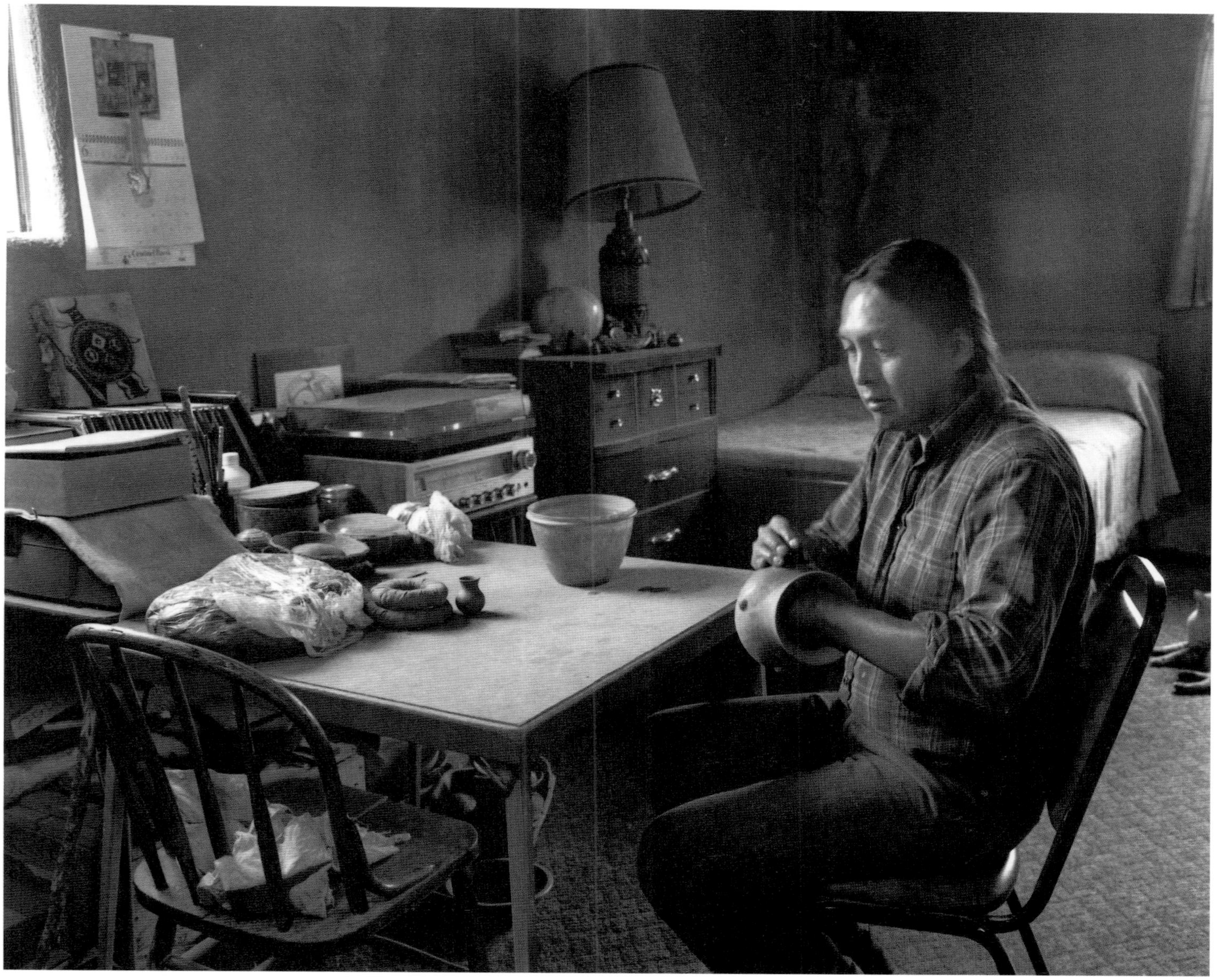

ANTHONY DURAND
polishing pot
Picurís Pueblo

tional Pueblo premise that all things are interconnected. This ongoing philosophical shift occurring within the Pueblo world of accepting human superiority leads to artists who see creativity primarily as an economic activity, as a means to individual fame and recognition, and as a way to produce decorative items for racial identification. For instance, the individual identification with works of art to personally claim the power of cosmic creativity through the signing of names on art pieces is now commonplace in the Pueblo art world. This particular action attests to the human and individual focus occurring since the revival of Pueblo arts by non-Indian romantics around and before the turn of this century.

The tense relationship that has consequently developed between the historical and contemporary Pueblo world is illustrated by the present-day use of the words "art" and "artists." Much has been written about native languages not including "art" as a word because the individual creative act in the traditional world was about doing things in a way to feel oneness with other humans as well as with the earth, clouds, and wind. Achieving an understanding of the flow of life within which one participated was the goal. It was not to distinguish the self as an individual outside of the context of the human community or nature. Today, "art" and "artists" are words of positive distinction for Pueblo people because fame and individual recognition are accepted ways of trying to make human life meaningful. Distinction of the human individual within the human economic, social, and political realms are vitally important today to Pueblo people, Pueblo artists. Fame in the art world is becoming more important for a sense of self. How much money one's creation can be sold for determines the worth of the person. As Pueblo artists take on this way of thinking, continuity with the traditional belief system that upholds oneness and not separateness through possessiveness, competitiveness, and superiority is weakened.

The scenario of native peoples and artists still being in simple continuity with their traditional lifeways is not so clear anymore. Pueblo communities, in reality, are not separate from and in alignment with American economic and political systems. Everyday life within those communities is dependent on grocery stores and money for subsistence. Lifeways are dramatically different than they were before the turn of this century. In some of the people's faces shown in this volumn, we can grasp the tension of living in transition between this and the other. We can see the striving for personal recognition and fame, and we can also sense that these people, these Pueblo artists, are struggling with defining themselves and deriving meaningfulness within a complex, disparate world such that they are now like artists of the European strain who *consciously* strive for connectedness or a sense of wholeness.

Sue Hertel, an America painter of the non-Indian world whose writing reflects an understanding of the struggle for connection, talked about the need to "repair the spirit in disarray." Such artists of the European tradition consciously and deliberately search for spiritual meaning because the world that they come from does not generally acknowledge the spiritual in daily life. For the most part, the Western world expects artists to look for new and unknown truths as if truth and wholeness are things separate from themselves. Originality and uniqueness of subject and expression are desired over the confirmation of connectedness.

Today, many Indian artists can be seen as part of that effort to consciously take that magical complexity that exists in the world and lead it, as Sue Hertel has said, "into an inevitable, unquestionable simplicity." The effort, however, is usually not about *easily* flowing with the complexity that can lead to unquestionable simplicity or wholeness. It is generally seen to happen only through thorough human manipulation, and manipulation as only superior beings can imagine doing. Artists, then, see themselves as manipulators of color, texture, and form to express their individual vision, creativity, and power. They are then seen as special for their personal vision by the rest of the world. Indian artists, then, are presented as special people who have taken unto themselves the label of individuals with unique capabilites and special sensitivies rather than as people who share in the flow of universal creation where sensitivity is commonplace.

What does remain as a hope in the end is that we all—Indian, non-Indian, artists, nonartists, rural or urban—desire that genuine experience of oneness with the breath of life that forms the world we live in. And I do believe that however we express ourselves we all do yearn to feel the breath of the universe assuring us of our connection with the clouds, wind, rain, and mountains—and with ourselves and each other. The Pueblo Indian artists shown here are working, for the most part, consciously or unconsciously, to feel meaningfulness within a complex whole:

> Yet, on some sweet morning, one understands that it all comes together in the most intricate oneness. It fits together so perfectly, so exquisitely. It is so simple, so unassuming. Not glamorous. Ordinary and perfect (Hertel, 1994).

REFERENCES

Hertel, Susan. *All This Change*. Nobleboro, MA: Blackberry Books, 1994.

Swentzell, Rina. *Younger-Older Ones*. Santa Fe, NM: Weaselsleeves Press, n.d.

Pueblo Artists

PORTRAITS

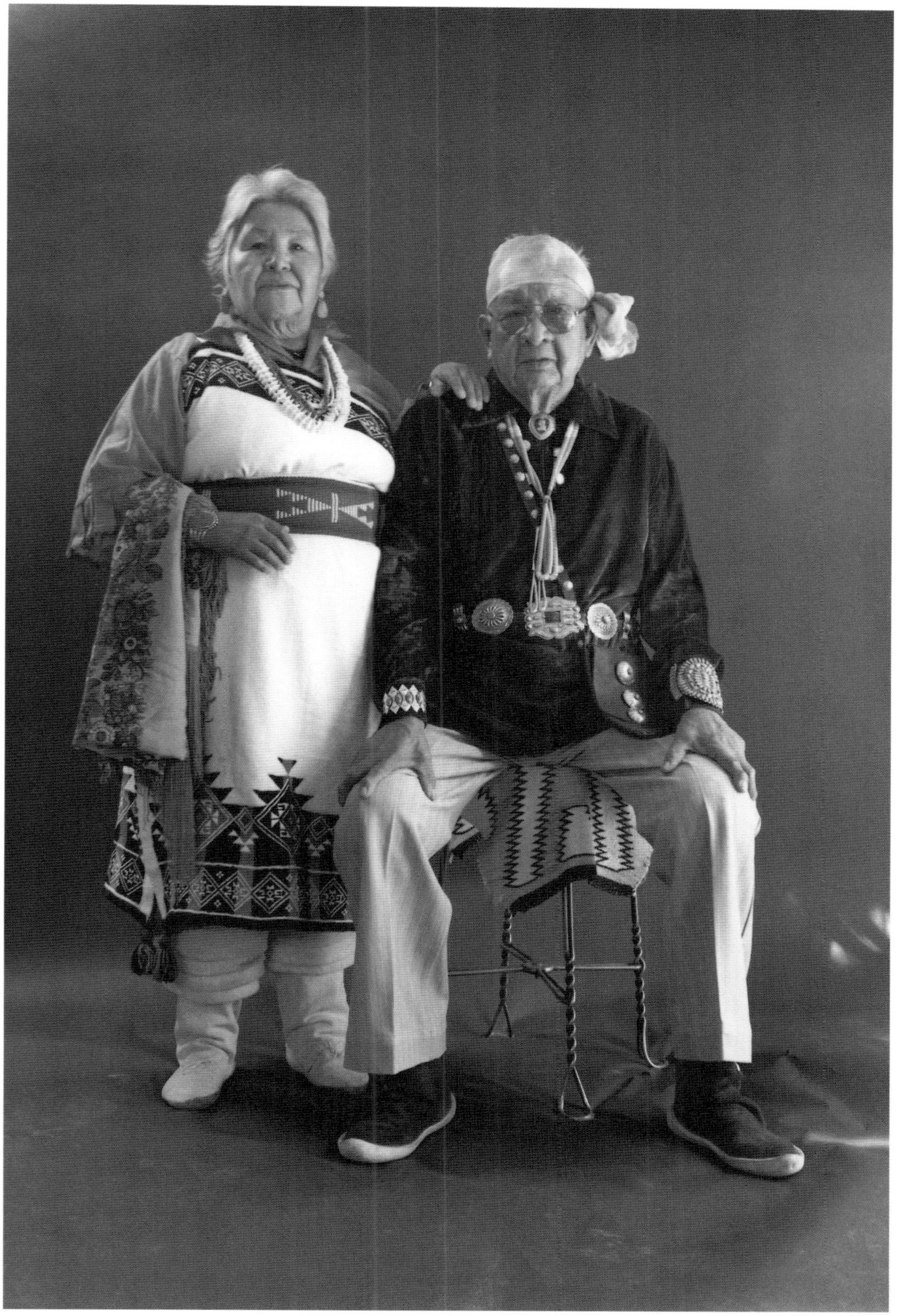

I

LYDIA TSOSIE, Traditional Pueblo Embroidery and Sewing, Picurís Pueblo,
CARL TSOSIE, Sr., Master Carpenter, Silversmith, Navajo
Wearing Purple Heart, Normandy Beach, World War II

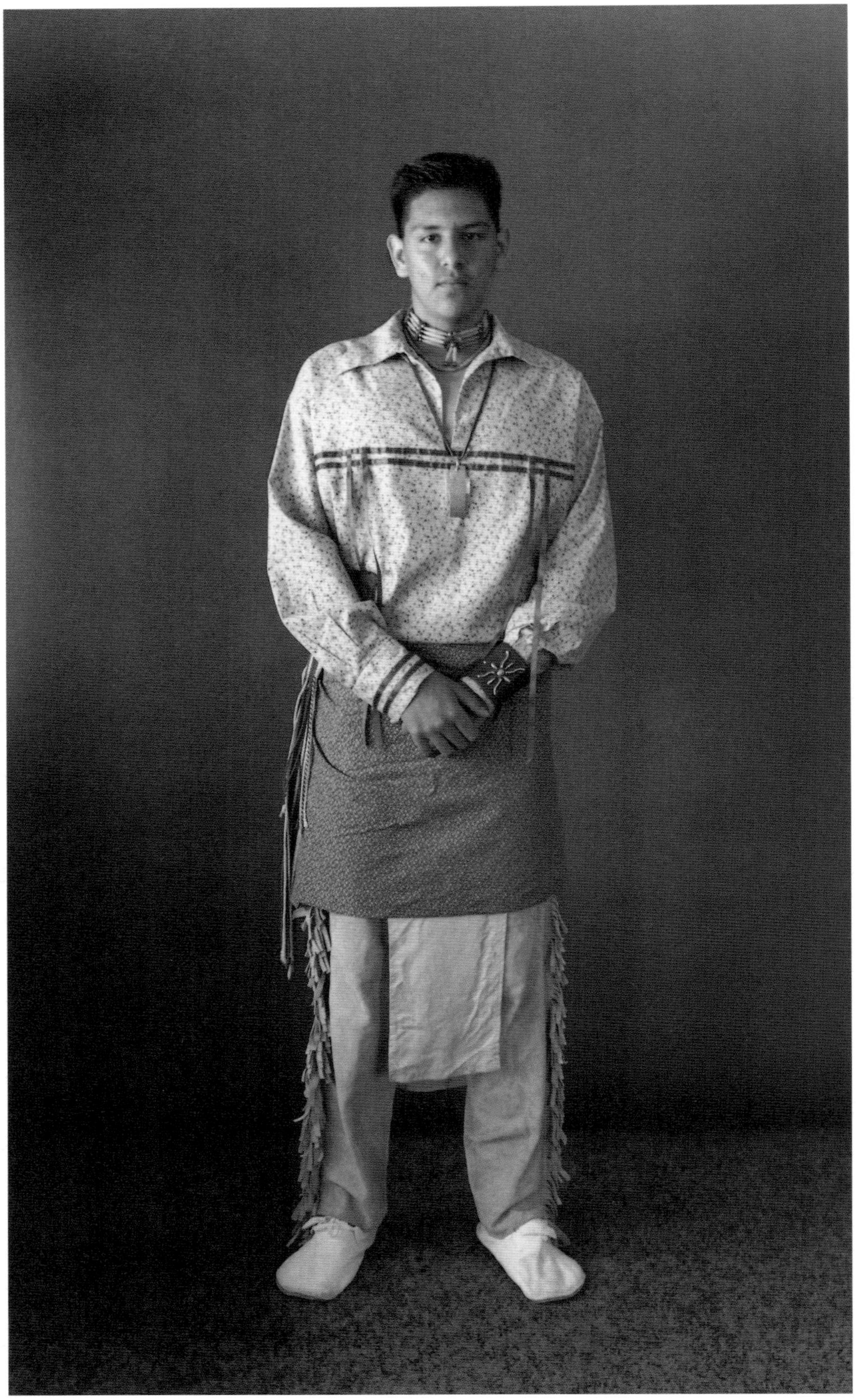

2

WAYNE NEZ GAUSSOIN

Connie Gaussoin's son

Traditional and Contemporary Jeweler

Picurís/Navajo

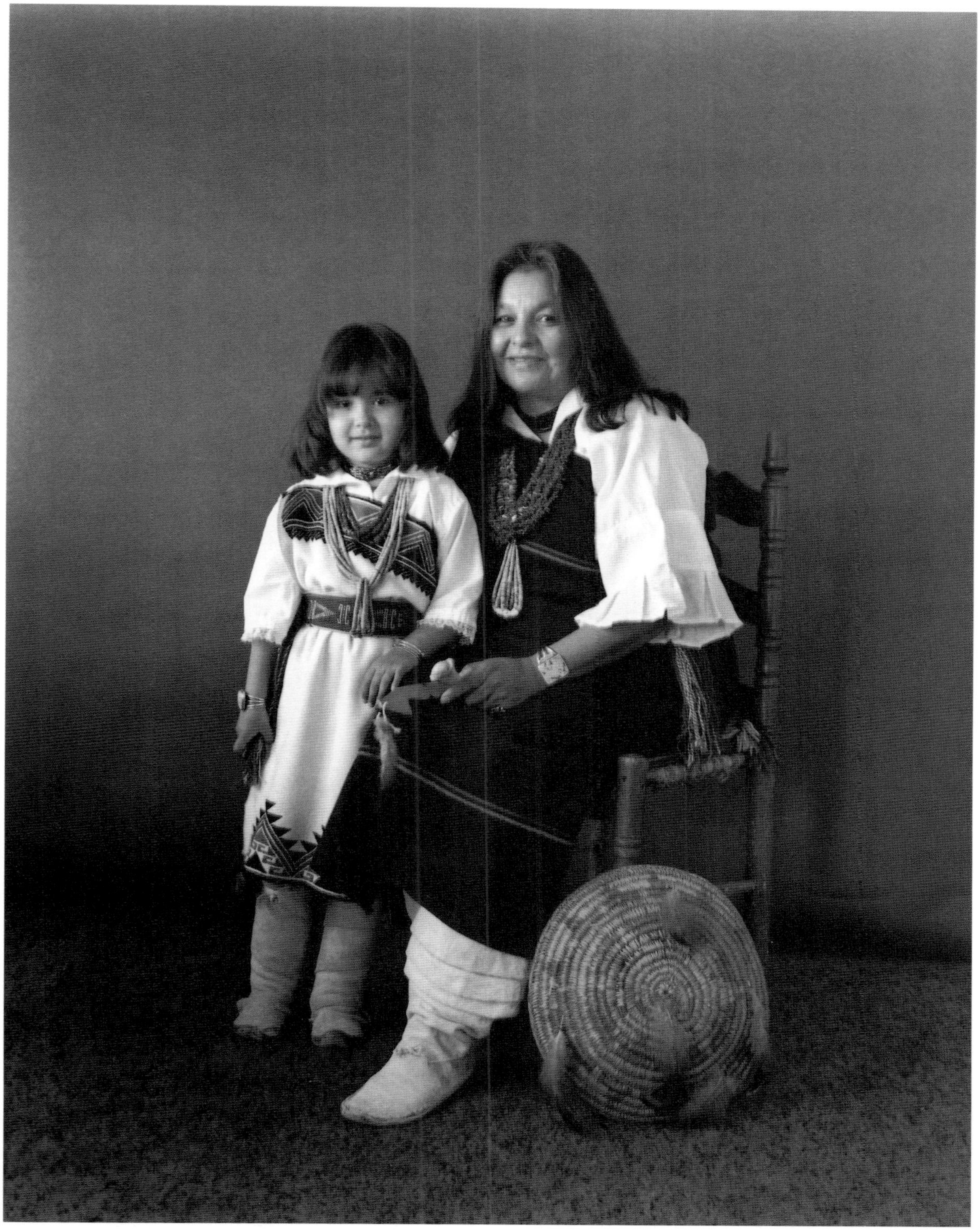

3
CONNIE GAUSSOIN
with daughter TAZBAH ANN GAUSSOIN
Lydia and Carl Tsosie's daughter and granddaughter
Traditional and Contemporary Jewelry
Picurís/Navajo

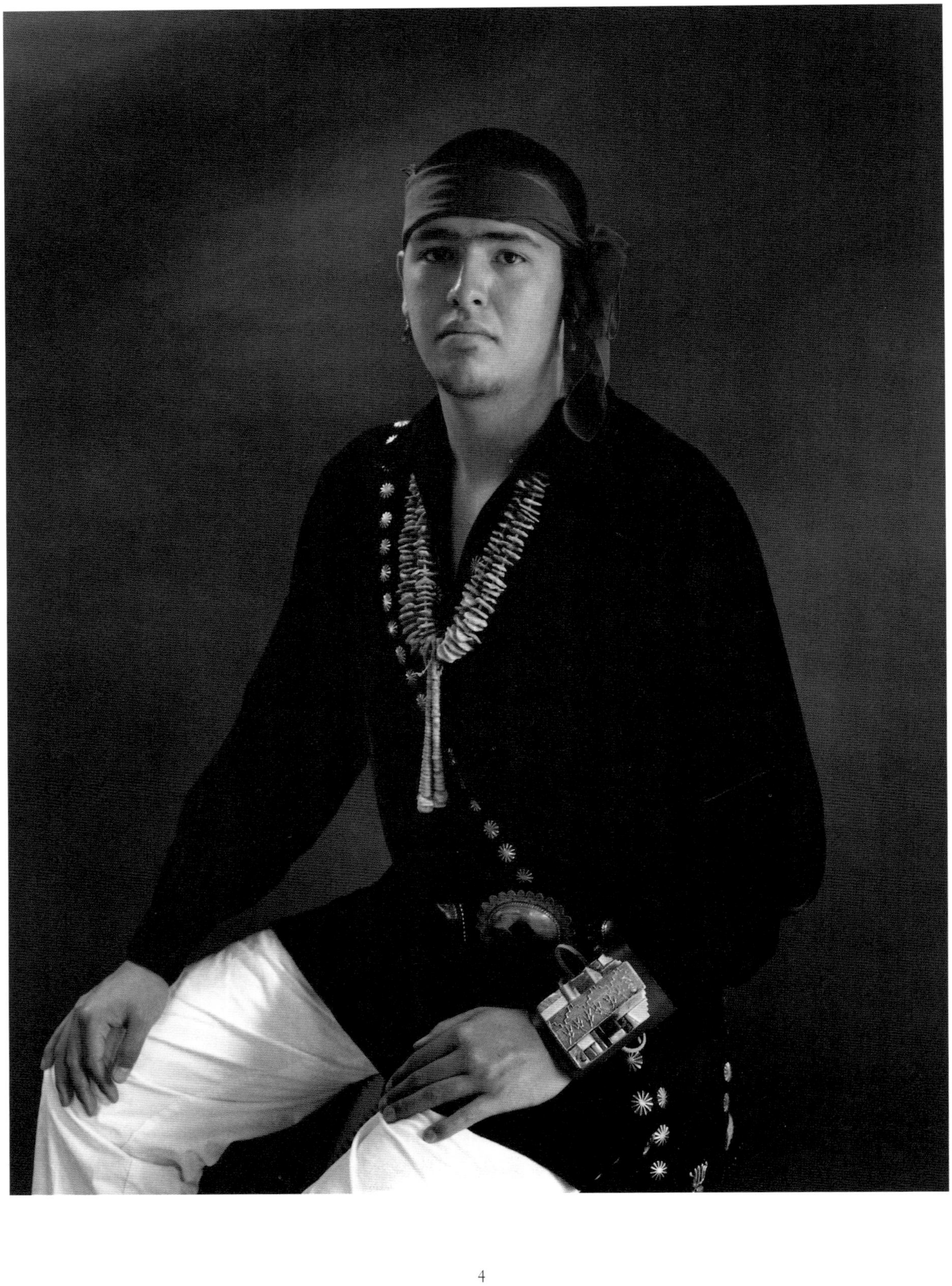

4

DAVID GAUSSOIN

Connie Gaussoin's son

Traditional and Contemporary Jewelry

Picurís/Navajo

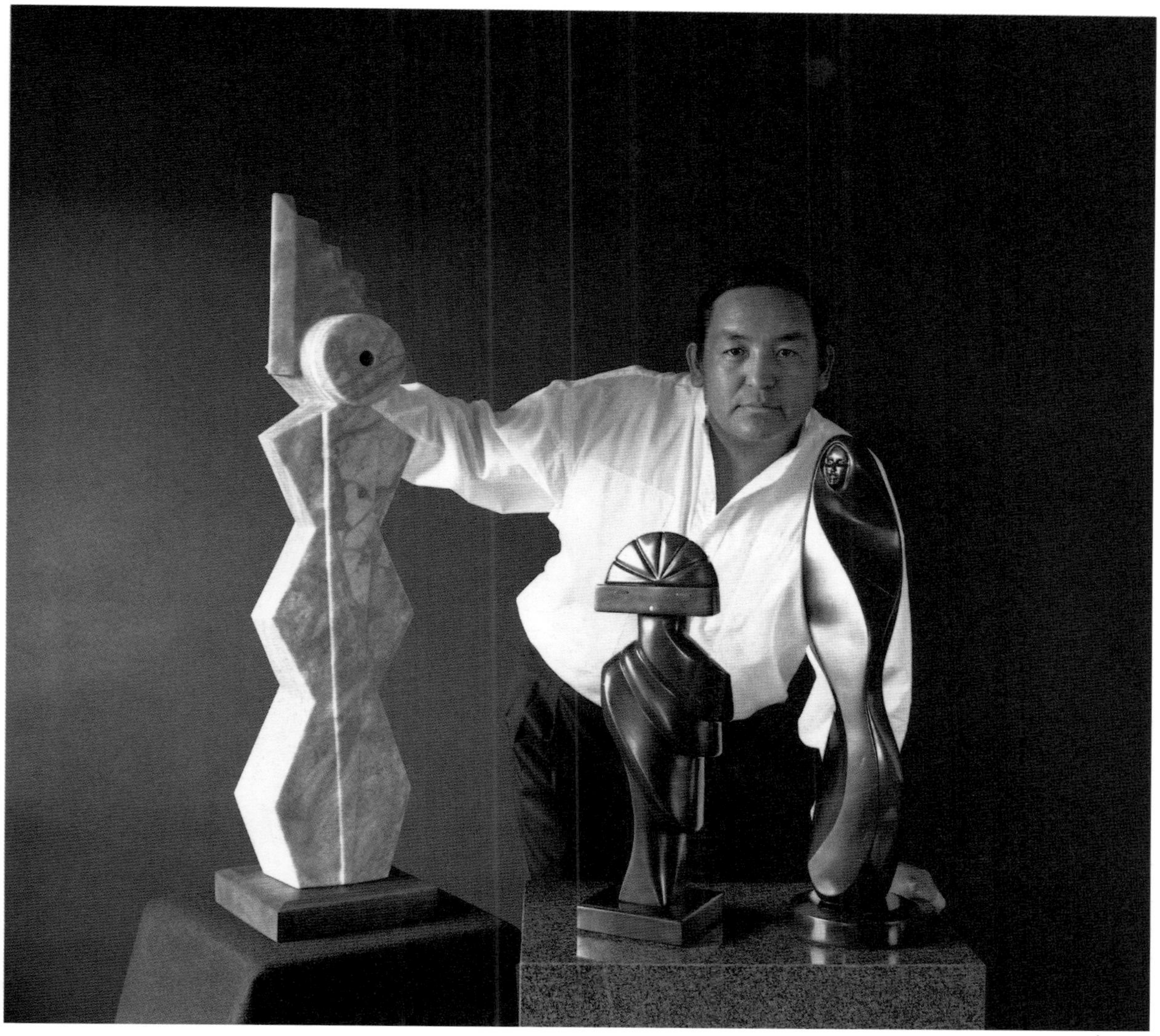

5

ROBERT DALE TSOSIE

Lydia and Carl Tsosie's son

Stone and Bronze Sculptor

Picurís/Navajo

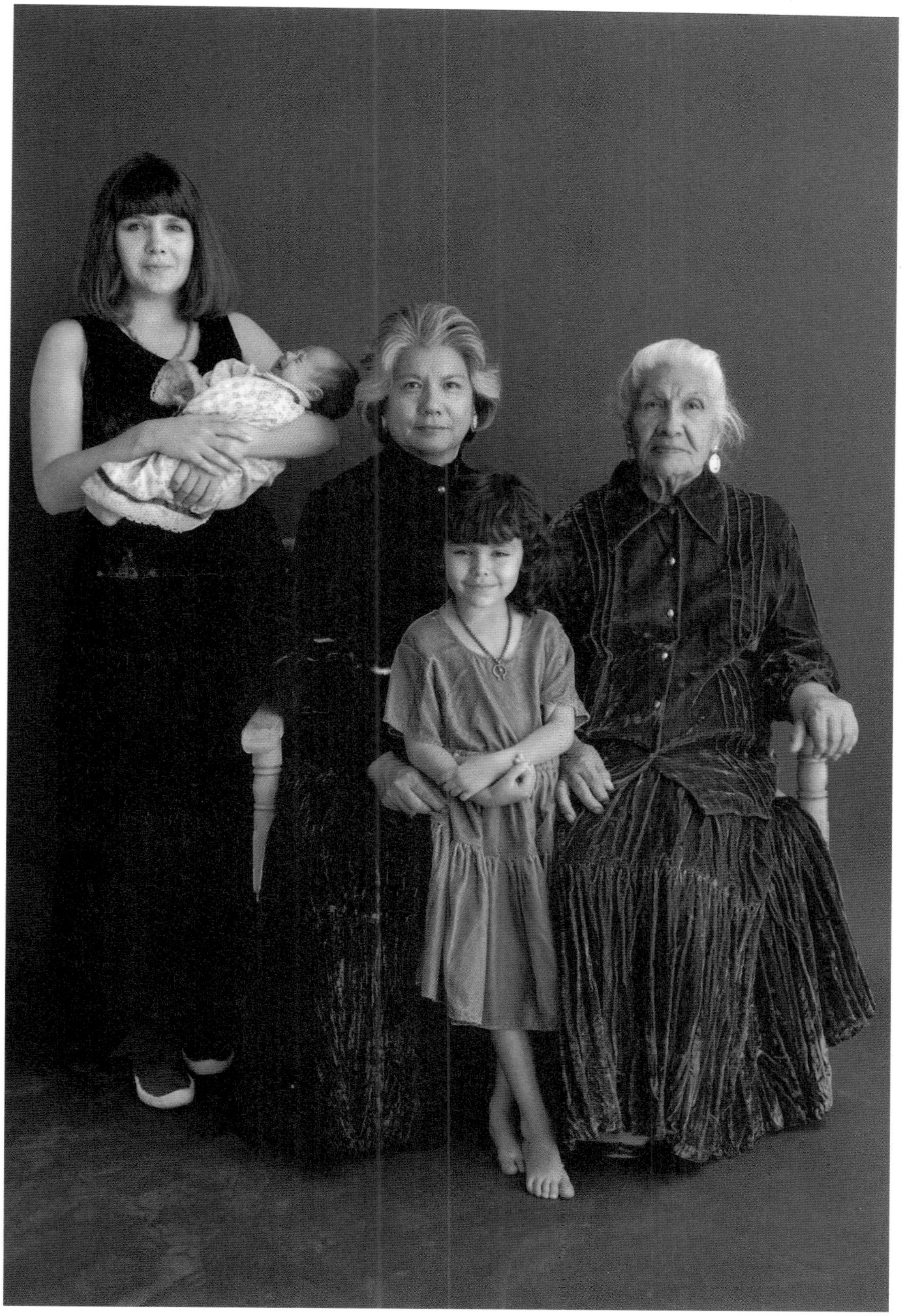

6

ROSE NARANJO, Traditional Potter,
with daughter DOLLY NARANJO-NEIKRUG, Contemporary Potter,
granddaughter JODY NARANJO, Contemporary Potter and Artist,
great-granddaughters JADE, Artist, and CORAL
Santa Clara Pueblo

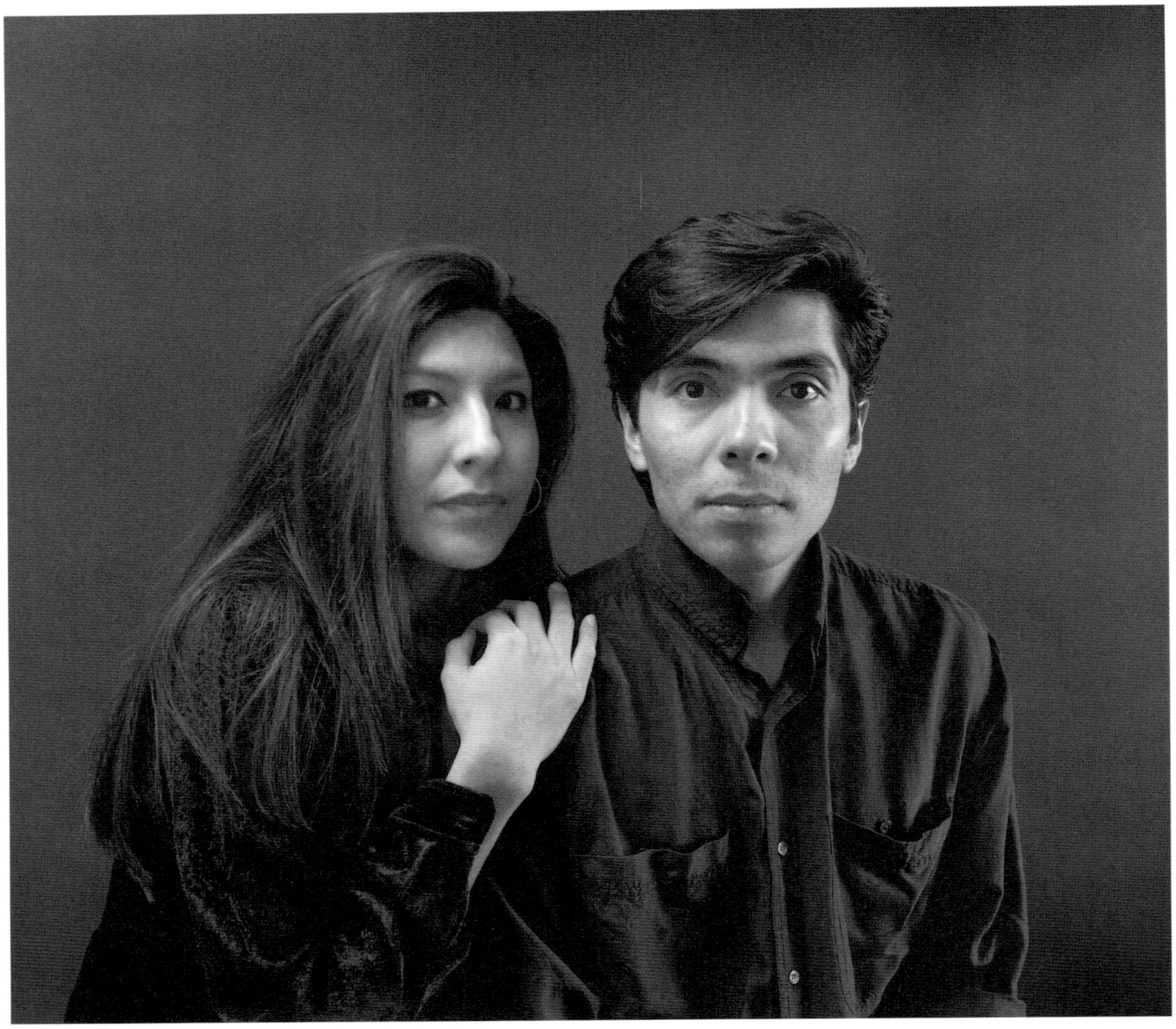

7

DUSTY NARANJO with brother FORREST NARANJO

Rose Naranjo's grandchildren

Contemporary Potters

Santa Clara Pueblo

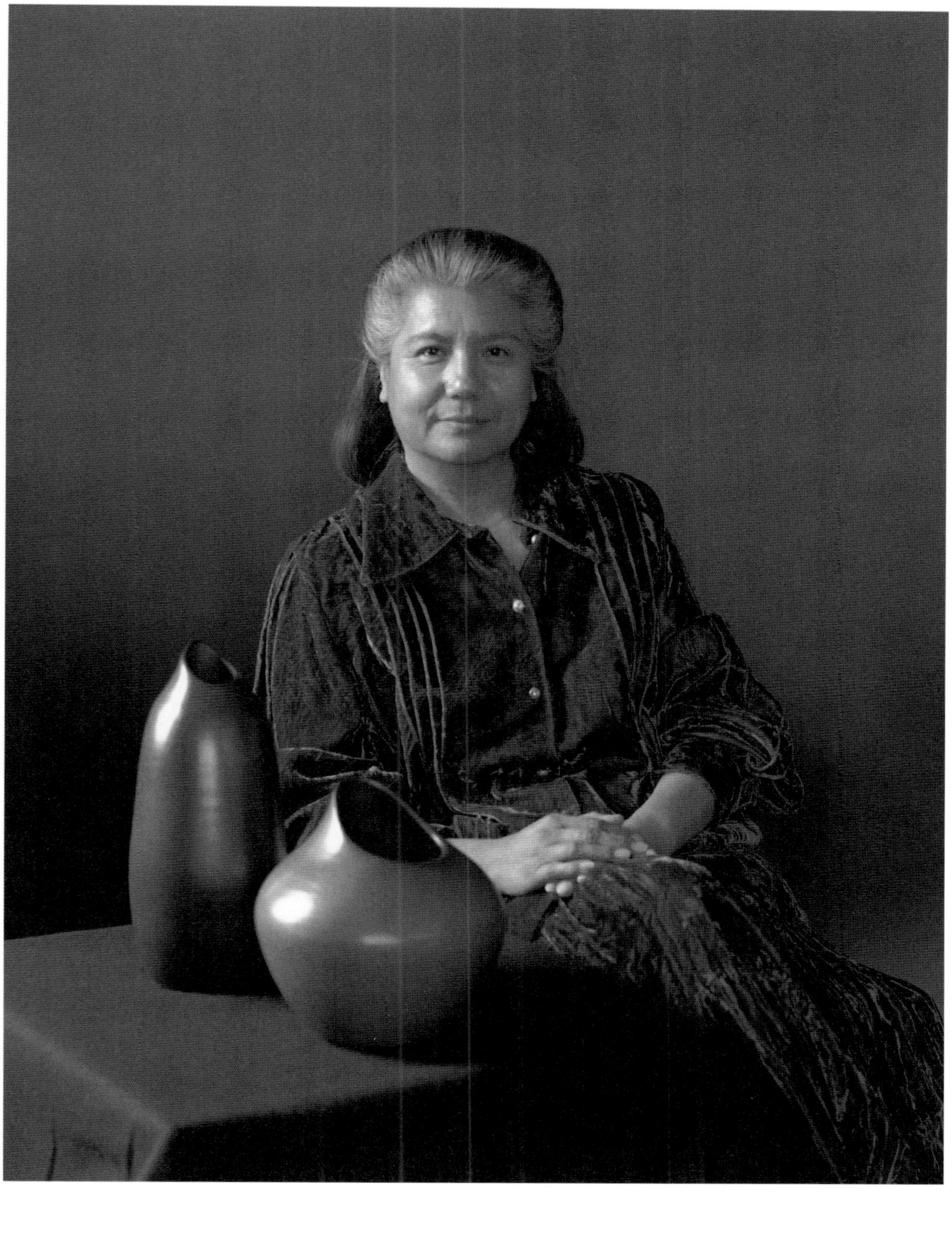

8
DOLLY NARANJO-NEIKRUG
Rose Naranjo's daughter
Contemporary Potter
Santa Clara Pueblo

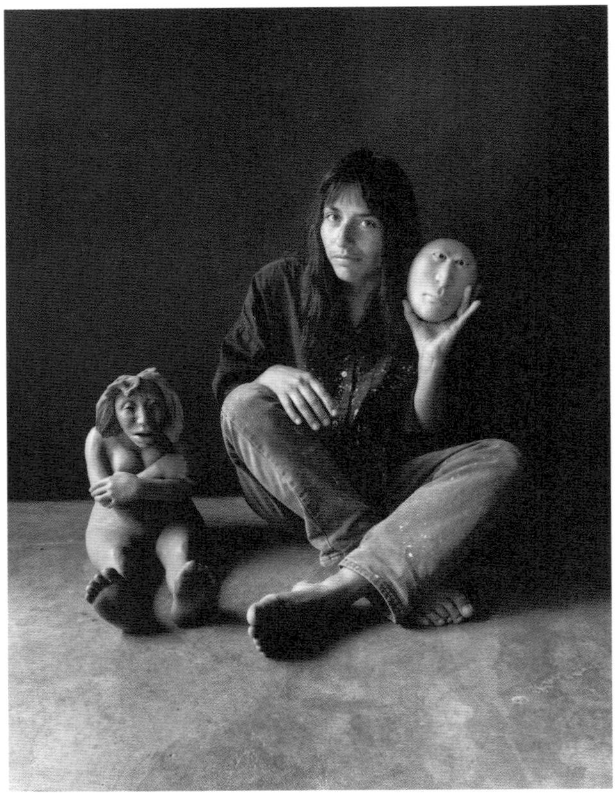
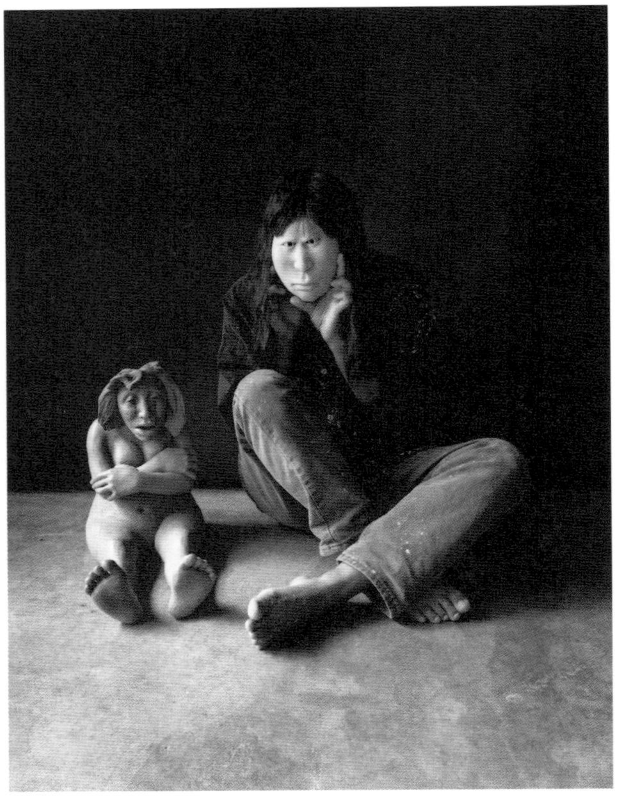

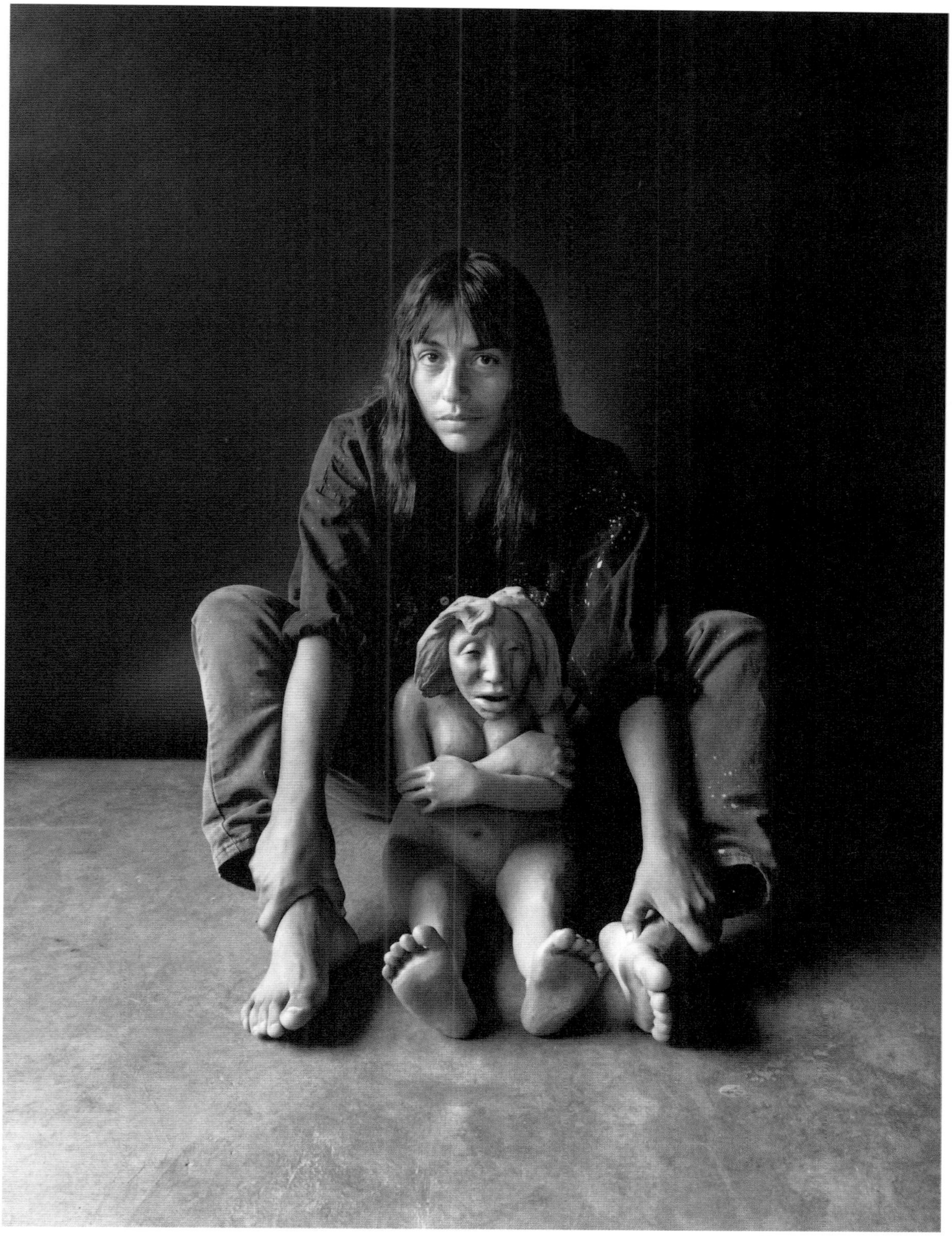

9, 10, 11

ROXANNE SWENTZELL

Rina Swentzell's daughter

Rose Naranjo's granddaughter

"I am a sculptor of human emotions"

Santa Clara Pueblo

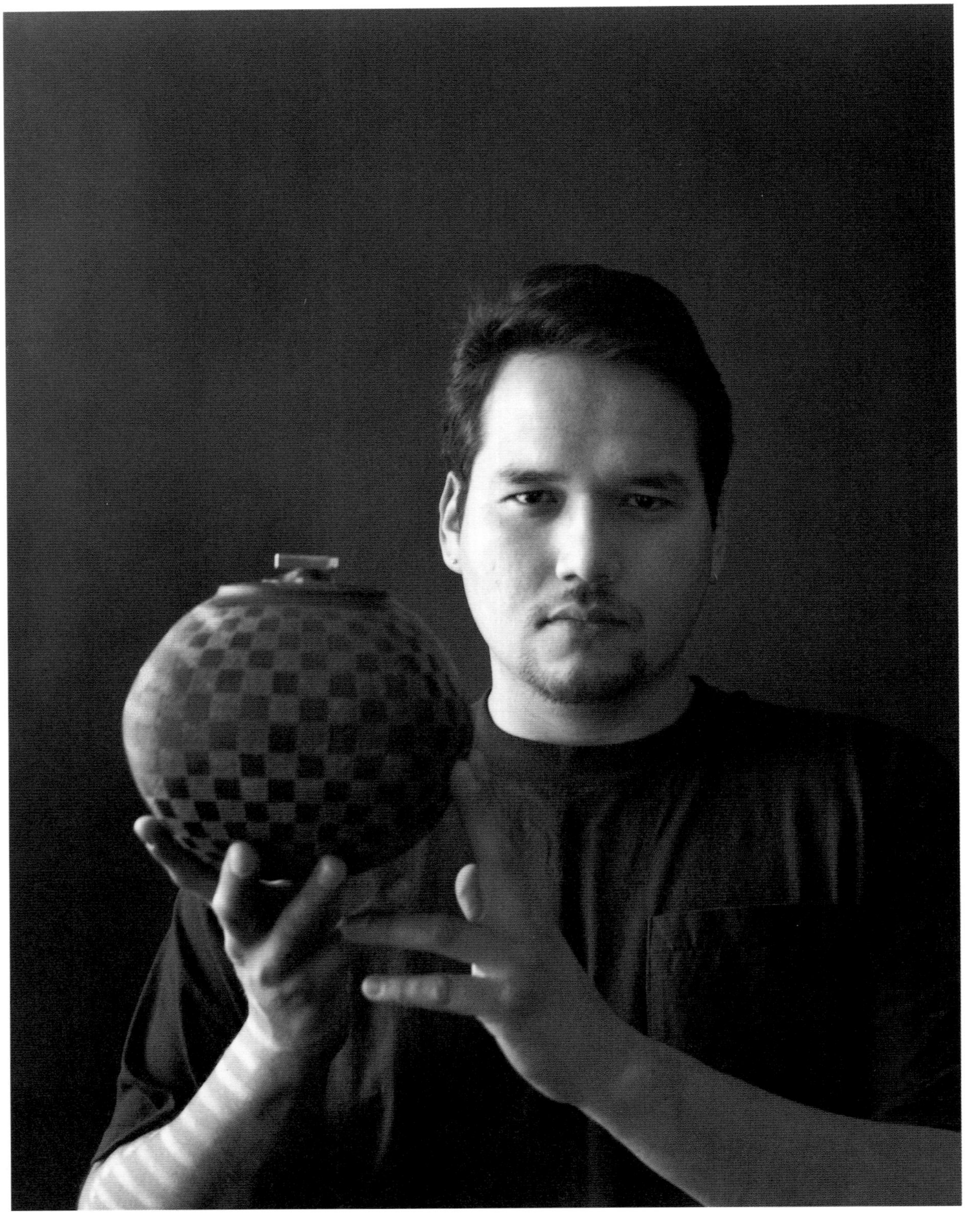

12

JOEL McHORSE

Christine McHorse's son

Contemporary Micaceous Pottery and Silver

Navajo/Taos Pueblo

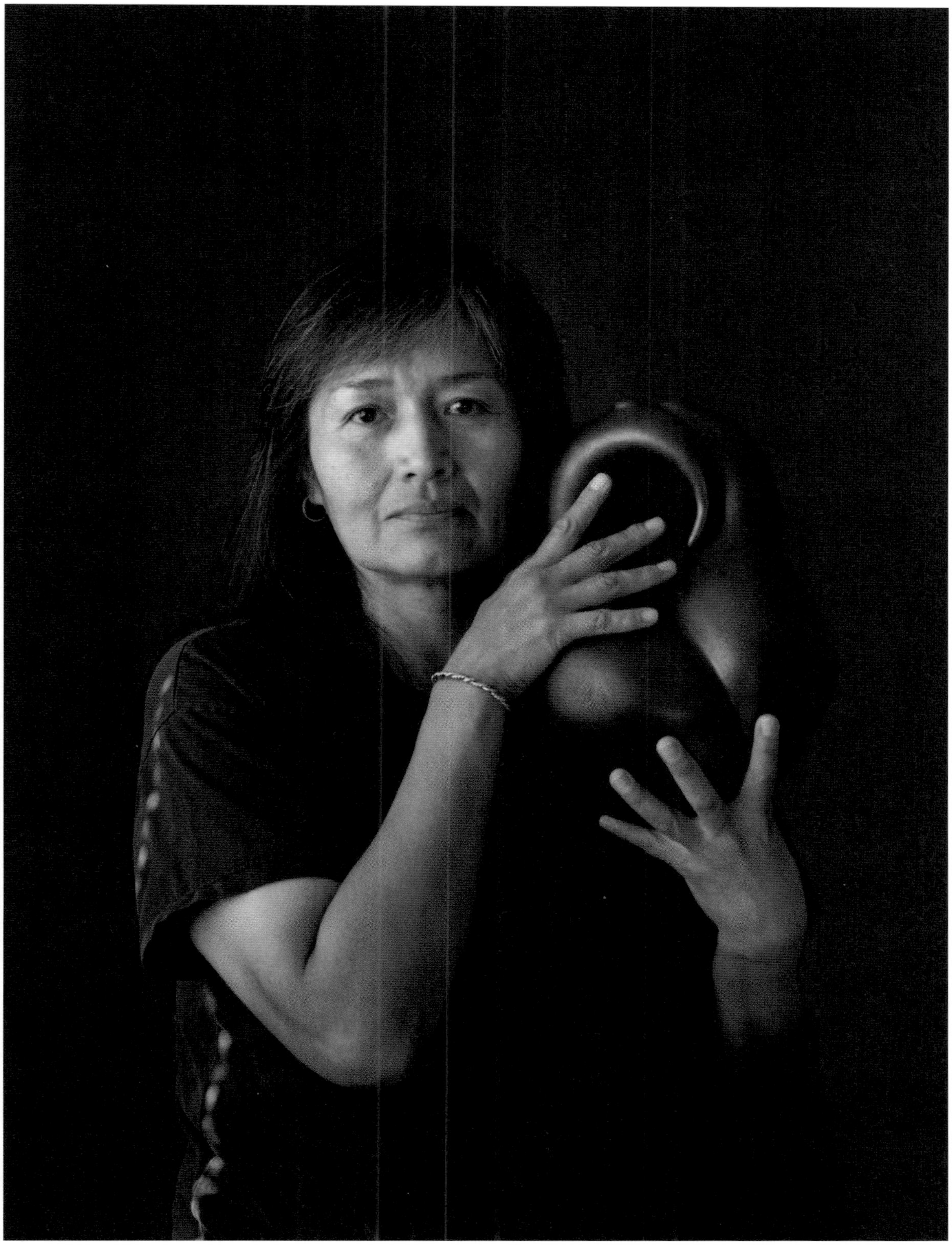

13

CHRISTINE McHORSE

Traditional and Contemporary Micaceous Potter

Navajo

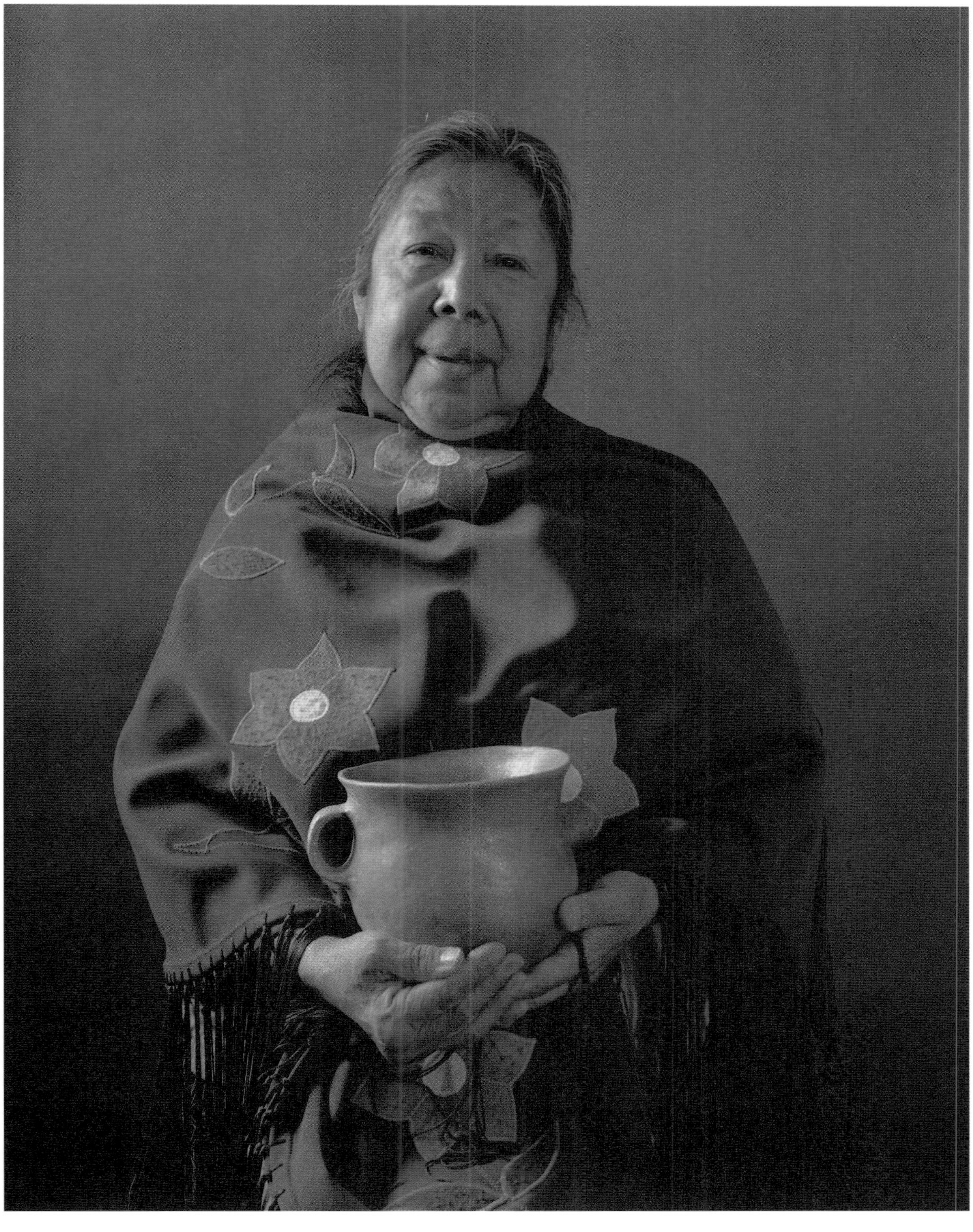

14

MARGARET ARCHULETA

Traditional Micaceous Potter, Weaving, Beadwork

Picurís Pueblo

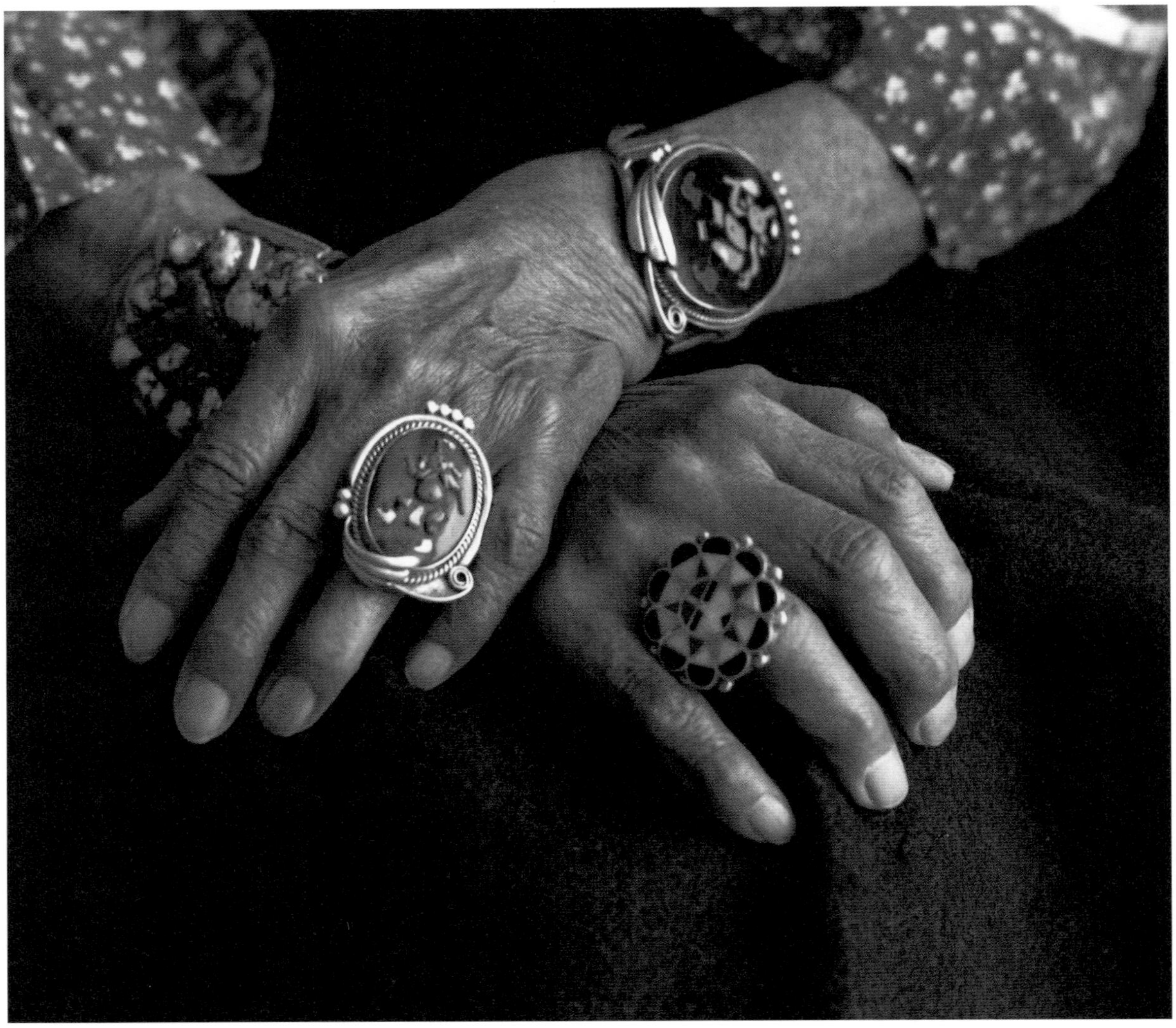

15

PABLITA VELARDE'S hands

Santa Clara Pueblo

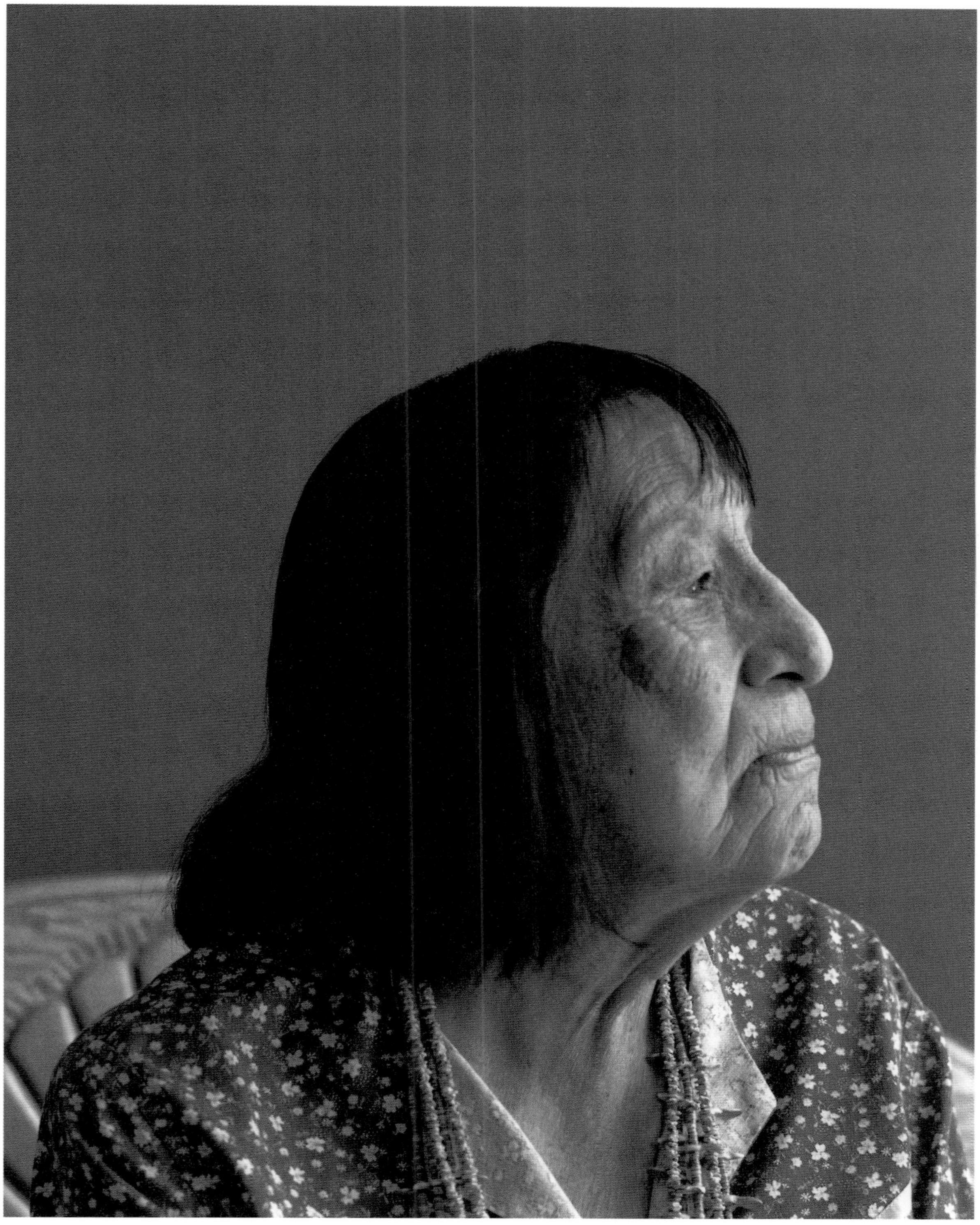

16

PABLITA VELARDE

Painter, Dorothy Dunn School of Southwest Indian Painting

Santa Clara Pueblo

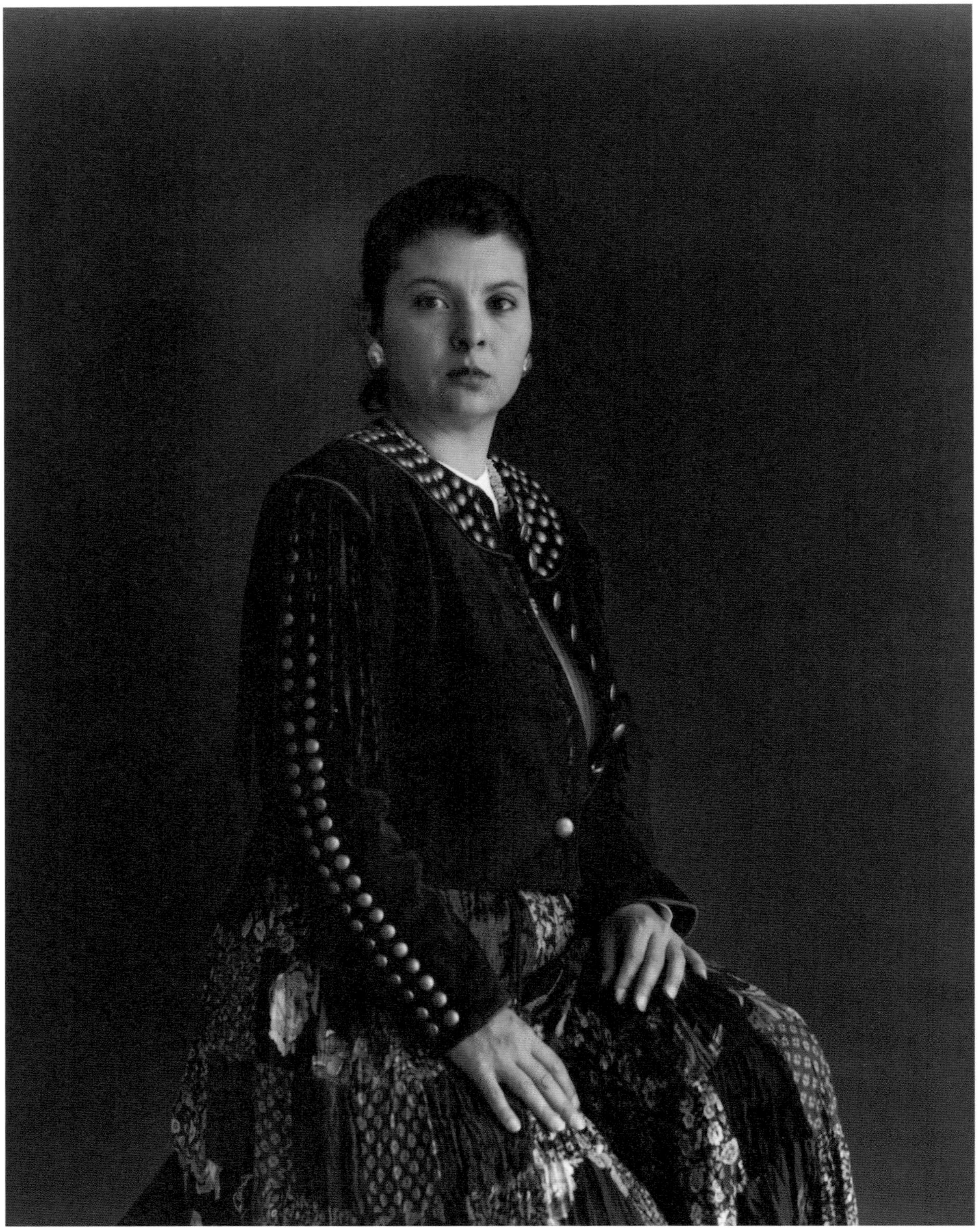

17

MARGARETE BAGSHAW-TINDEL

Pablita Velarde's granddaughter

Abstract Artist

Santa Clara Pueblo

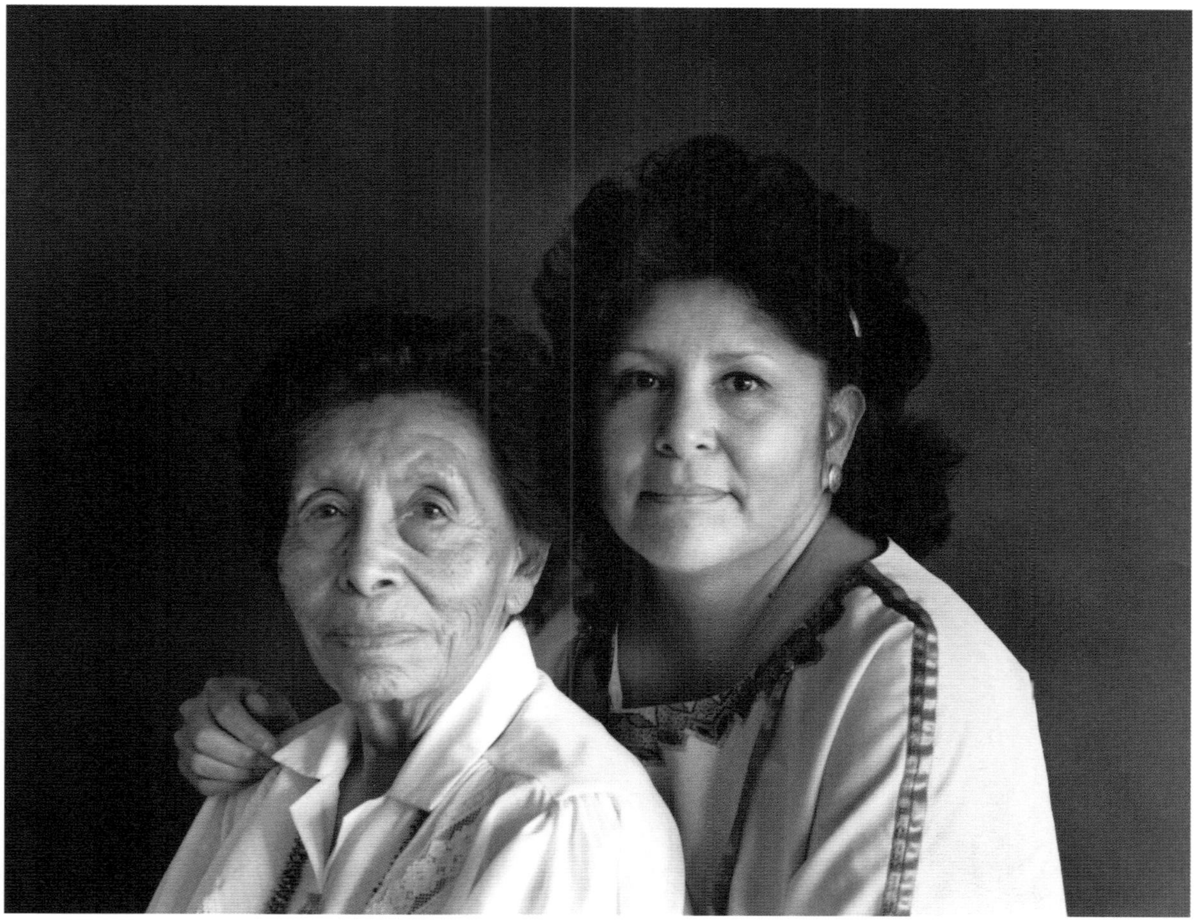

18

JANE BACA
Pablita Velarde's sister
with daughter STARR TAFOYA
Traditional Potters
Santa Clara Pueblo

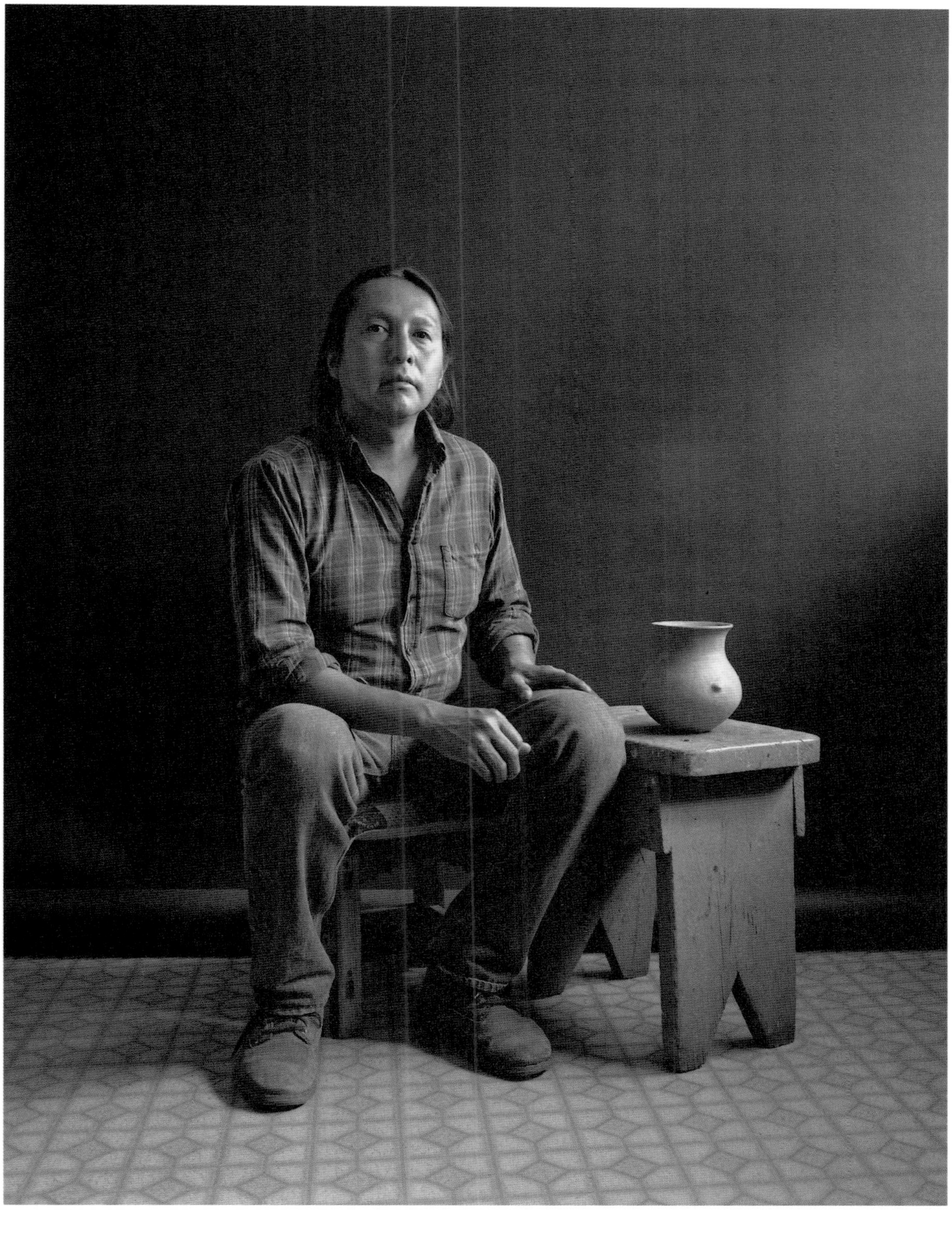

19

ANTHONY DURAND

Traditional and Contemporary Micaceous Potter

Picurís Pueblo

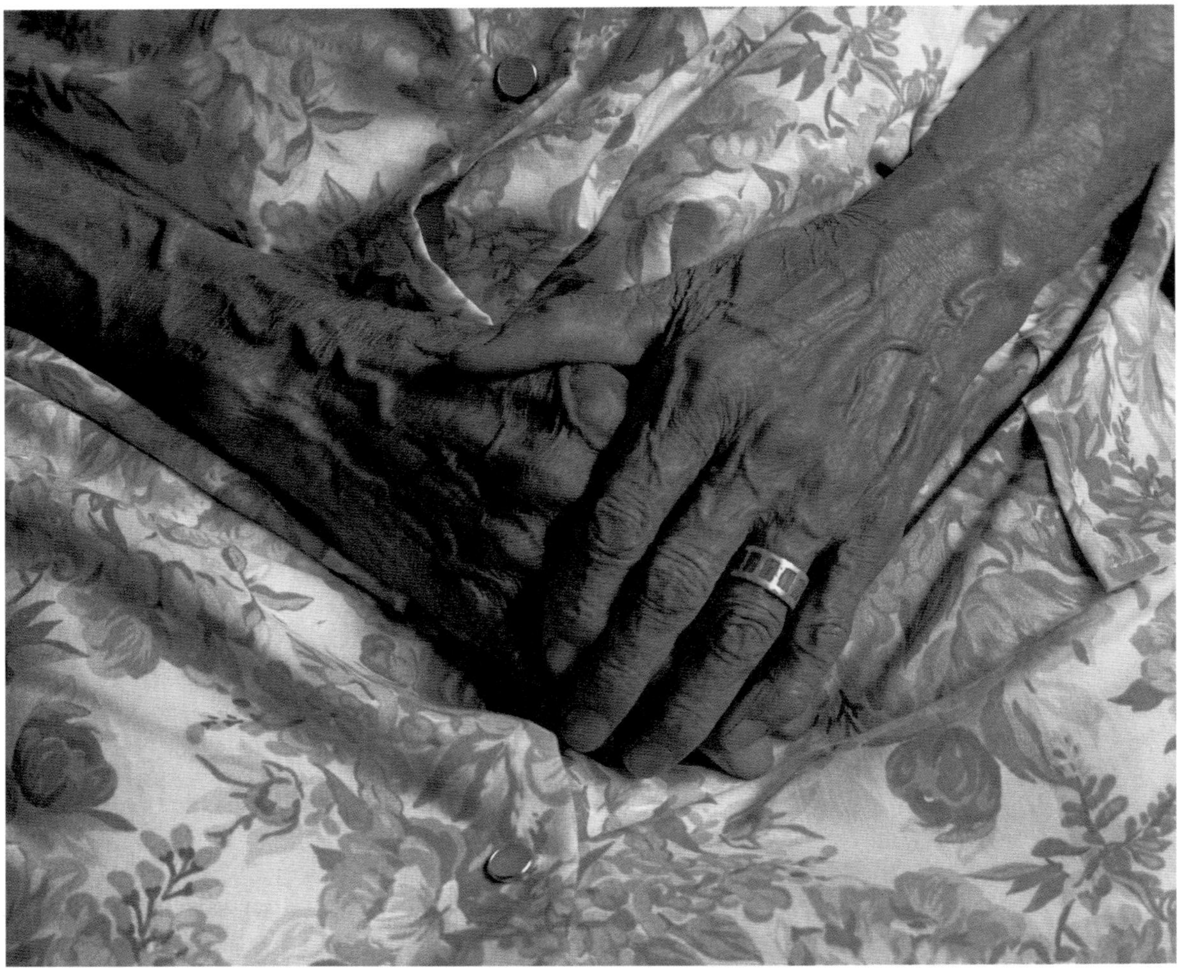

20

CORA L. DURAND'S hands

Traditional Micaceous Potter

Picurís Pueblo

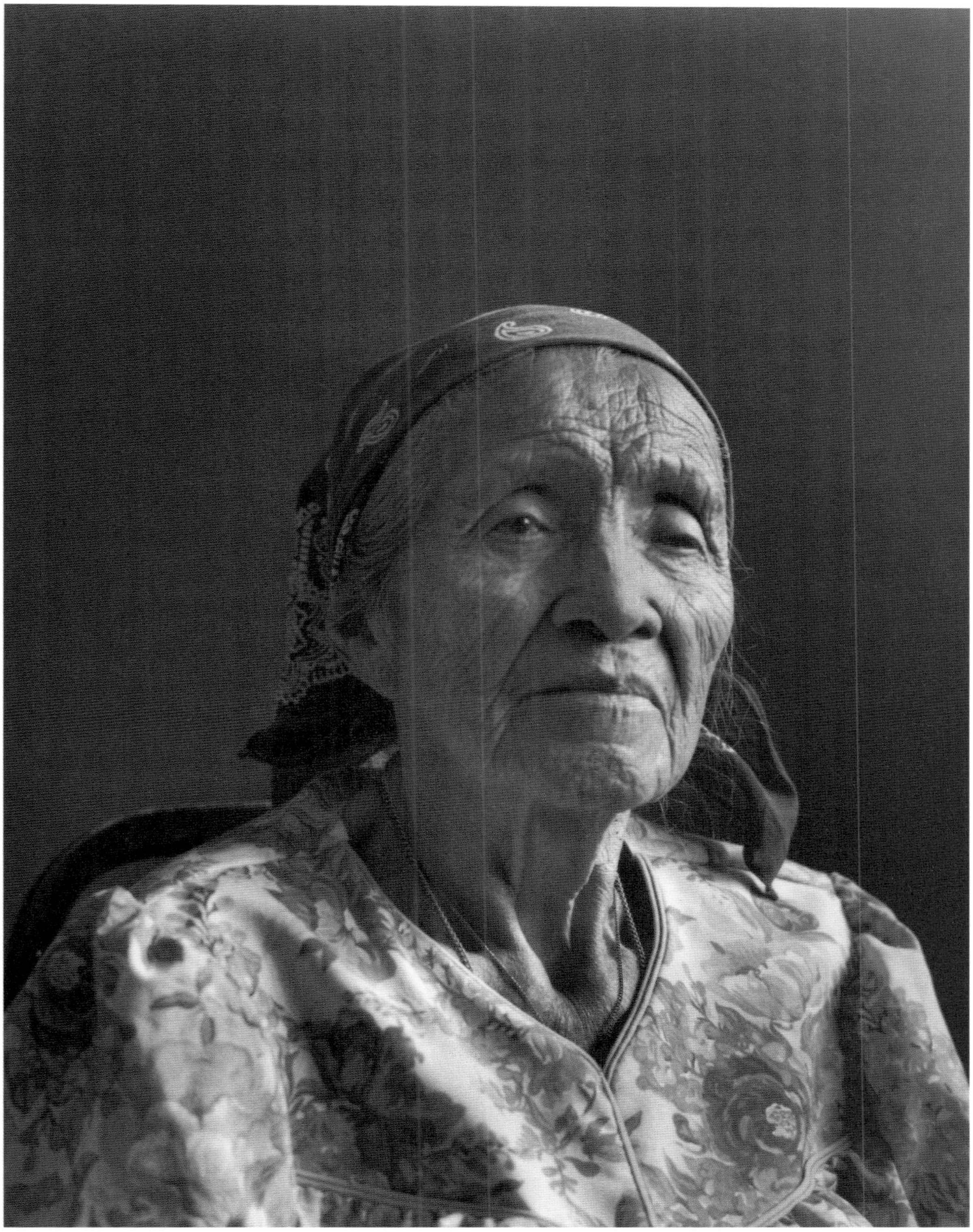

21

CORA L. DURAND, age ninety-three

Anthony Durand's grandmother

Traditional Micaceous Potter

Picurís Pueblo

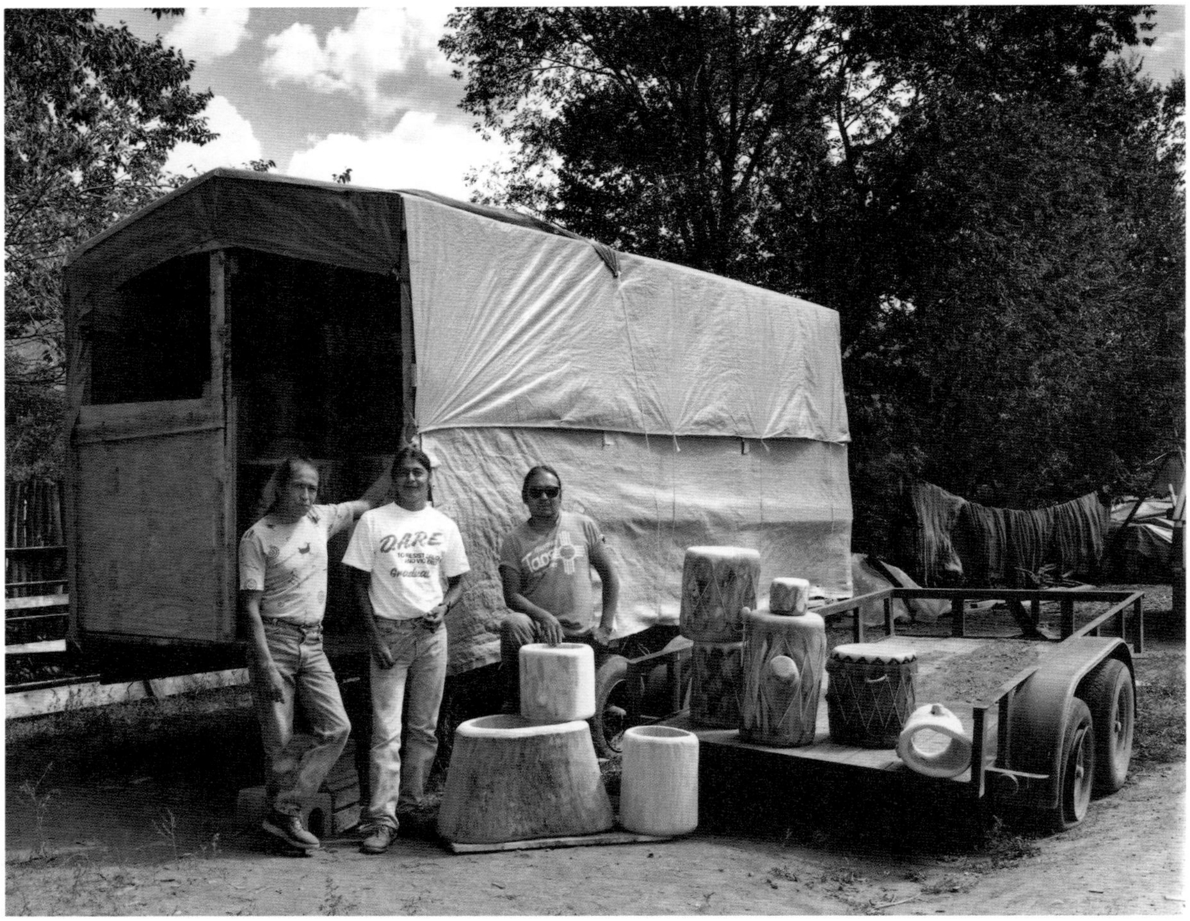

22

PHILLIP C. MARTINEZ

with brothers DAVID and BENITO MARTINEZ

Traditional Drum Makers

Taos Pueblo

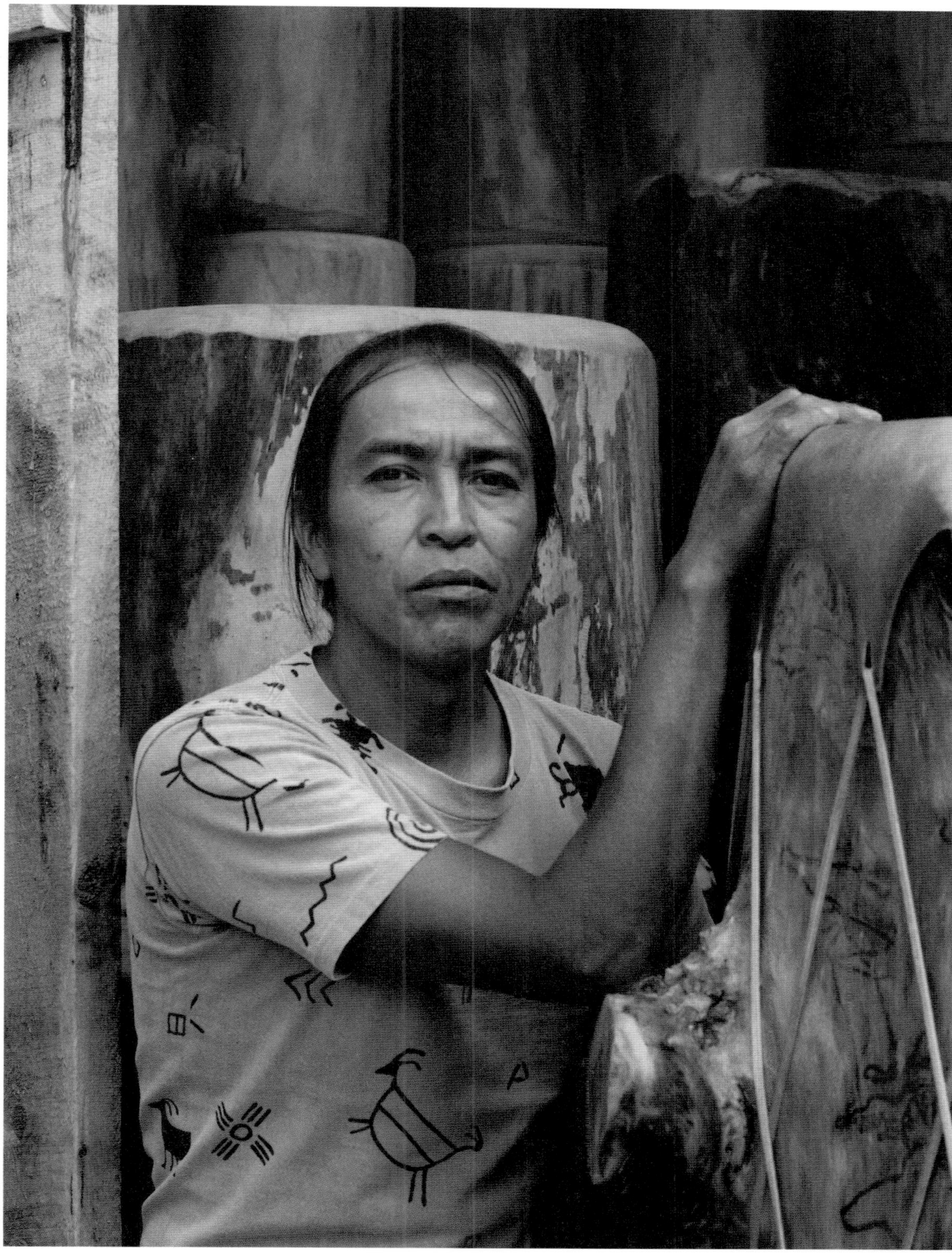

23
PHILLIP C. MARTINEZ
Traditional Drum Maker
Taos Pueblo

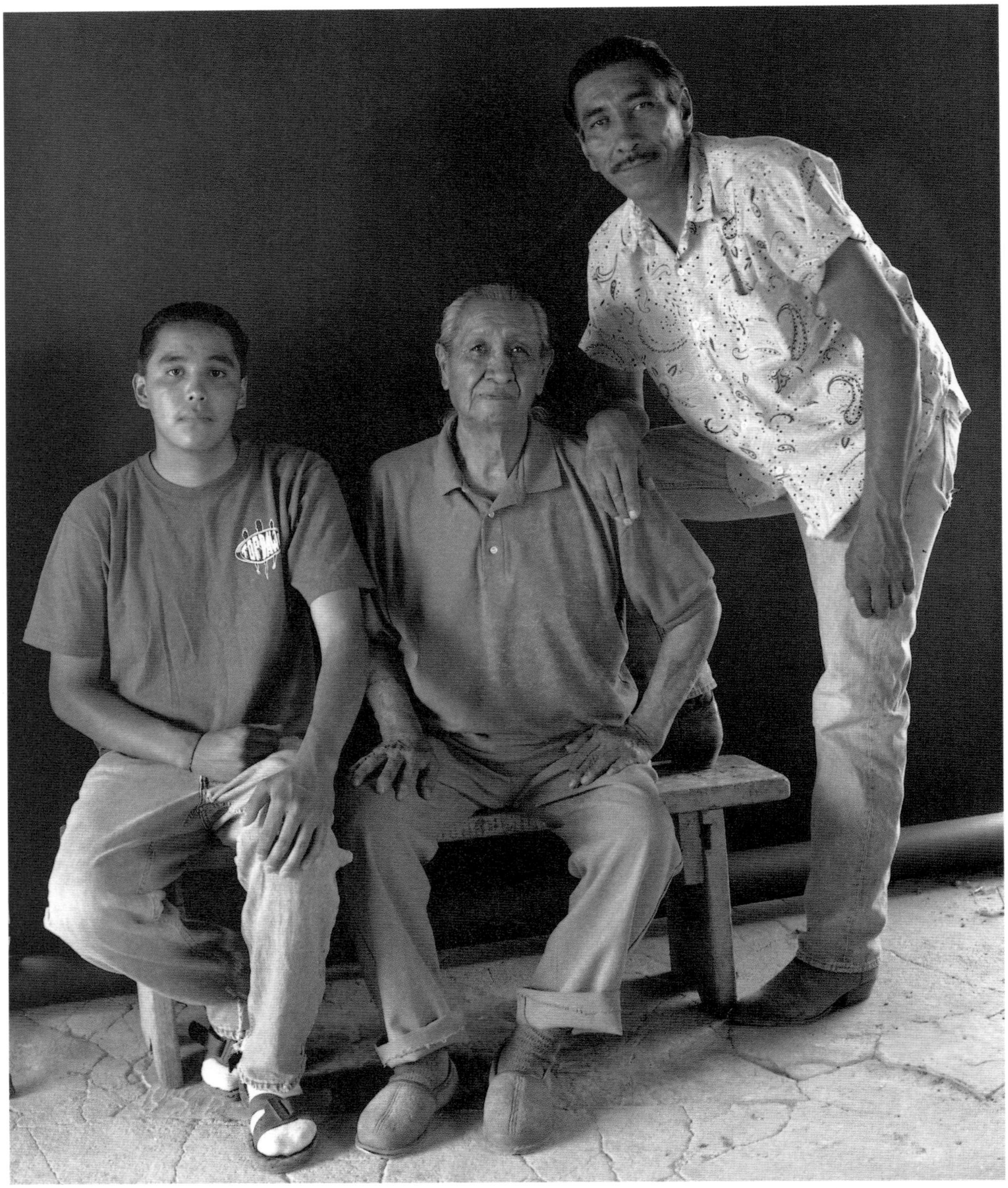

24

RALPH SUAZO

with nephew JOHN SUAZO and John's son SHAW SUAZO

Wood-carvers, Stone Sculptors

Taos Pueblo

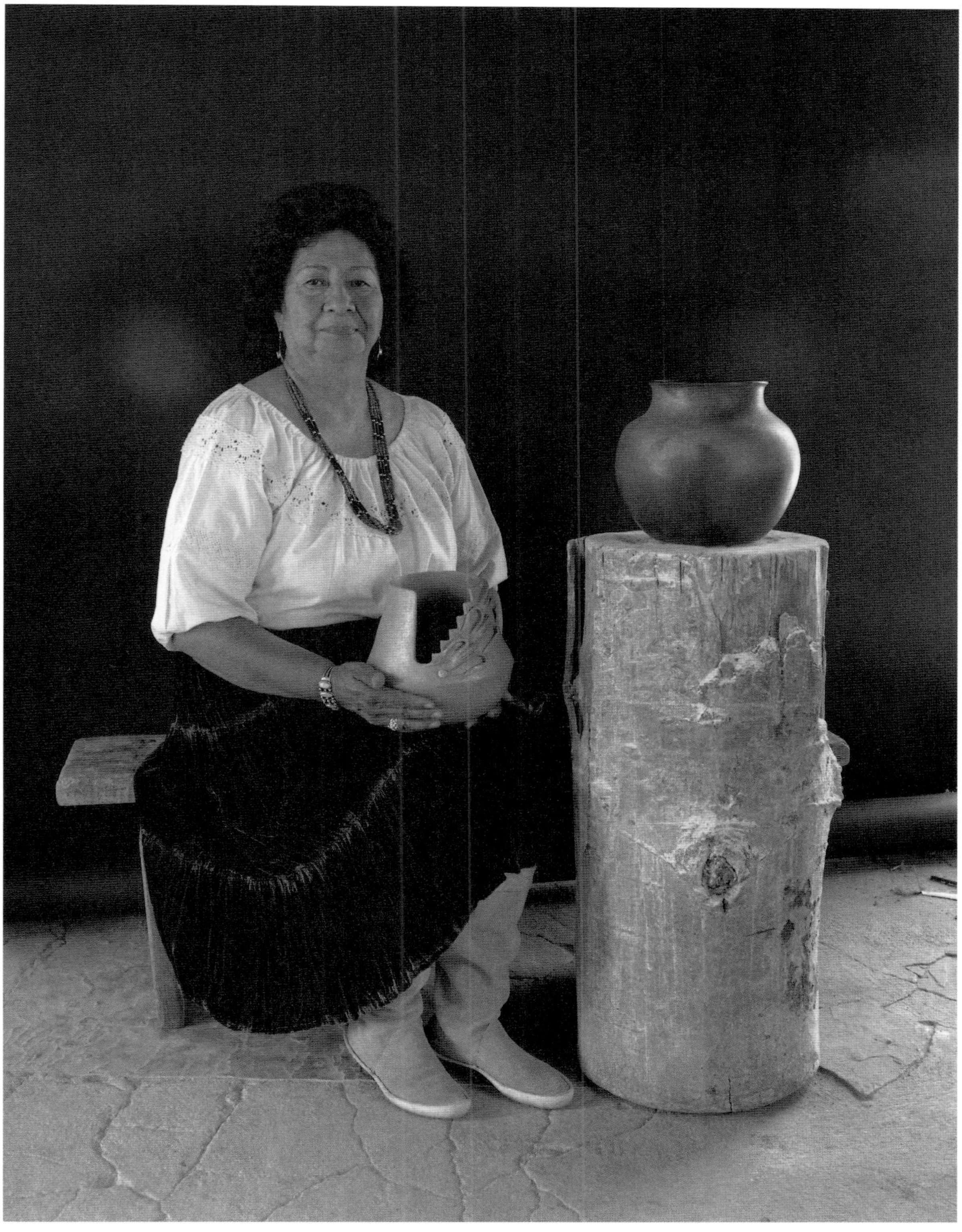

25

JUANITA SUAZO-DUBRAY

John Suazo's mother

Traditional Micaceous Potter

Taos Pueblo

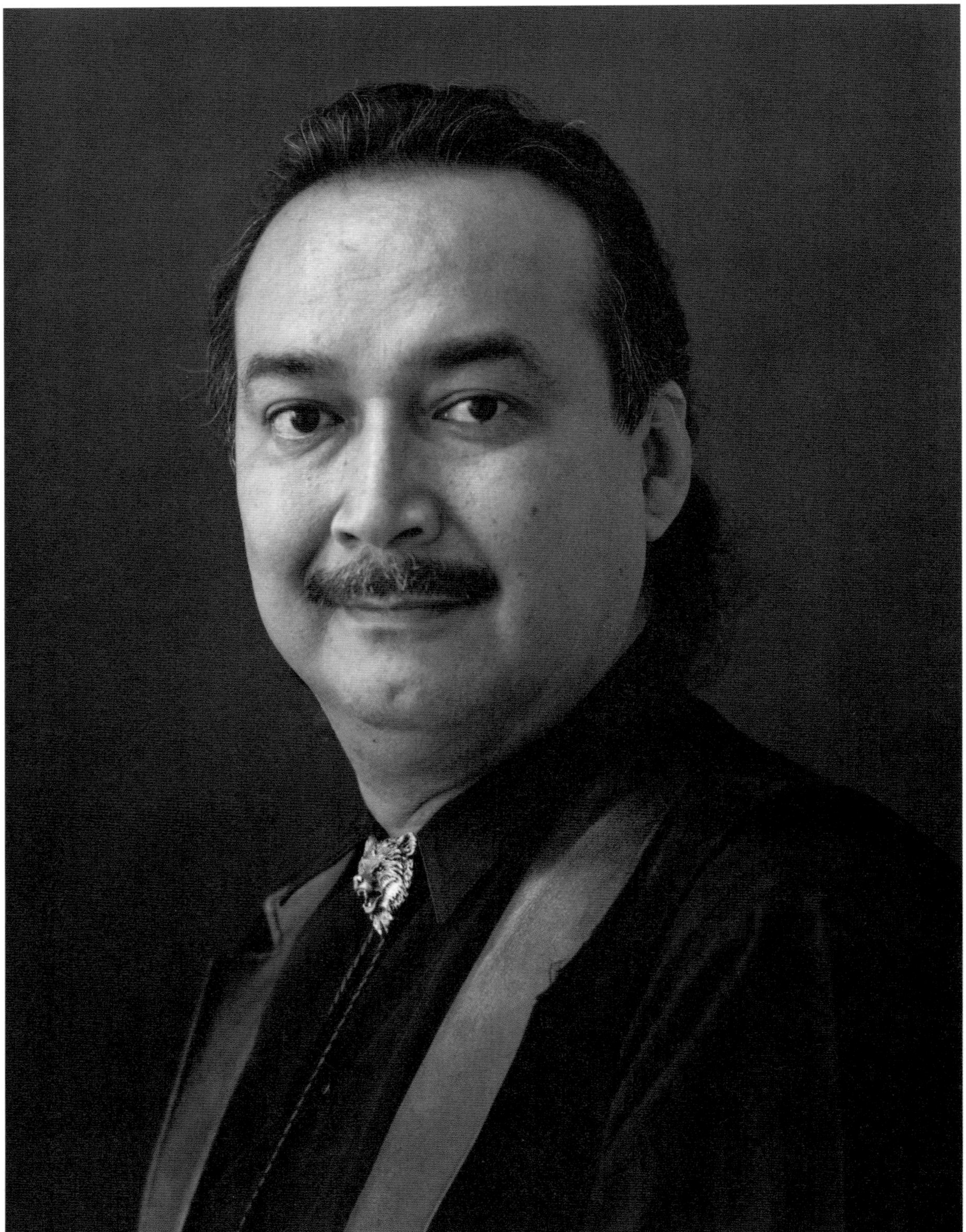

26

NORMAN PACHECO

Artist — Painter, Murals, Woodcarver

San Juan Pueblo

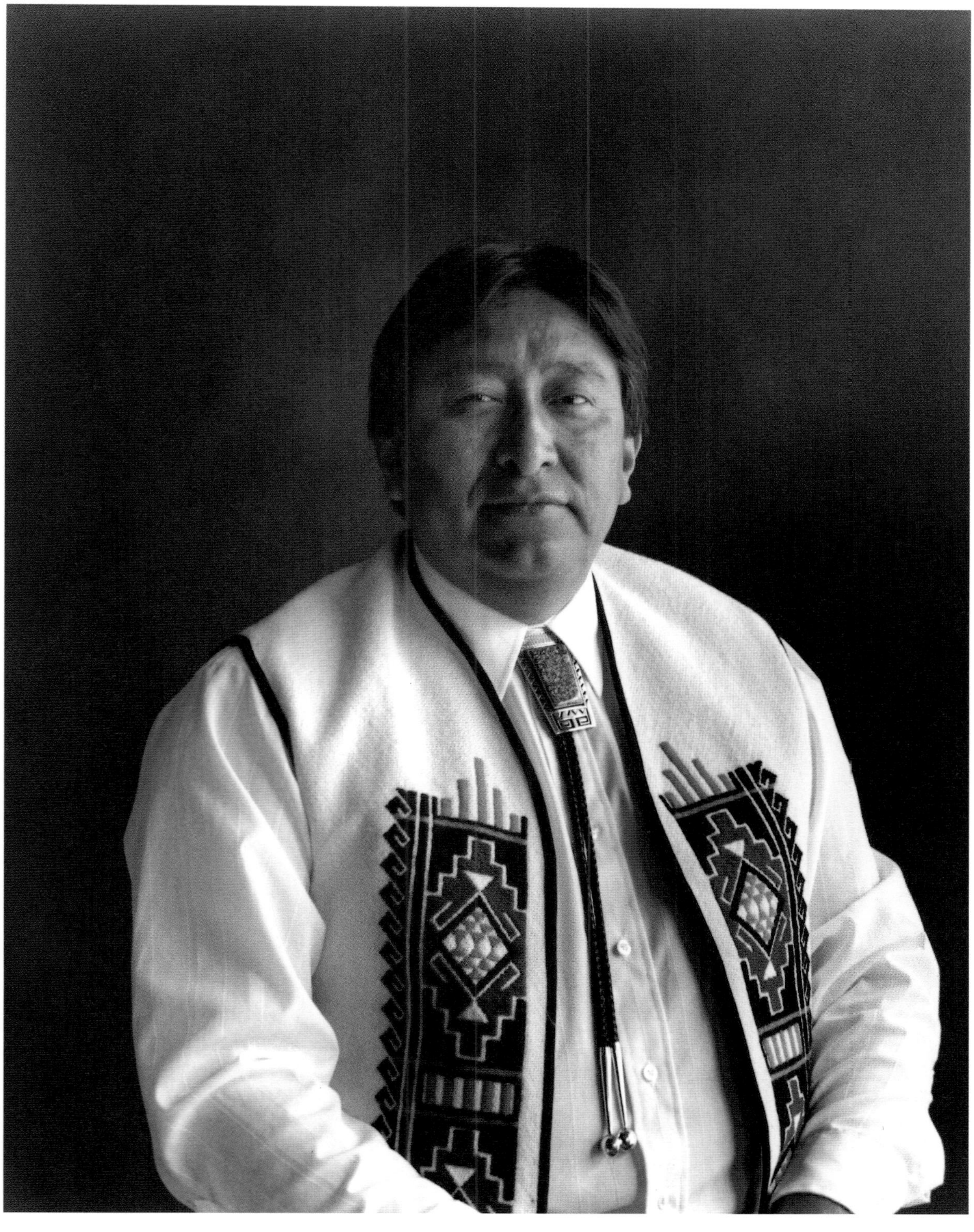

27

MIKE BIRD-ROMERO

Silversmith

San Juan Pueblo

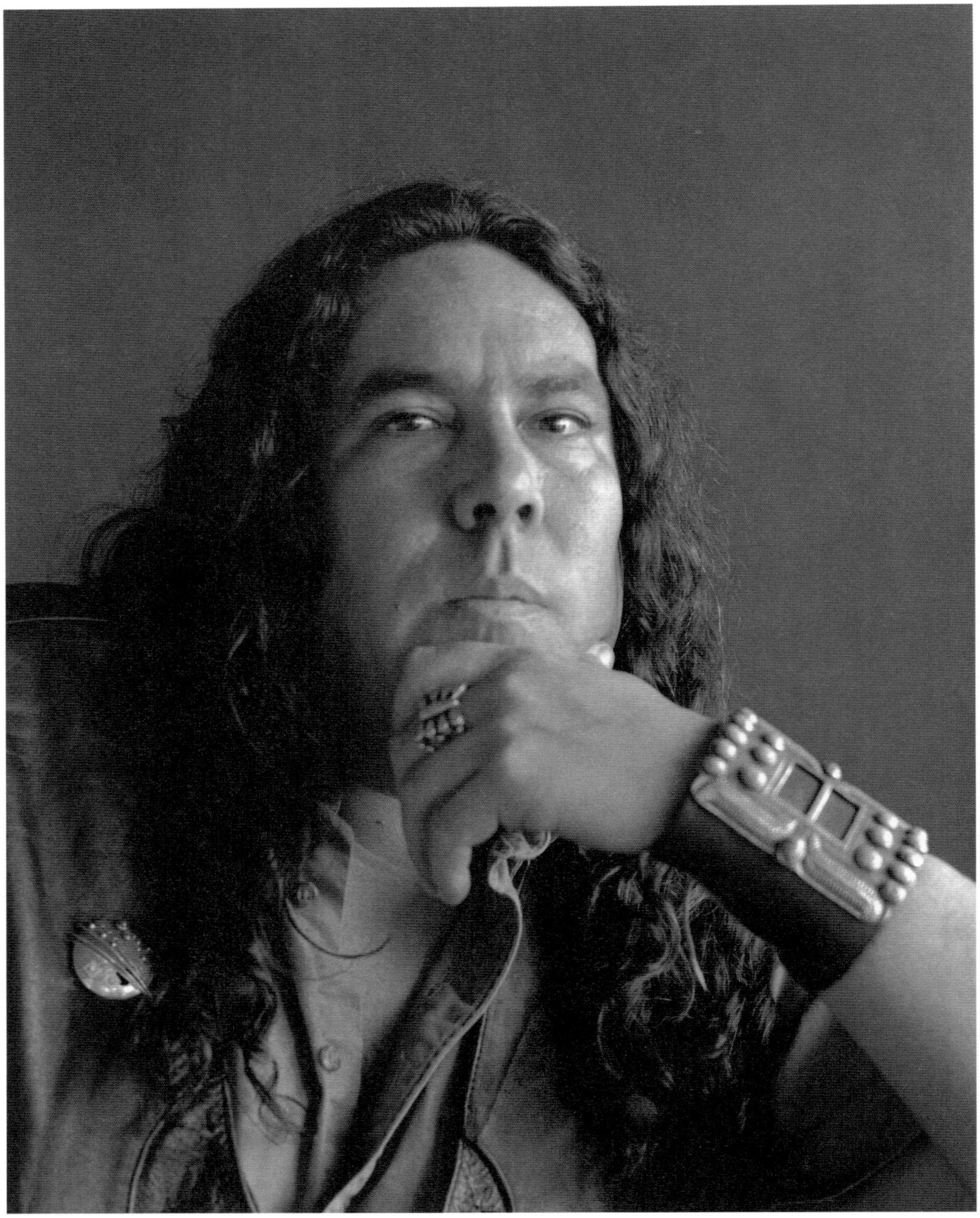

28

MARK SWAZO-HINDS

Artist, Sculptor

Tesuque Pueblo

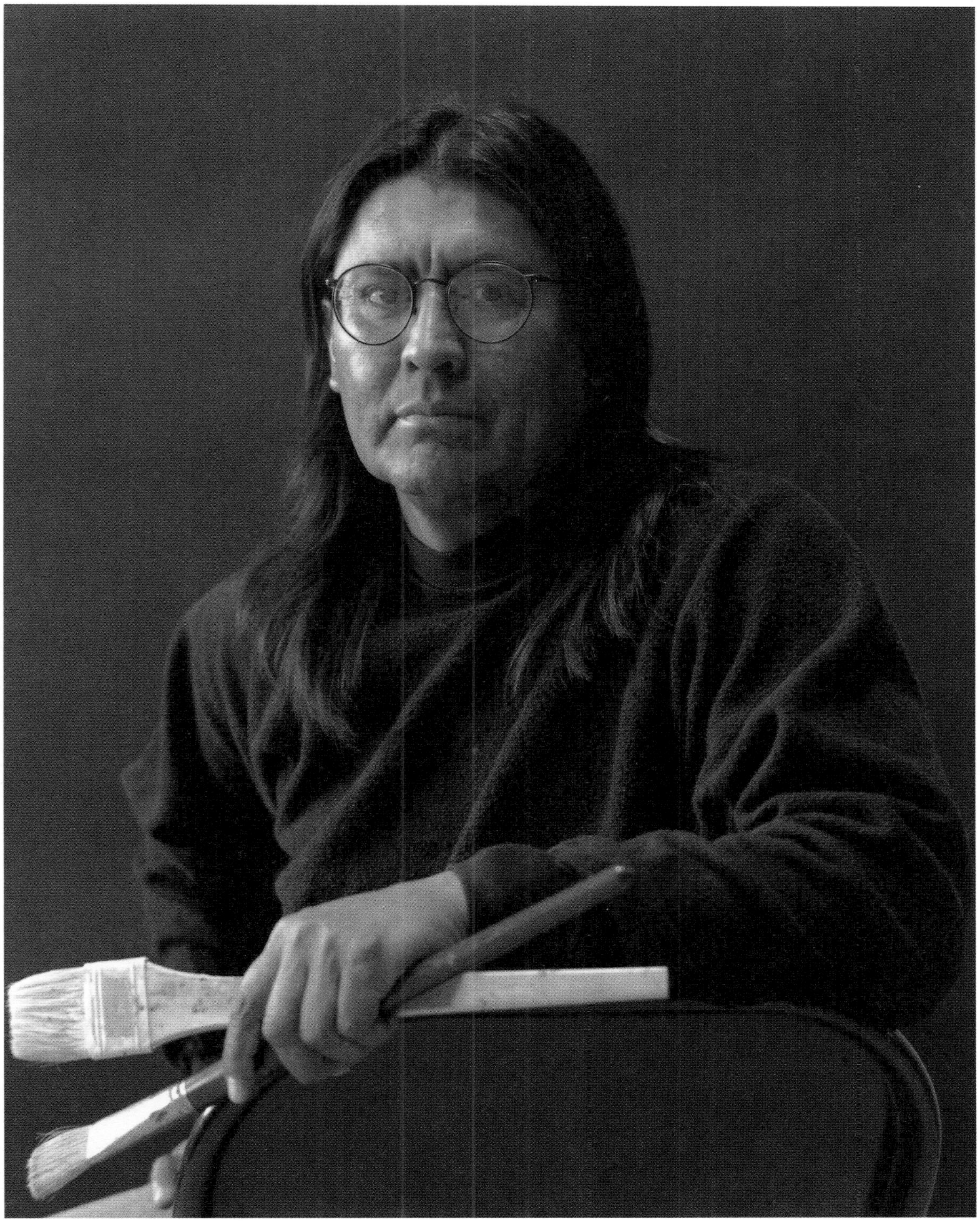

29

FELIX VIGIL

Contemporary Painter in Mixed Media and Oil Paints

Jicarilla Apache/Jémez Pueblo

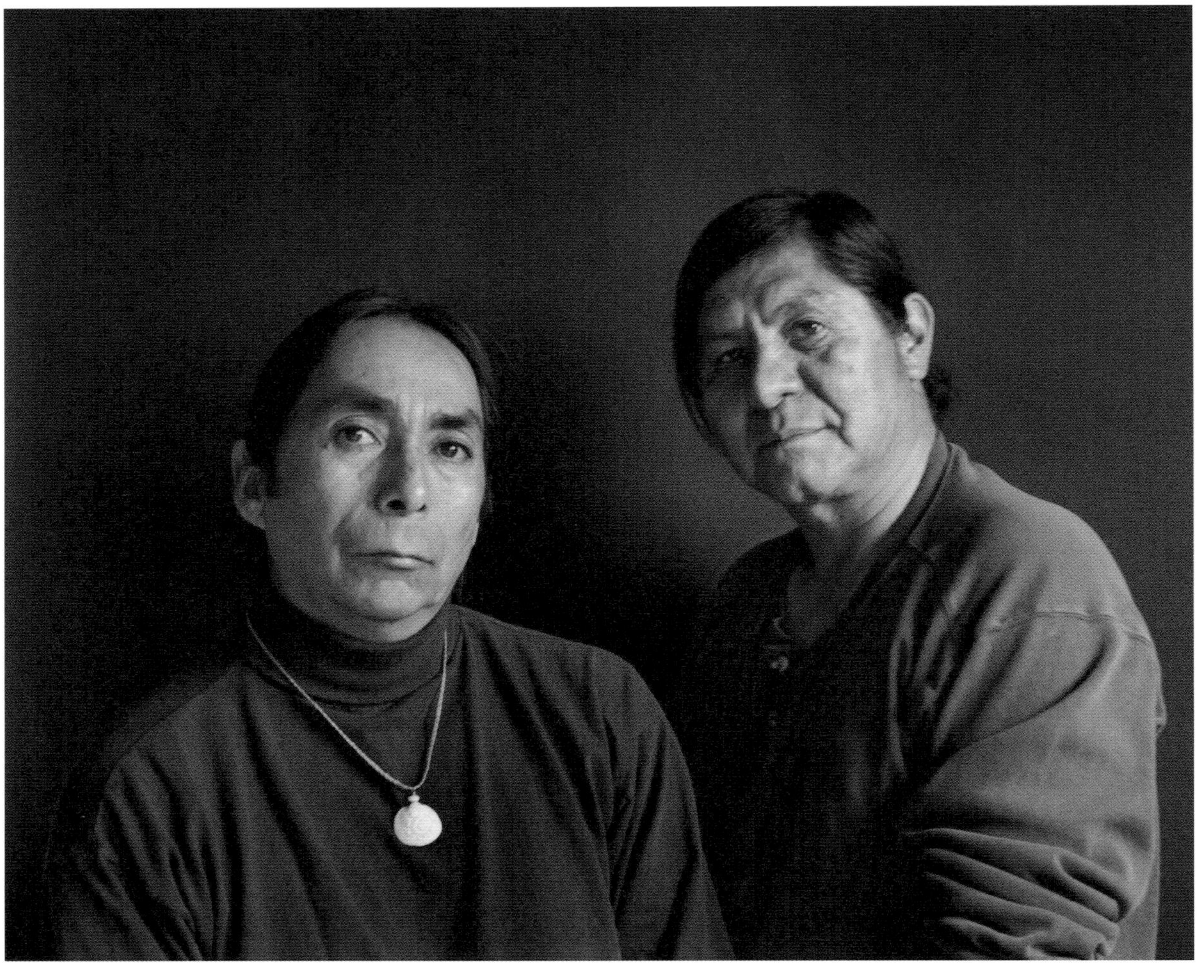

30

JONATHAN WARM DAY, Painter,

with friend DAWN ANTELOPE, Traditional Micaceous Potter

Taos Pueblo

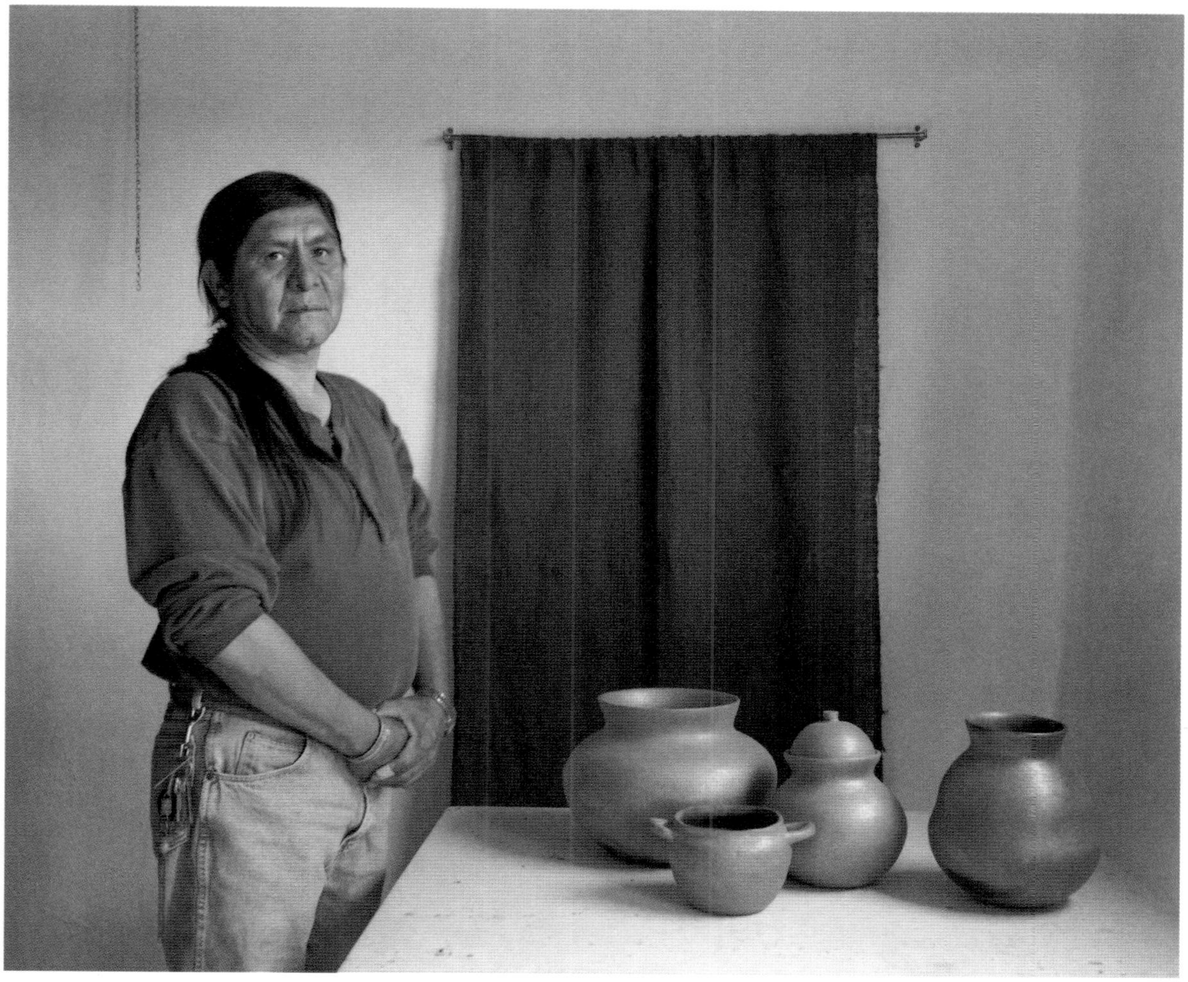

31

DAWN ANTELOPE

Traditional Micaceous Potter

Taos Pueblo

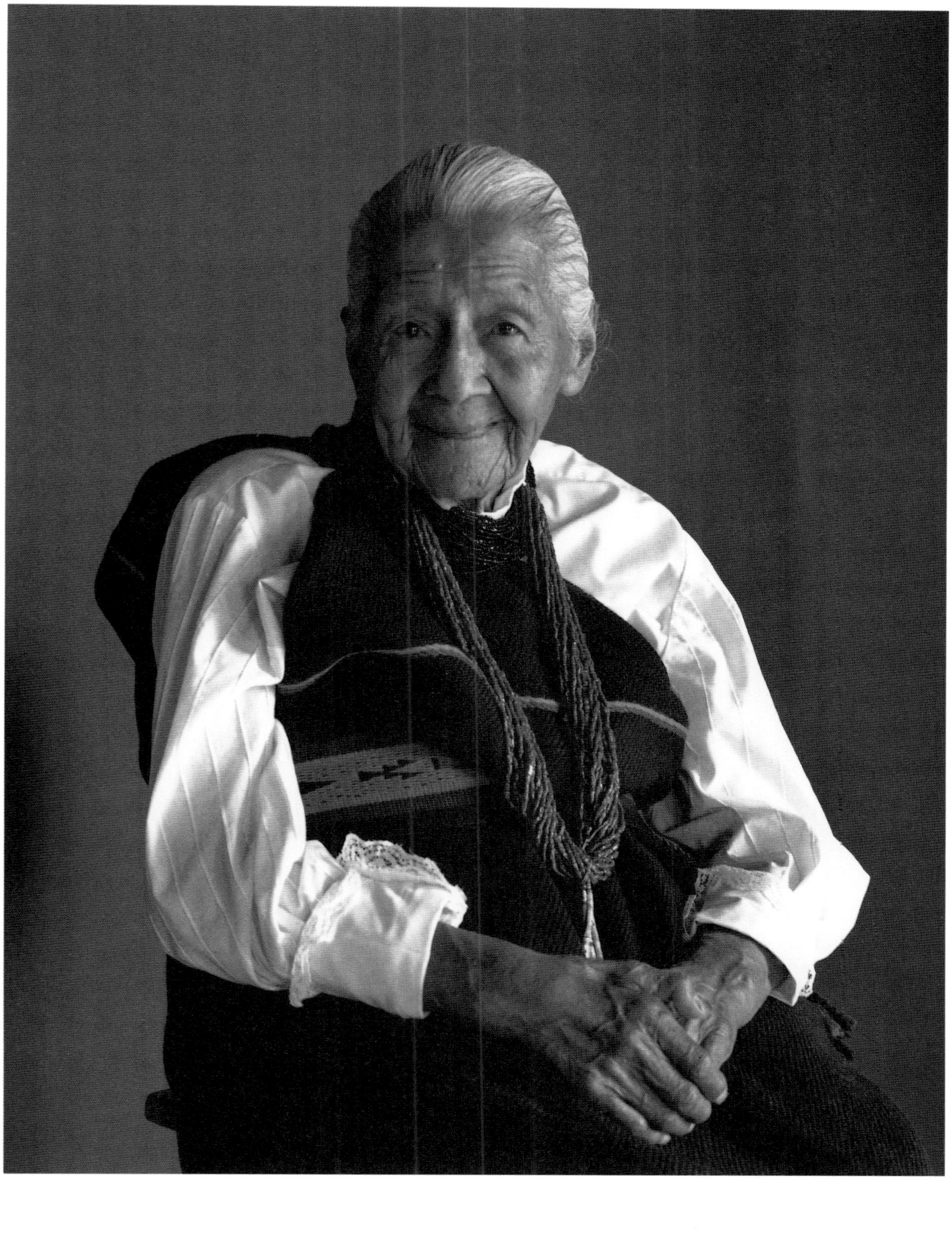

32

MARGARET TAFOYA, age ninety-one

Matriarch of Tafoya Family

Artist of Traditional Pottery

Santa Clara Pueblo

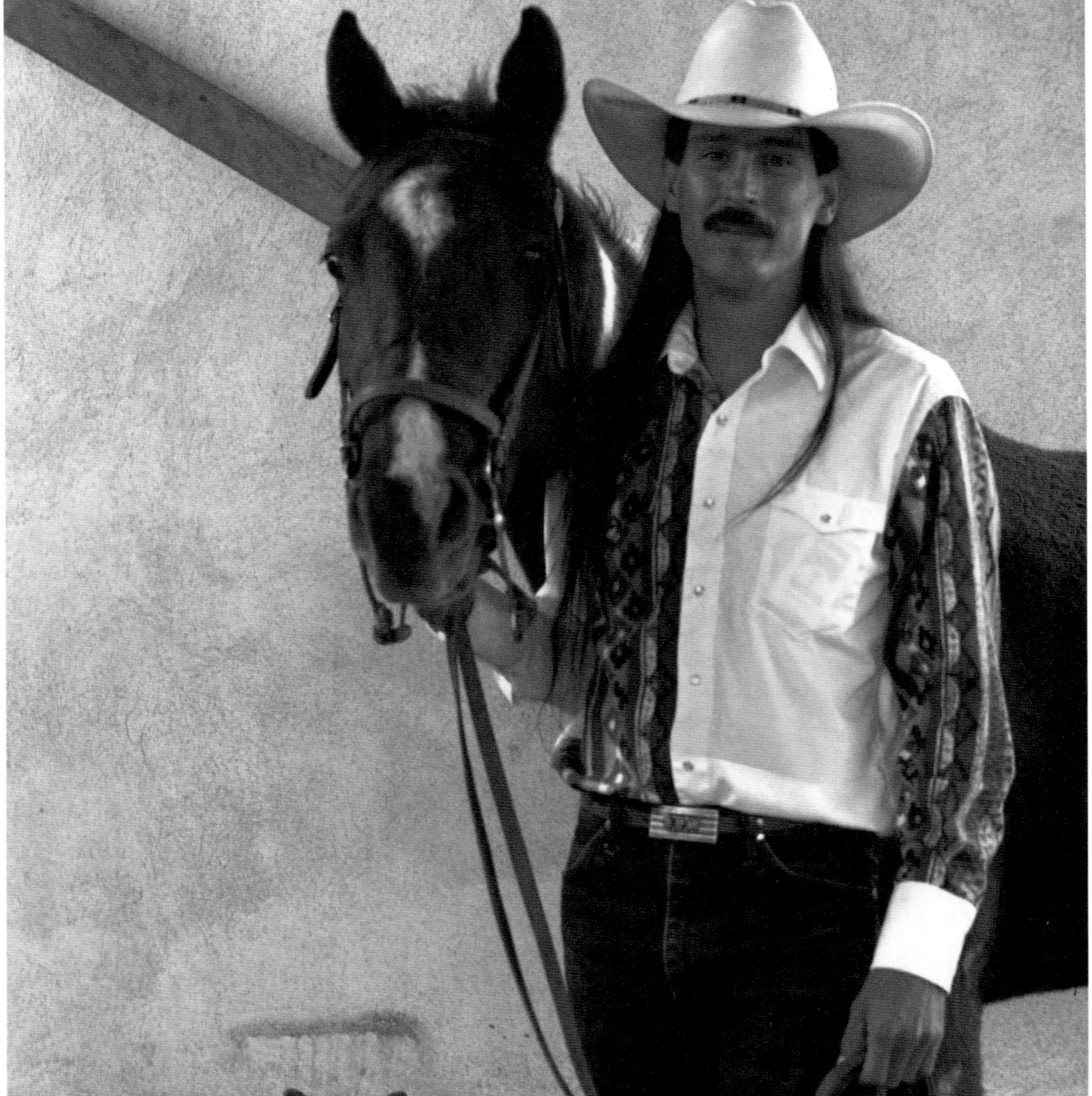

33
JEFF ROLLER
with horse "Baby" and dog "Saga"
Margaret Tafoya's grandson
Traditional and Contemporary Potter
Santa Clara Pueblo

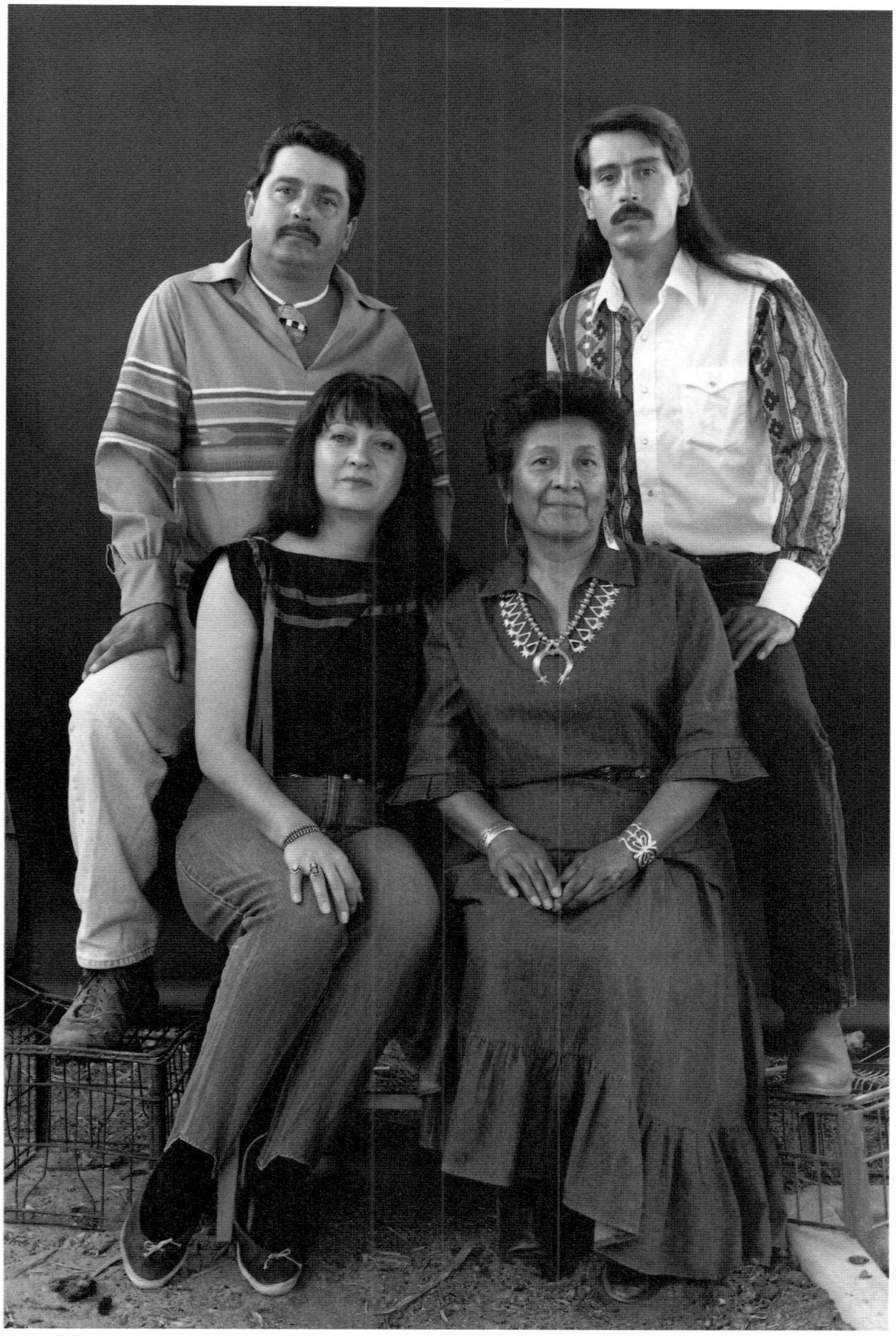

34

TONI ROLLER

Margaret Tafoya's daughter

with children CLIFF, JEFF, and SUSAN ROLLER

Traditional and Contemporary Potters

Santa Clara Pueblo

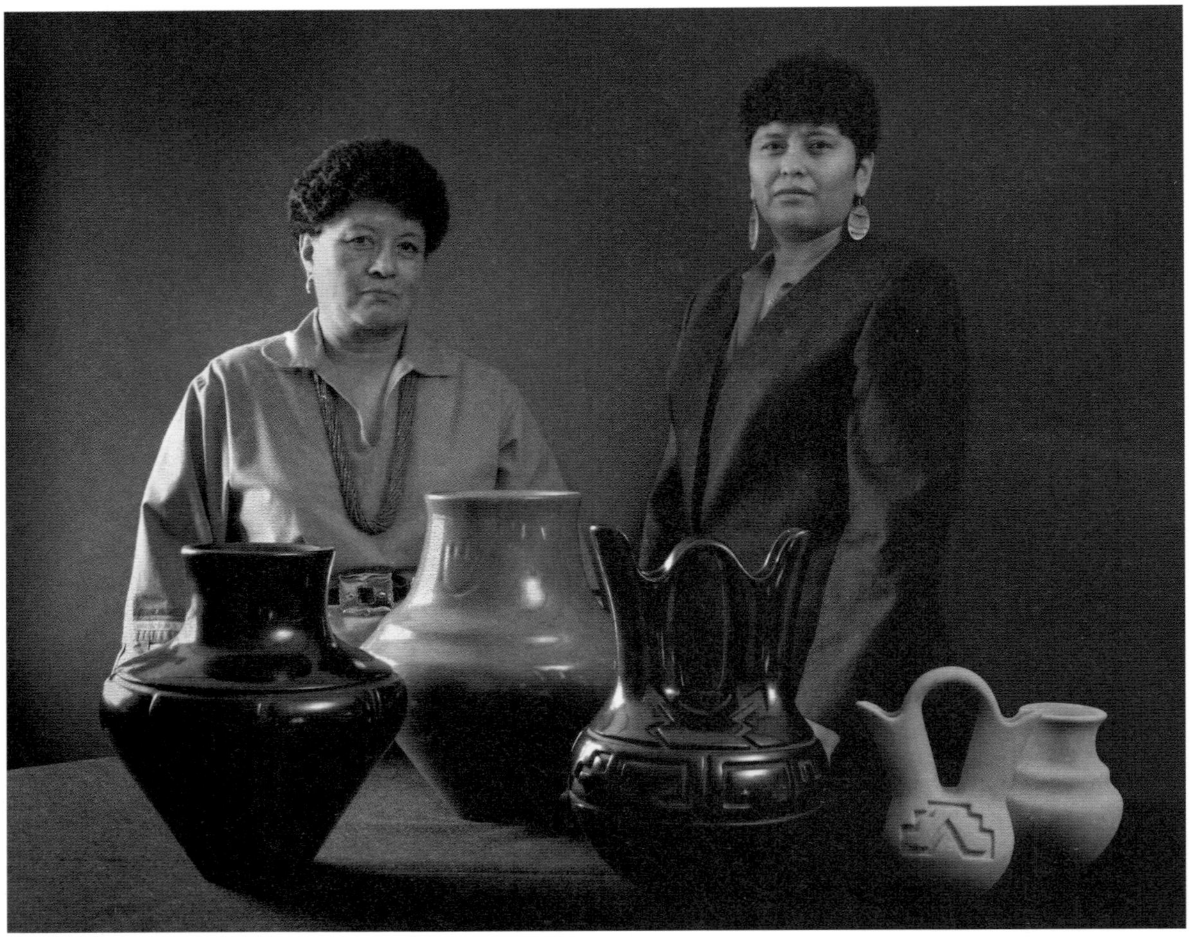

35
LU ANN TAFOYA
with daughter MICHELE Y. BROWNING
Margaret Tafoya's daughter and granddaughter
Traditional Potters
Santa Clara Pueblo

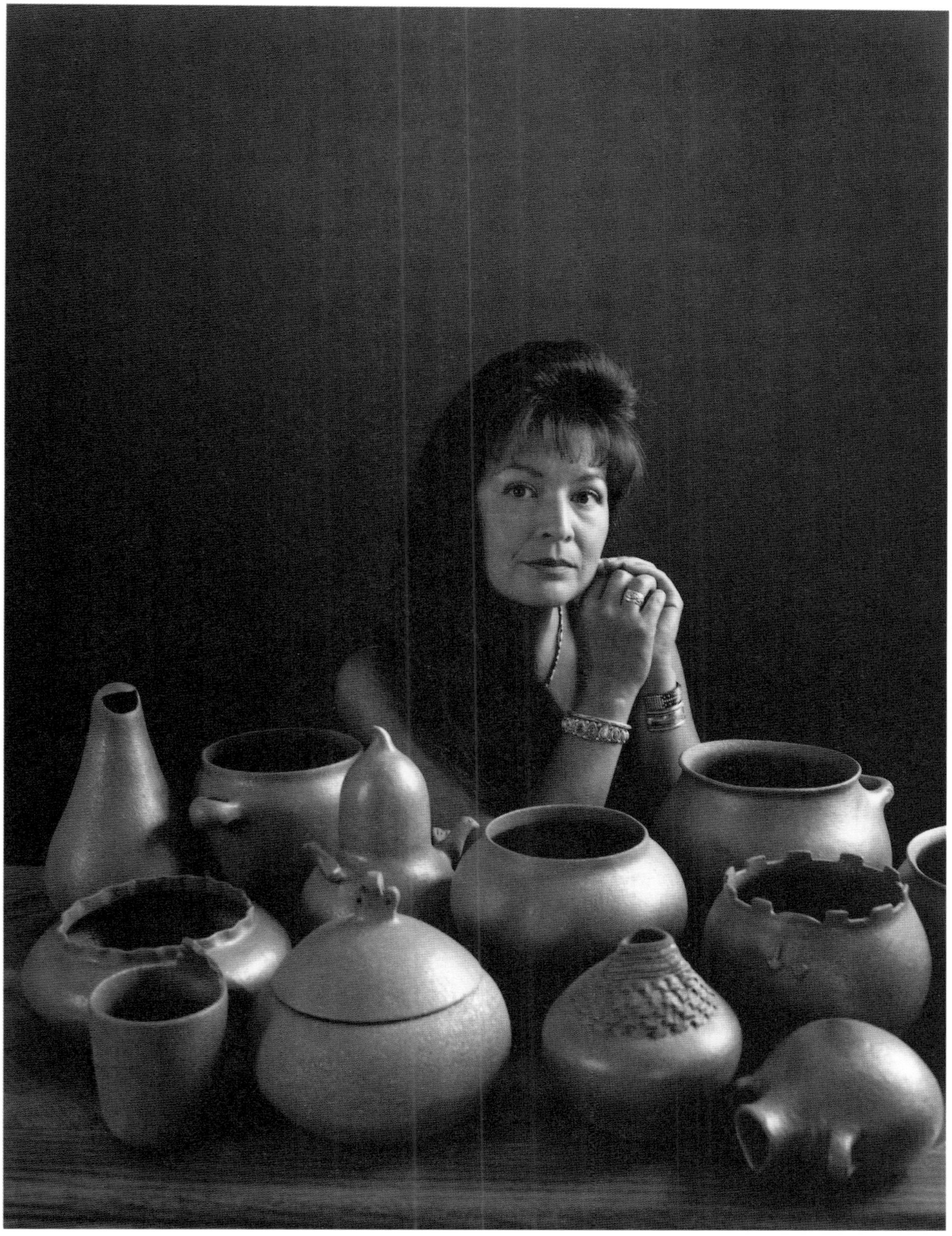

36

QUELLA (Yôe Povi) ROMERO MUSGRAVE

Traditional Micaceous Potter

Nambé Pueblo

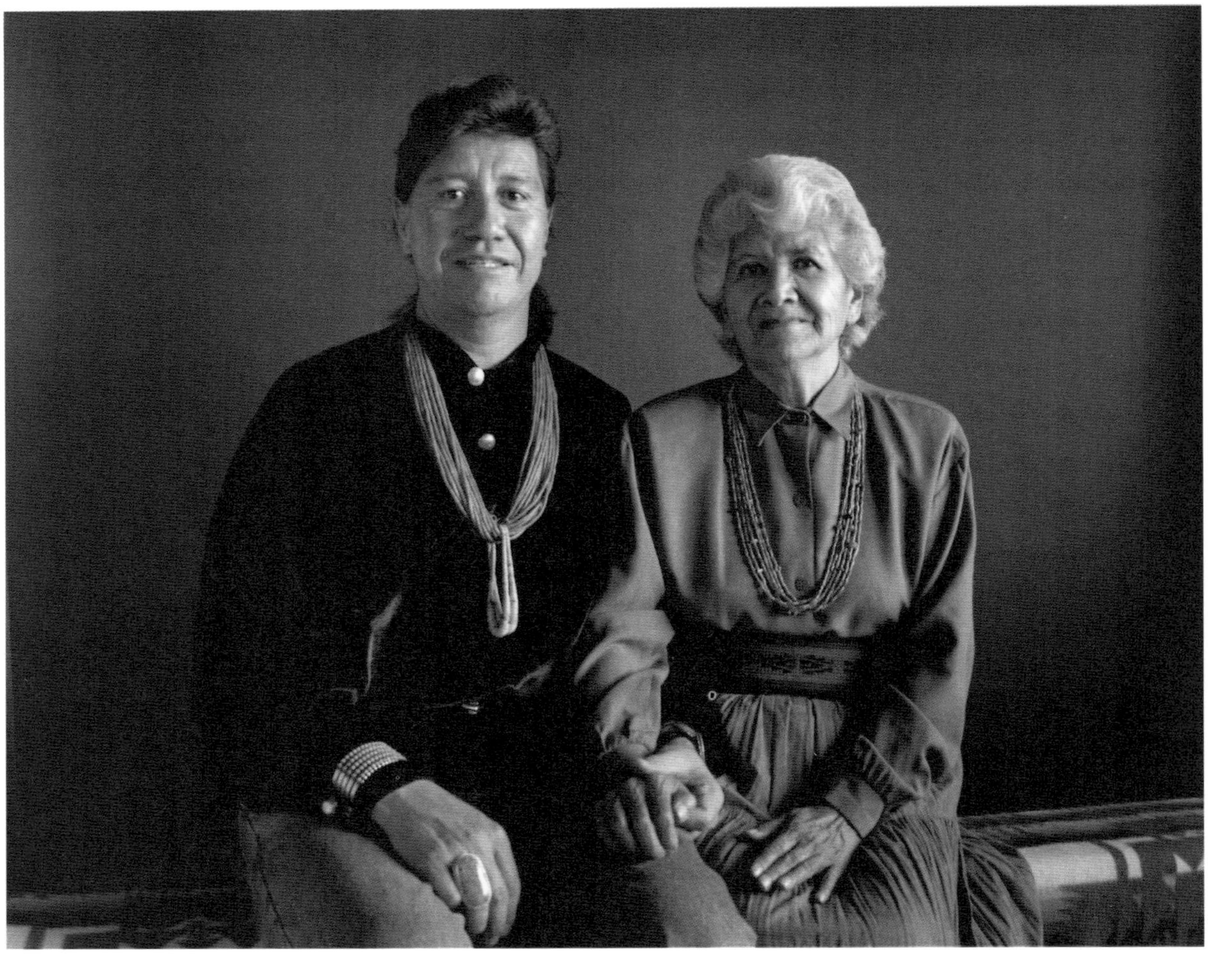

37
LONNIE VIGIL
with mother MELINDA VIGIL
Tewa Micaceous Potter
Nambé Pueblo

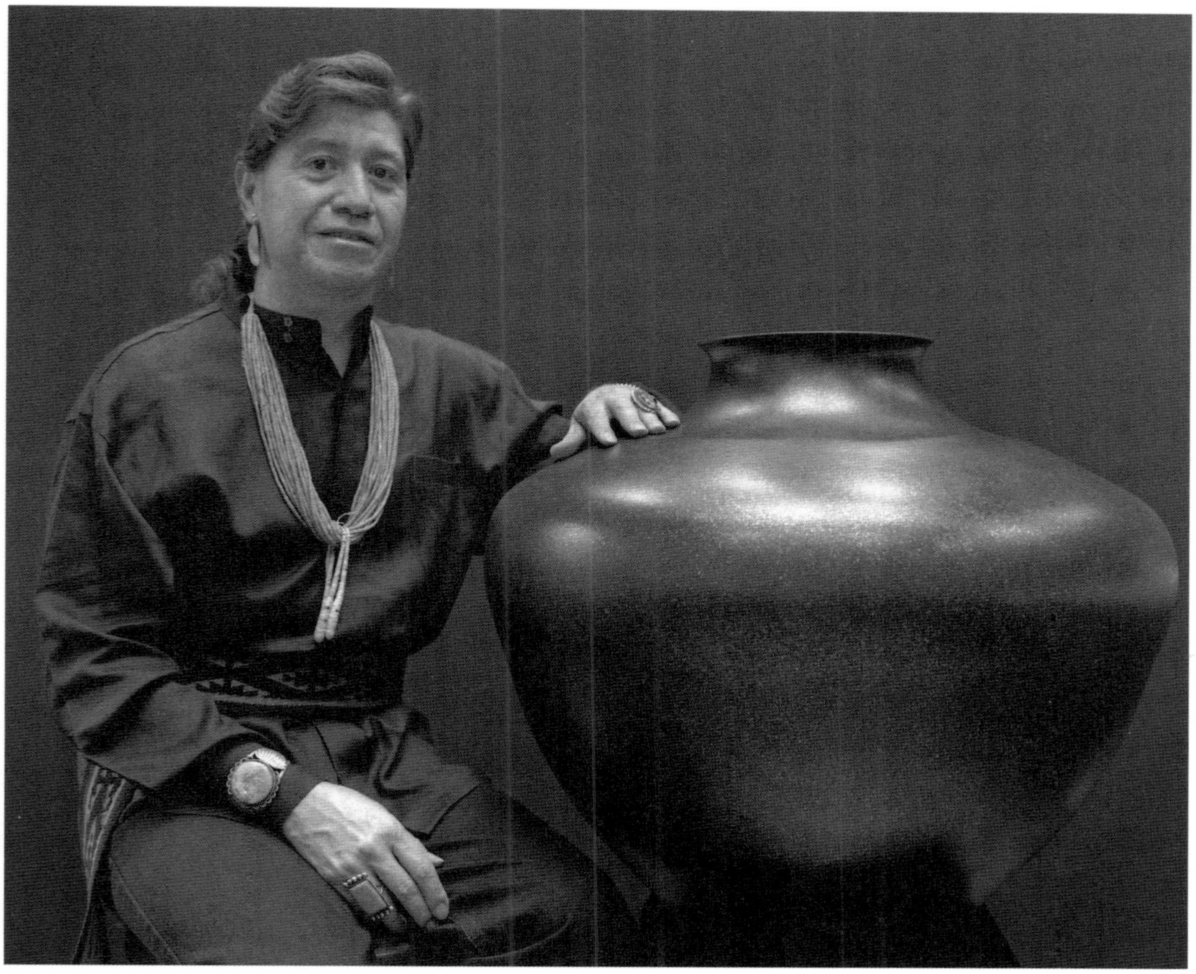

38

LONNIE VIGIL

Tewa Micaceous Potter

Nambé Pueblo

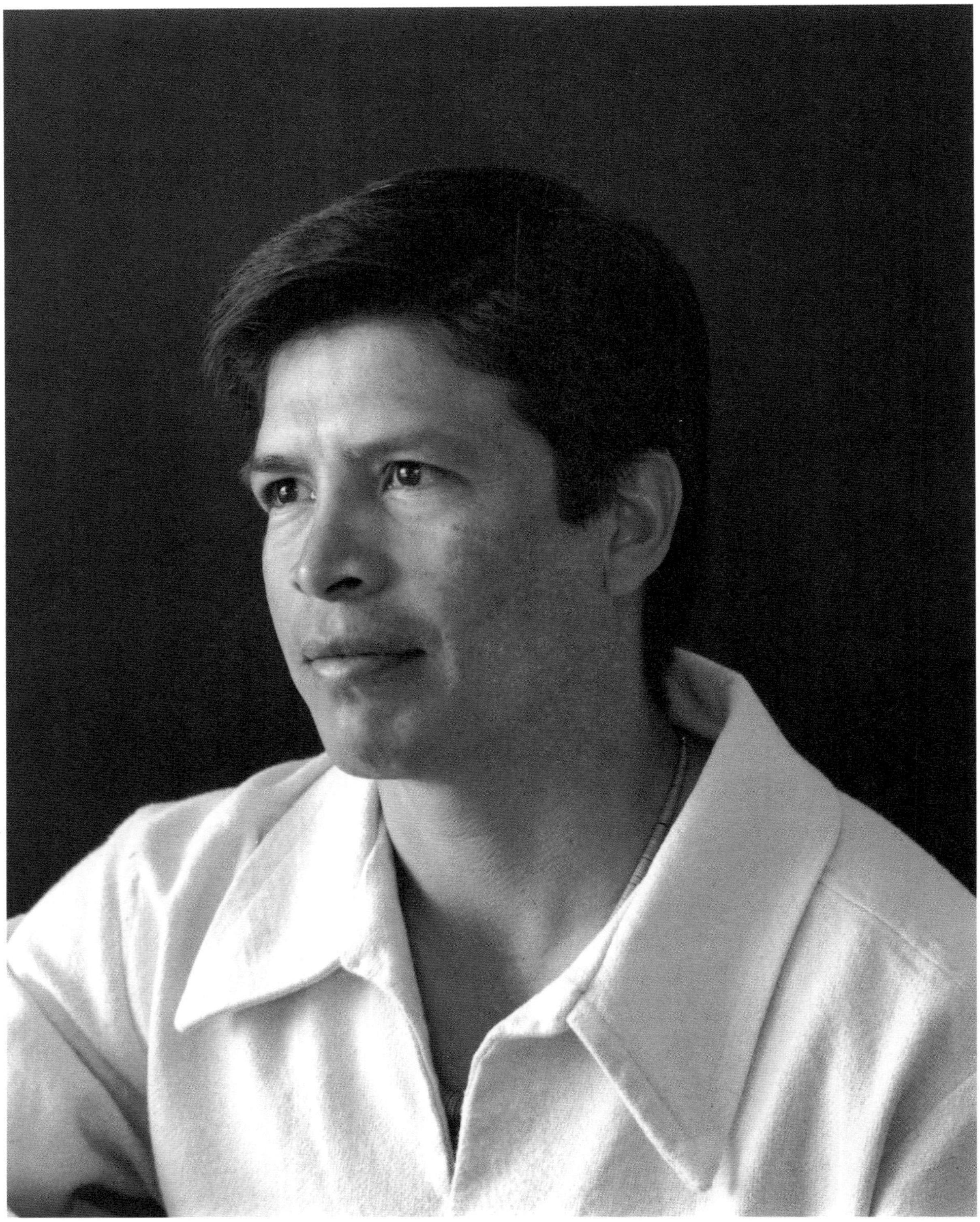

39

LT. GOVERNOR GEORGE RIVERA

Stone and Bronze Sculptor

Pojoaque Pueblo

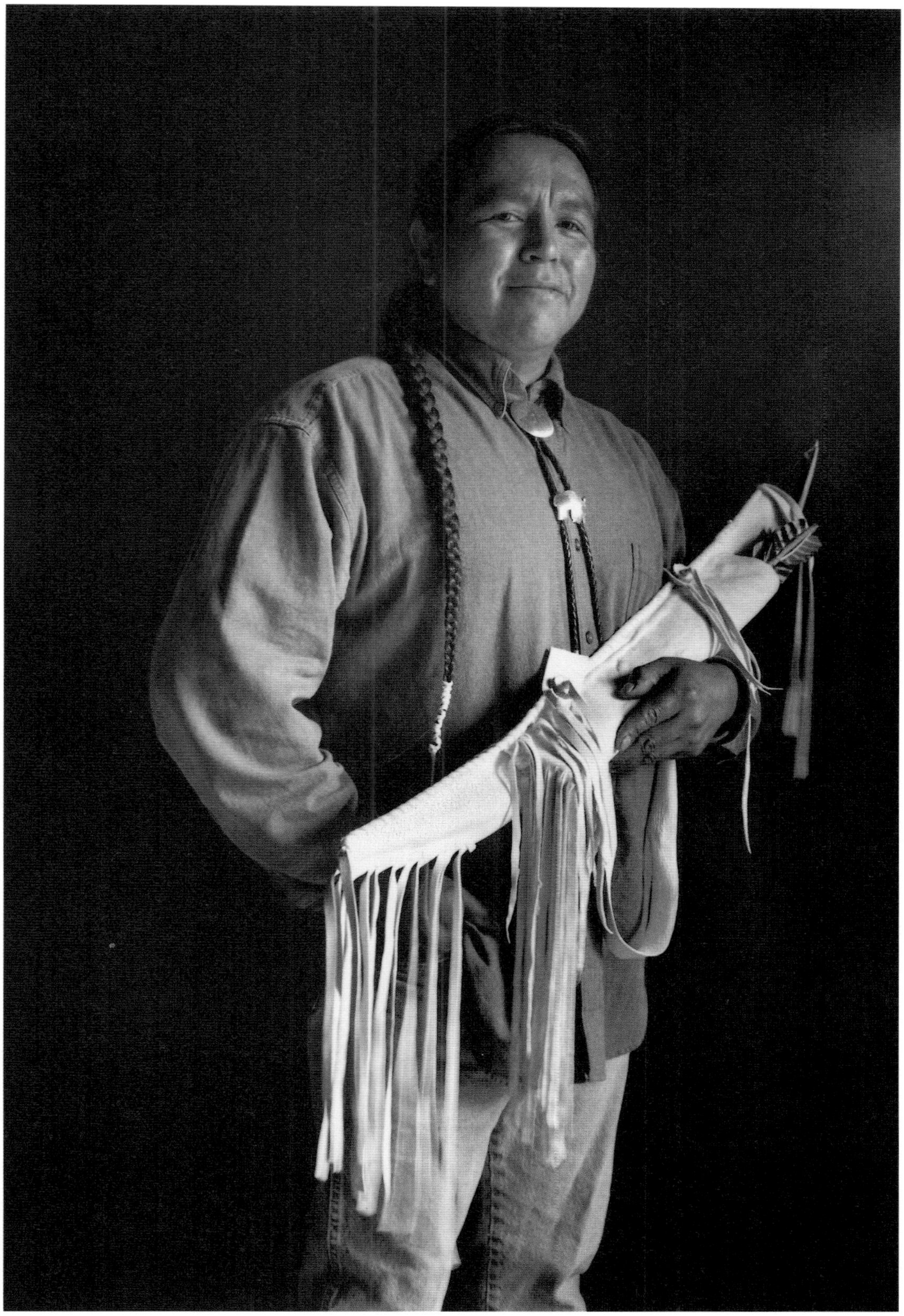

40

TOM READY-TO-HUNT

Silver and Goldsmith

Taos Pueblo

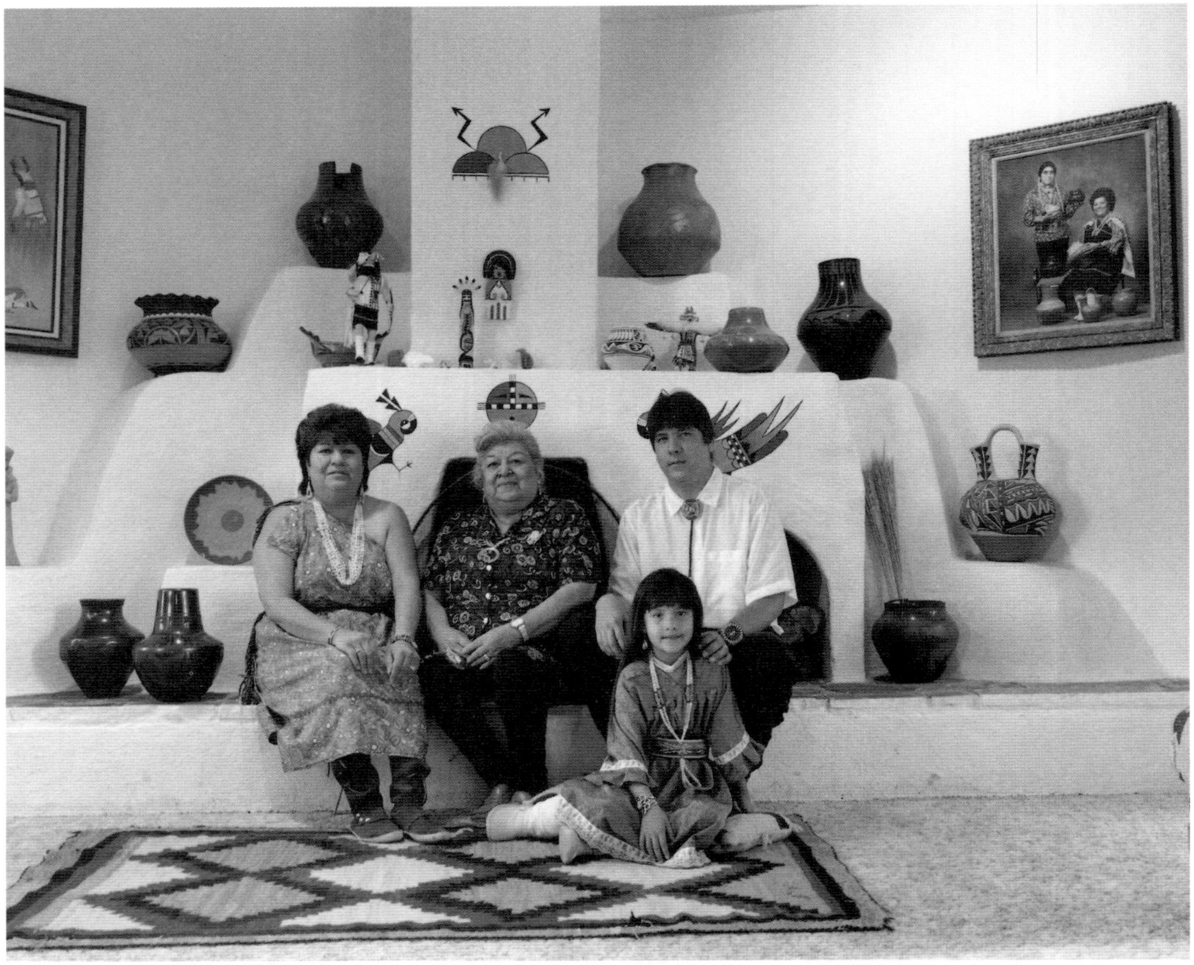

41

CARMELITA DUNLAP

with daughter MARTHA APPLELEAF FENDER,

grandson ERIK (Than Tsid̲éh) FENDER,

and granddaughter JUSTINE FENDER

Traditional Potters

San Ildefonso Pueblo

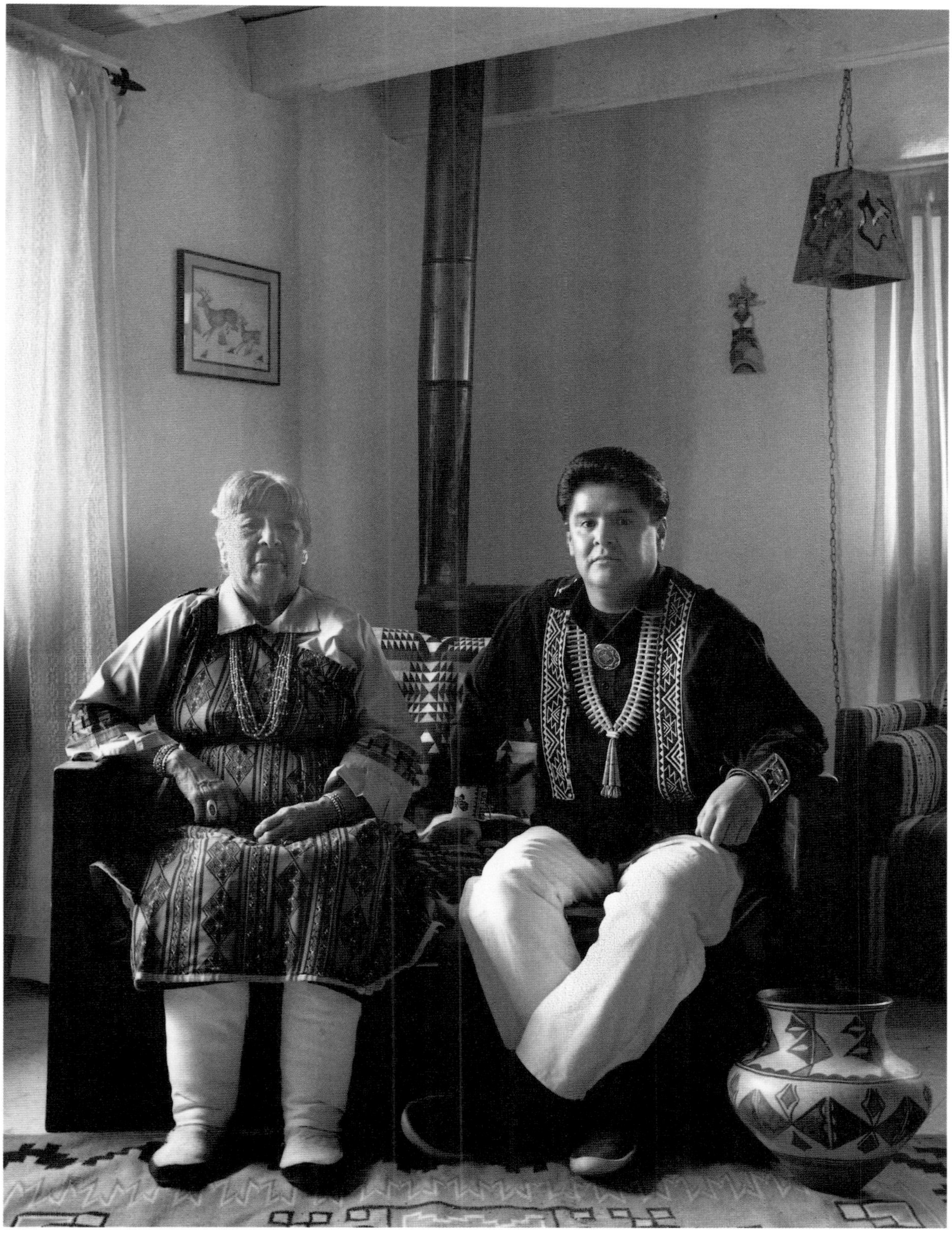

42
PHILOPITA TORRES
with son ELVIS TORRES
Traditional Potters
San Ildefonso Pueblo

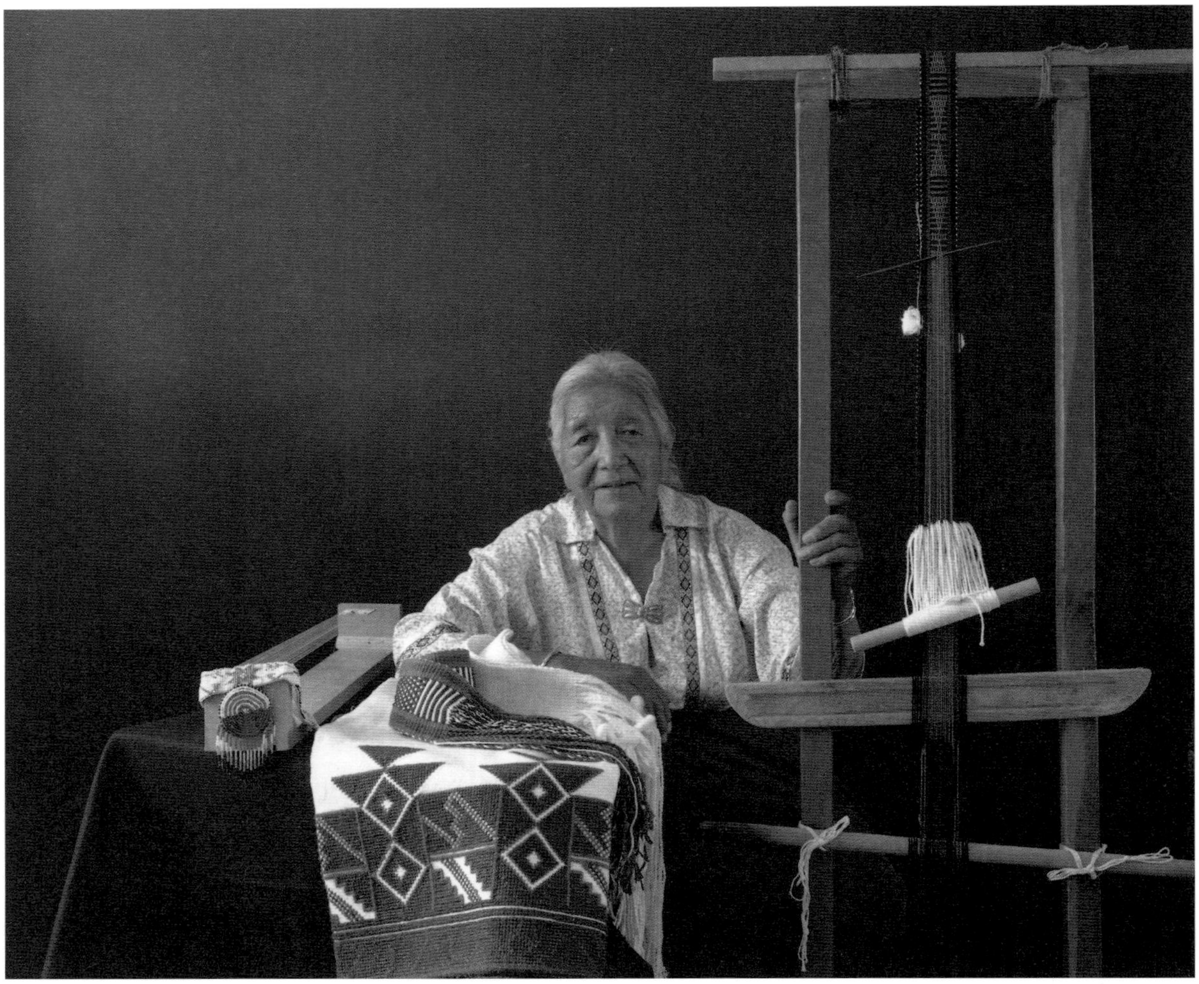

43
FRANCES MARTINEZ
Traditional Micaceous Potter, Weaving, Embroidery
Picurís Pueblo

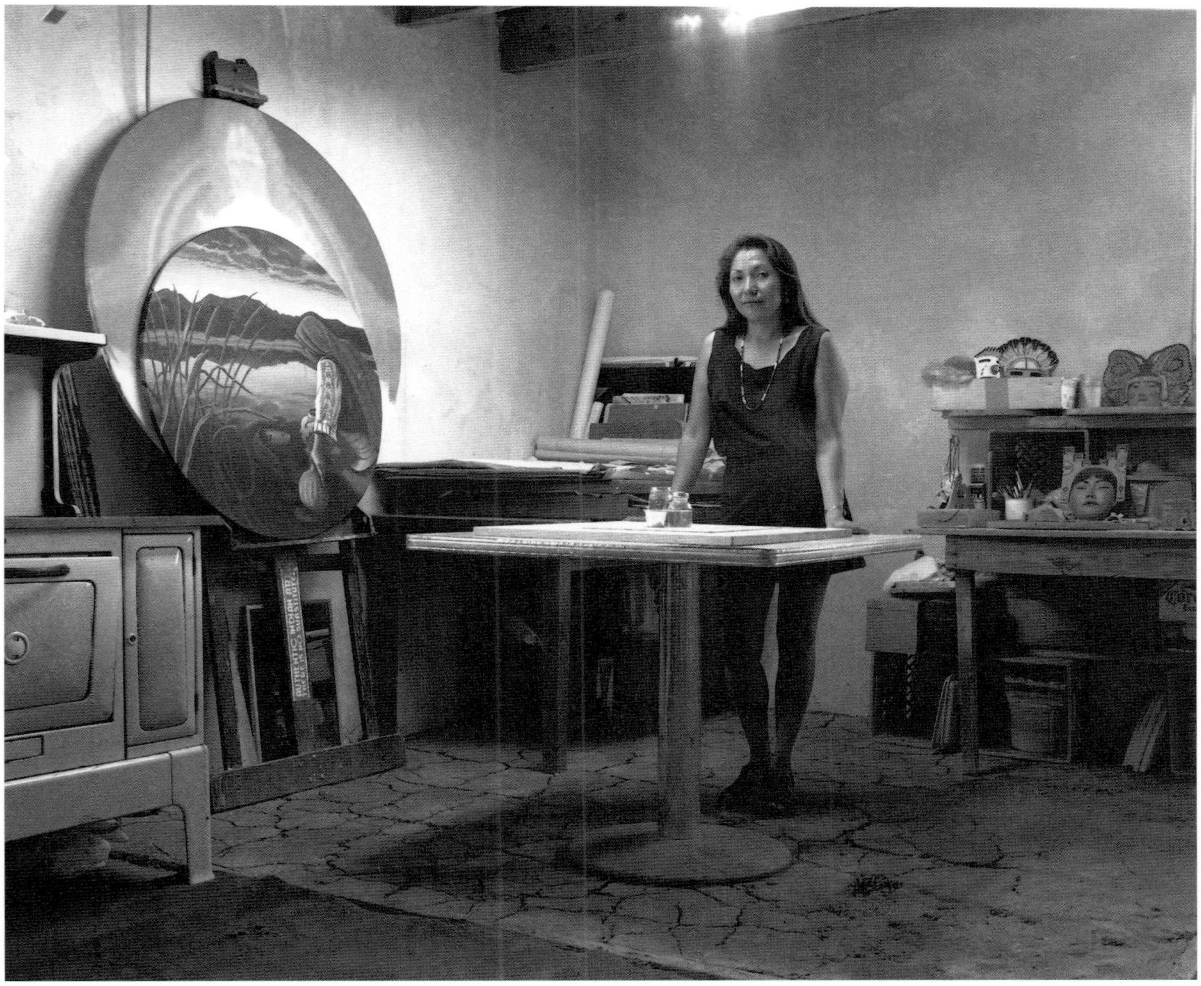

44

DEBORAH JOJOLA-SANCHEZ

Contemporary Painter, Printmaker, and Clay Work

Isleta/Jémez

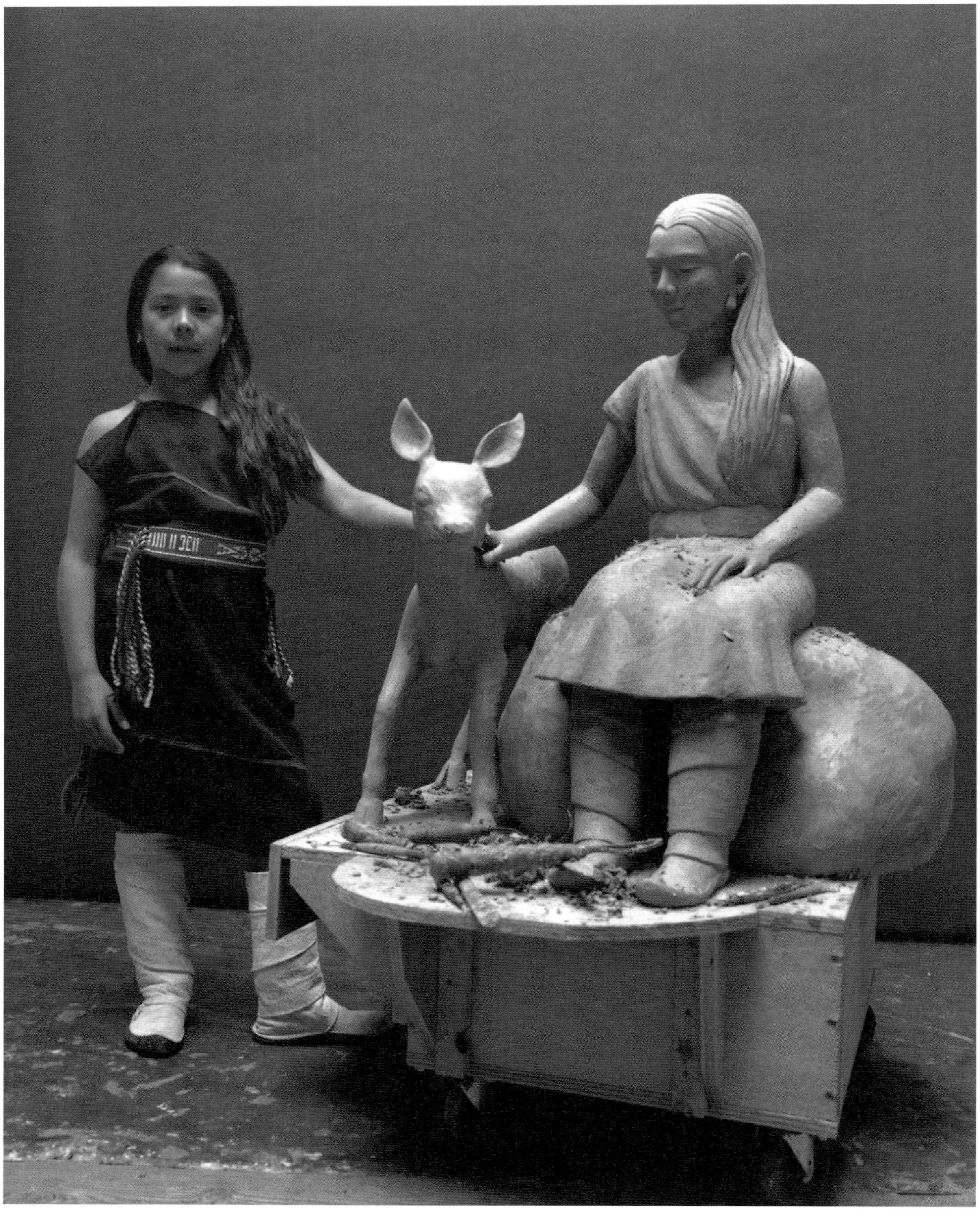

45

KATHERINE FAWN EAGLE-DAY LORETTO

with sculpture by mother Estella Loretto

Jémez Pueblo

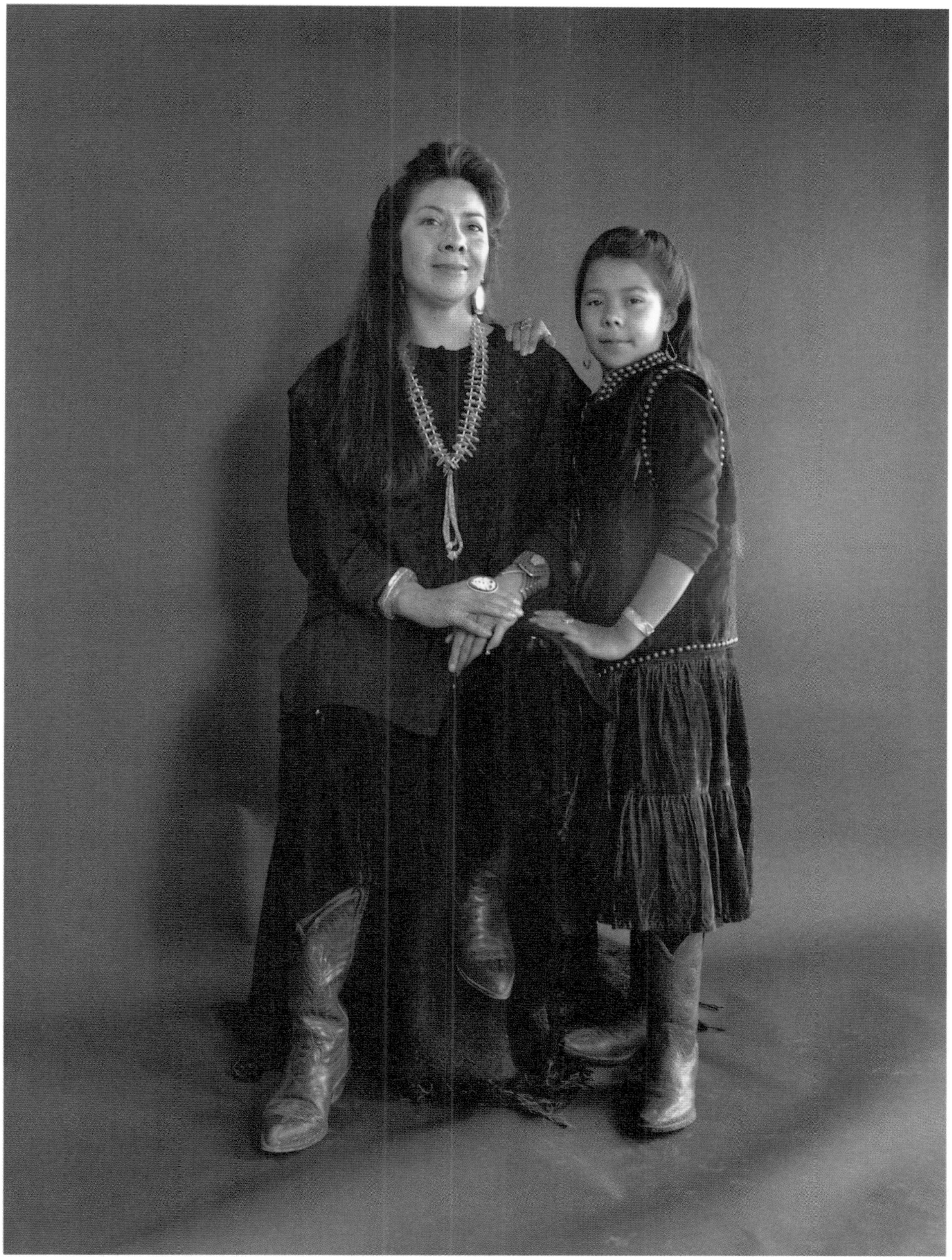

46

ESTELLA LORETTO

with daughter KATHERINE FAWN EAGLE-DAY LORETTO

Sculptor

Jémez Pueblo

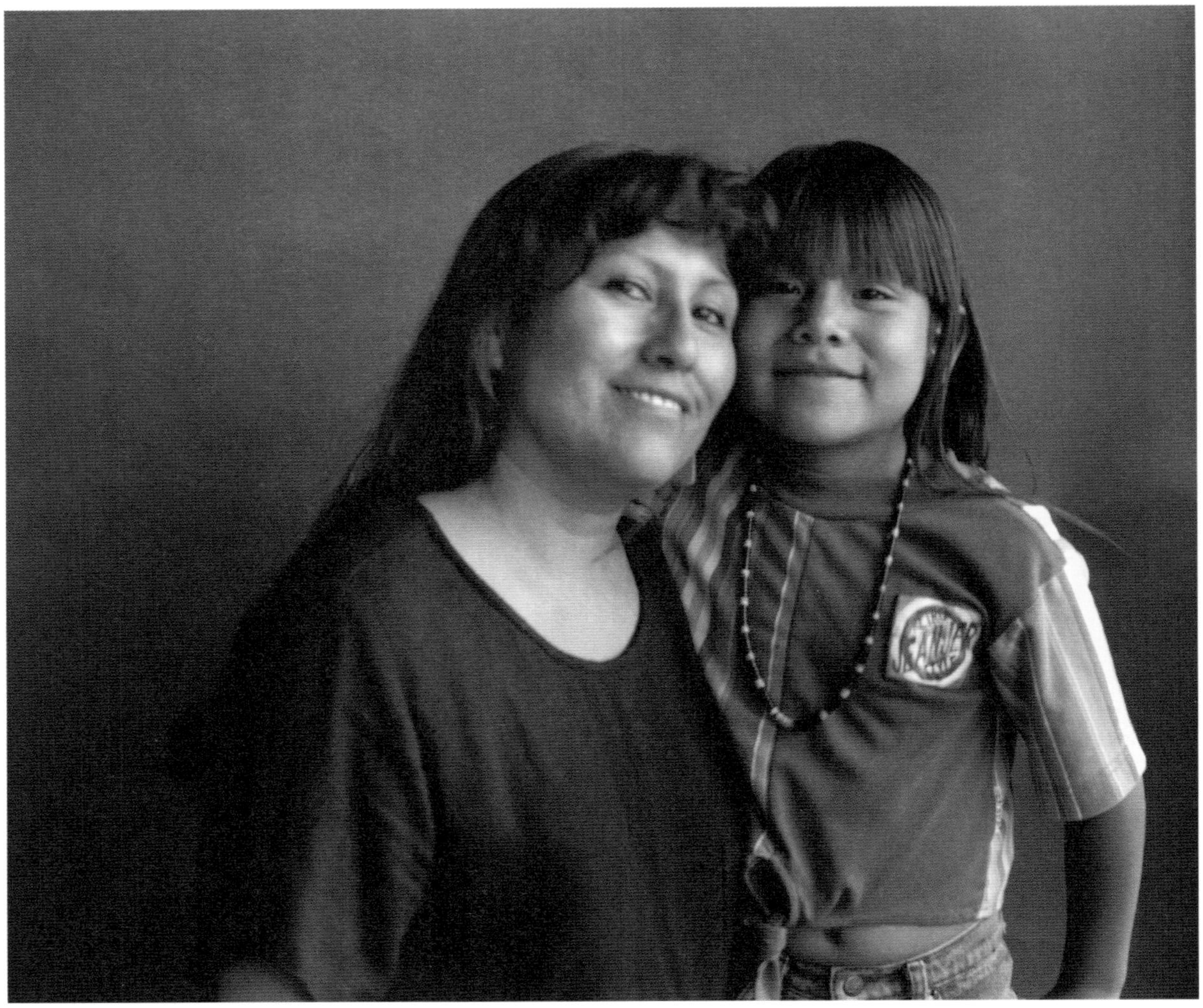

47
VIRGIE NUTIMA
Ignacia Duran's daughter
with daughter ERICA LENO
Traditional Micaceous Potter
Tesuque Pueblo

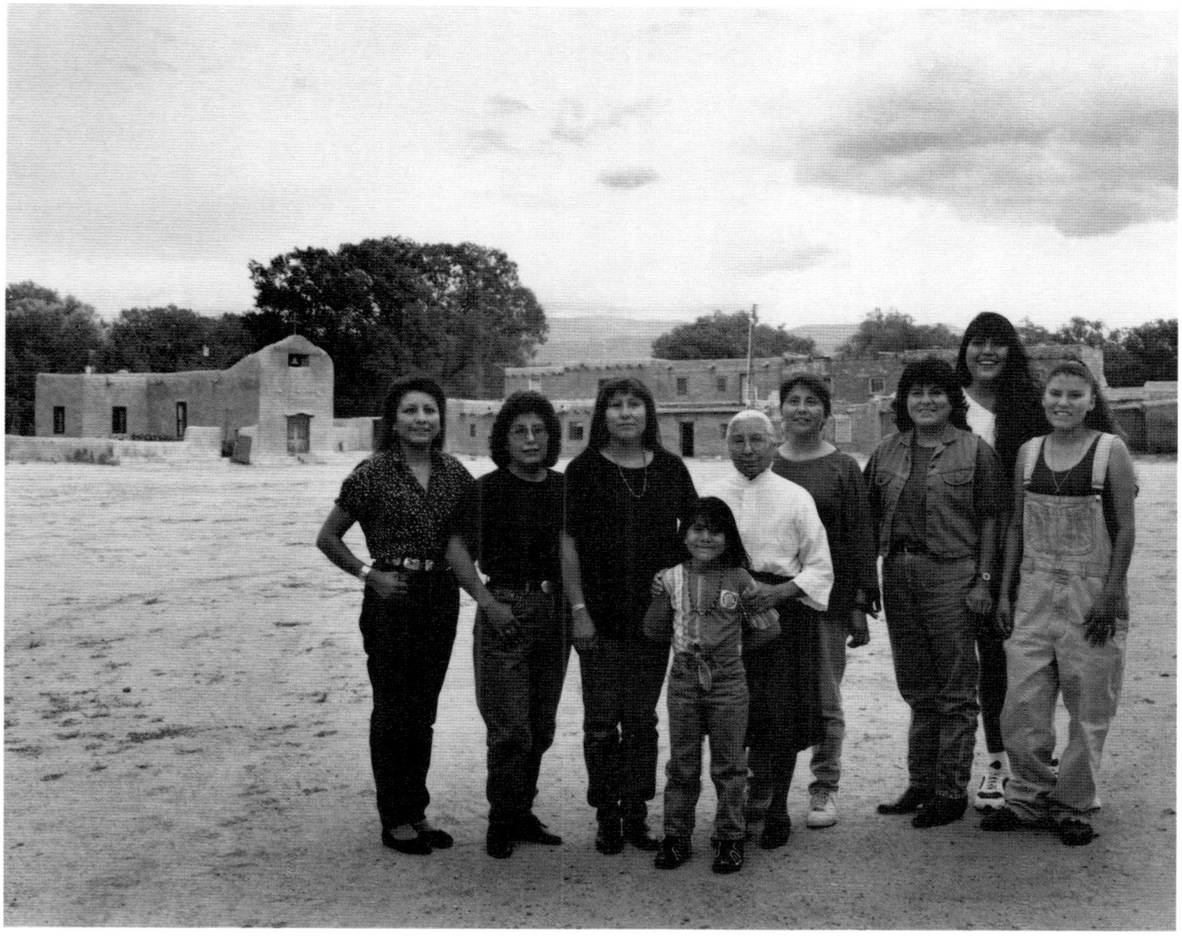

48

IGNACIA DURAN

with daughters STELLA TOLEDO, SUE DORAME,

VIRGIE NUTIMA, BEA DURAN-TIOUX, and REYES HERRERA,

and granddaughters ERICA LENO, RACHEL DURAN, and ROXANNE HERRERA

Traditional Micaceous Potters, Weaving, Sewing, and Beadwork

Tesuque Pueblo

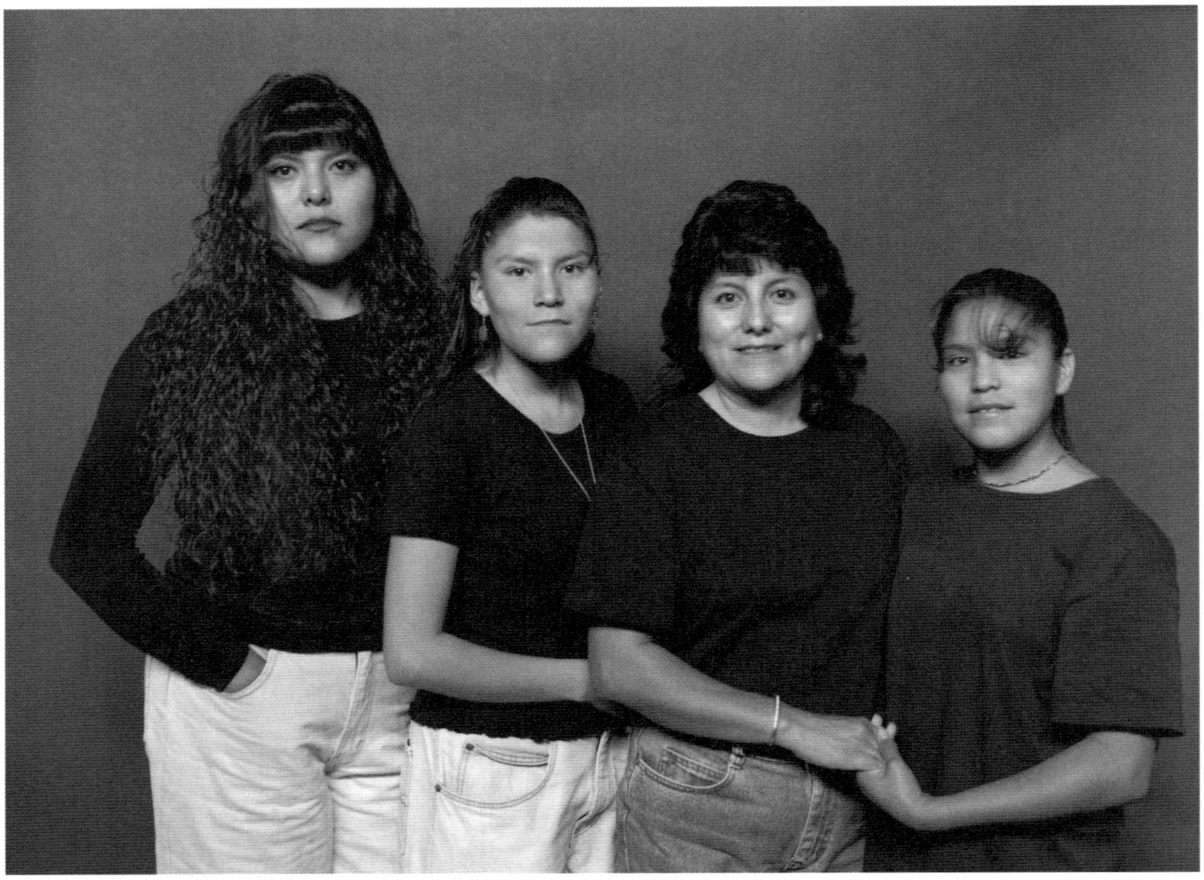

REYES HERRERA

with daughters RACHEL DURAN, ROXANNE, and RAEANN REYES

Traditional Micaceous Potter

Tesuque Pueblo

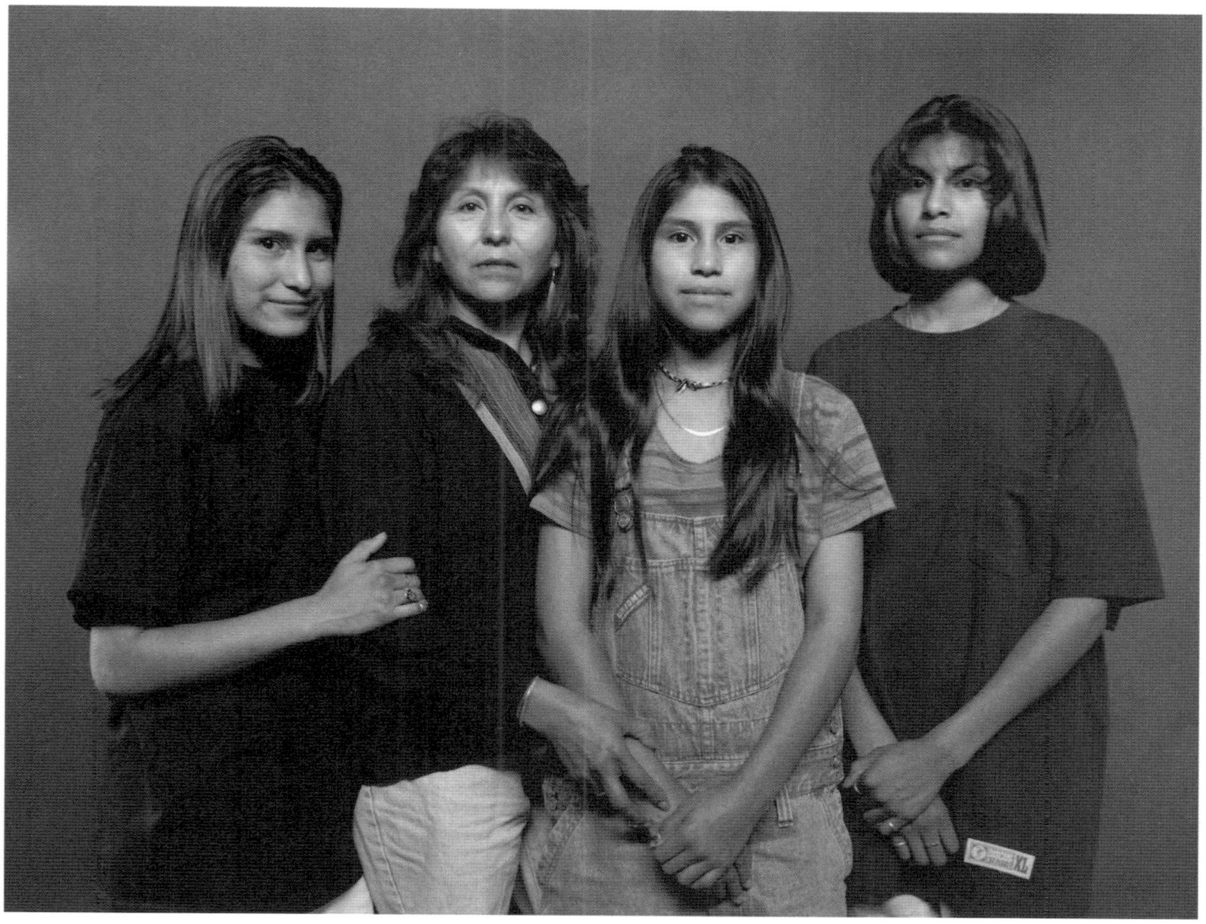

50

BEA DURAN-TIOUX

with daughters BAY-POVI, NANA, and SUMMER TIOUX

Traditional Micaceous Pottery, Drum Making, Weaving

Tesuque Pueblo

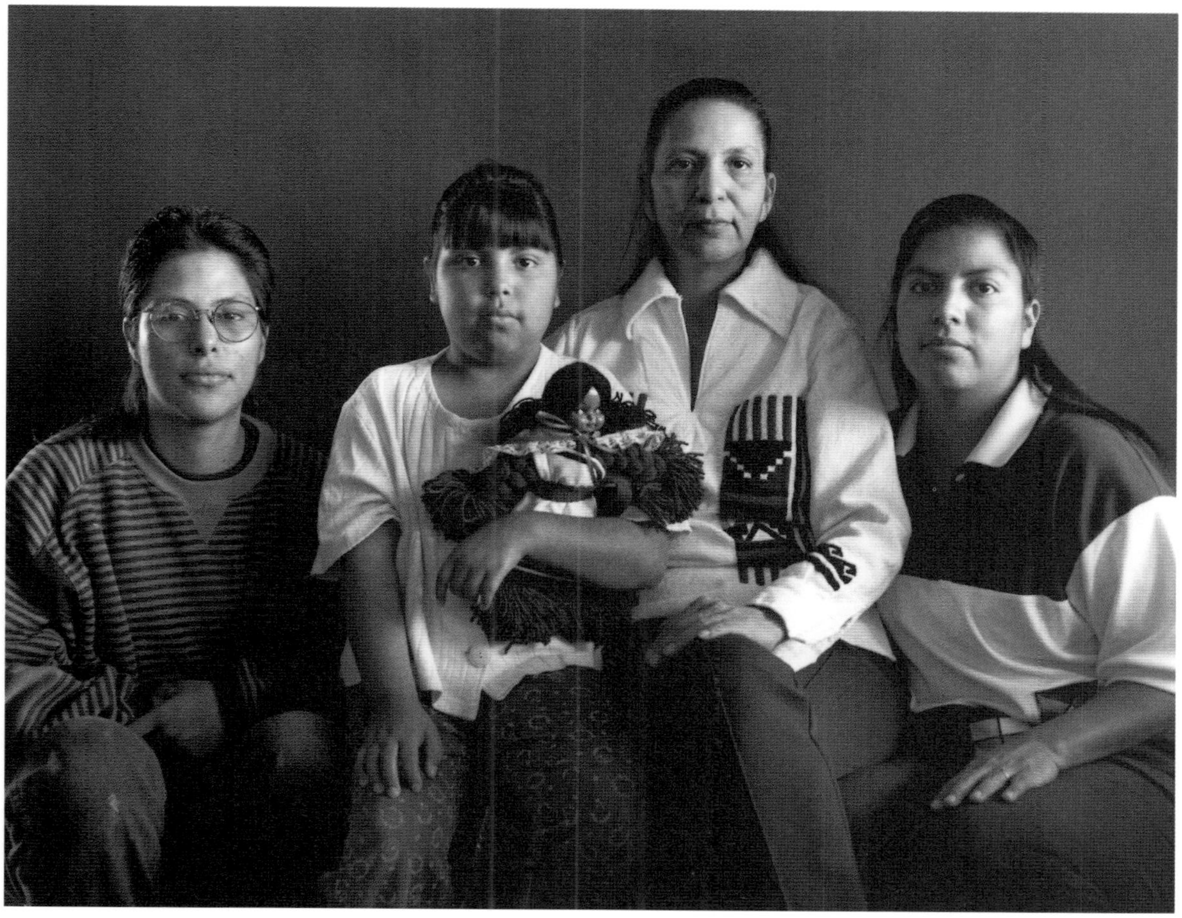

51

ELIZABETH MONTOYA

with daughters MARGIE MONTOYA and MICHELLE SANDOVAL

and granddaughter SARAH SANDOVAL

Traditional Pueblo Embroidery

Kiowa-Tewa/San Juan Pueblo

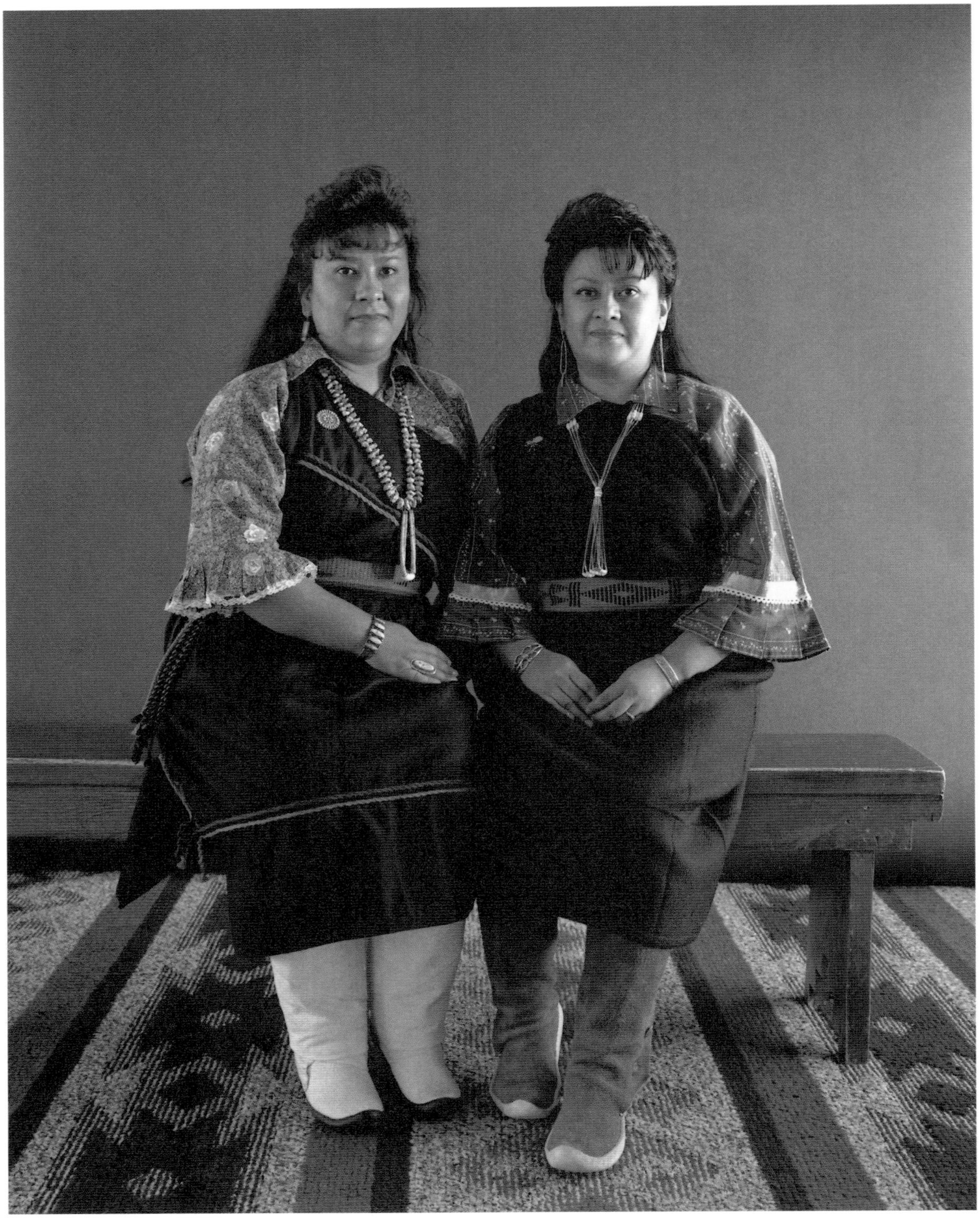

52

CAROL GUTTIEREZ-NARANJO

with sister KATHY GUTTIEREZ-NARANJO

(and sisters, opposite)

Traditional Potters

San Ildefonso Pueblo

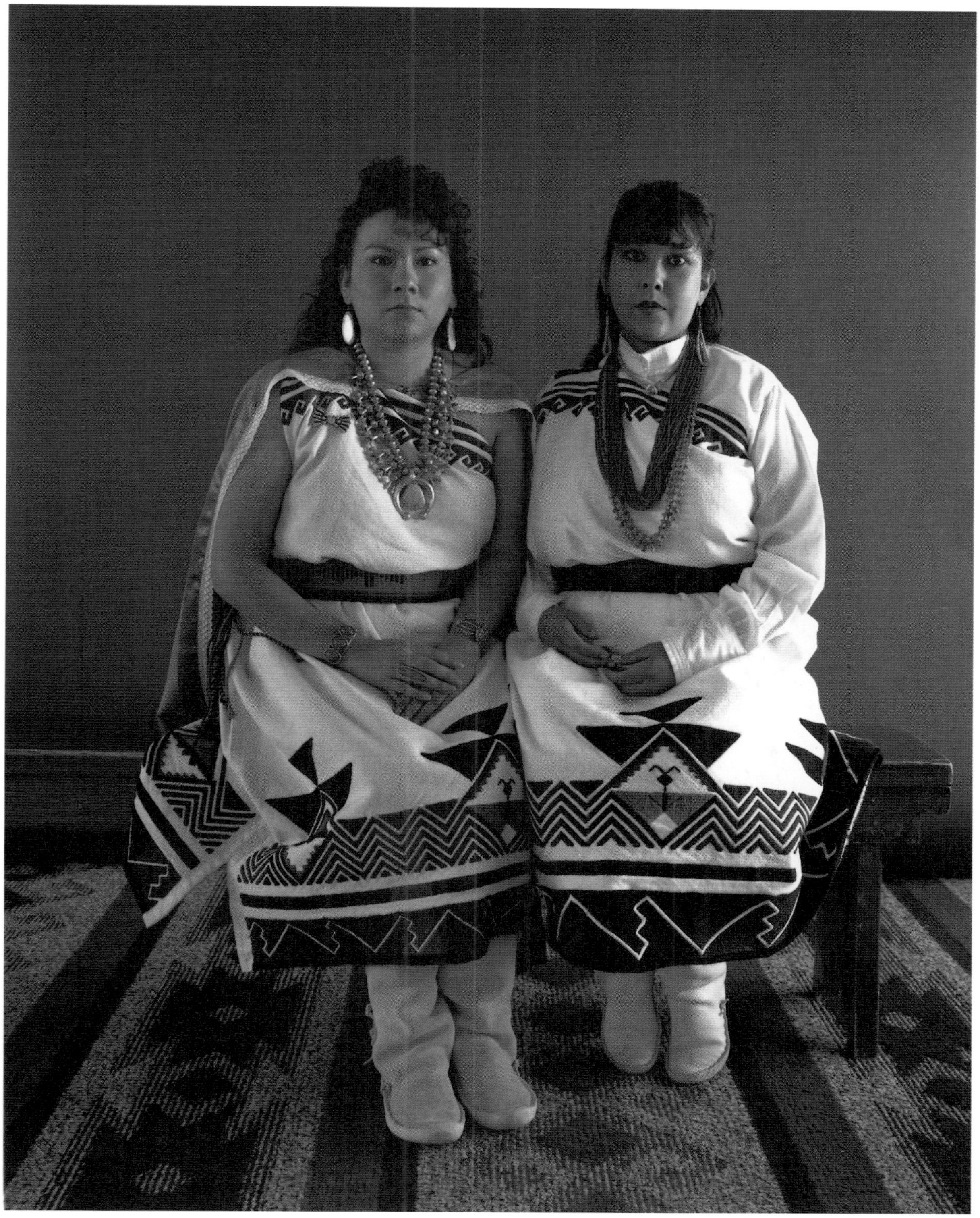

53
ROSE GUTTIEREZ, Traditional Potter,
with sister GERALDINE GUTTIEREZ, Traditional Potter and Painter
San Ildefonso Pueblo

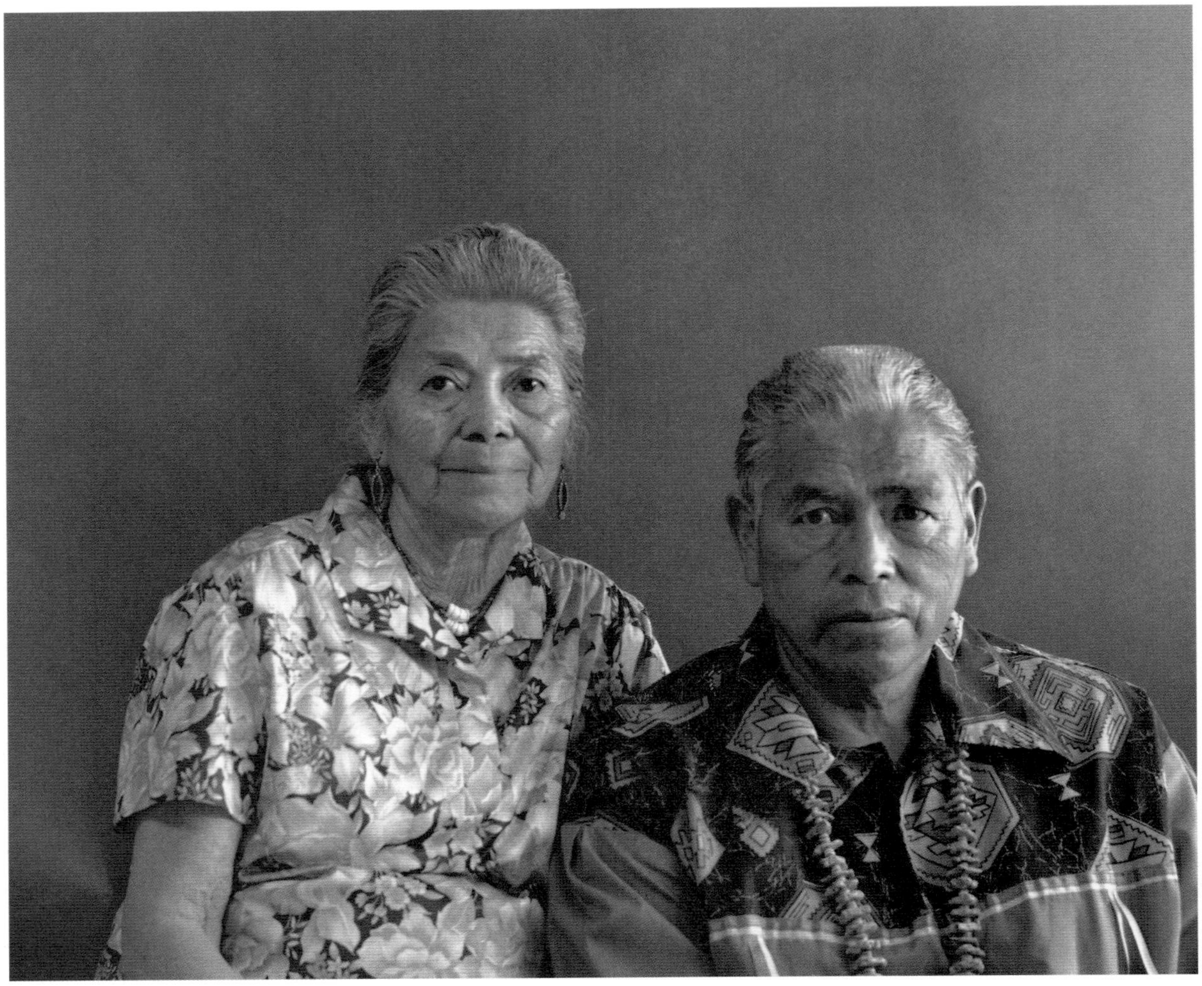

54
ALFRED (Sä-Wä-Pin) AGUILAR
with sister FLORENCE NARANJO
Traditional Potters
San Ildefonso Pueblo

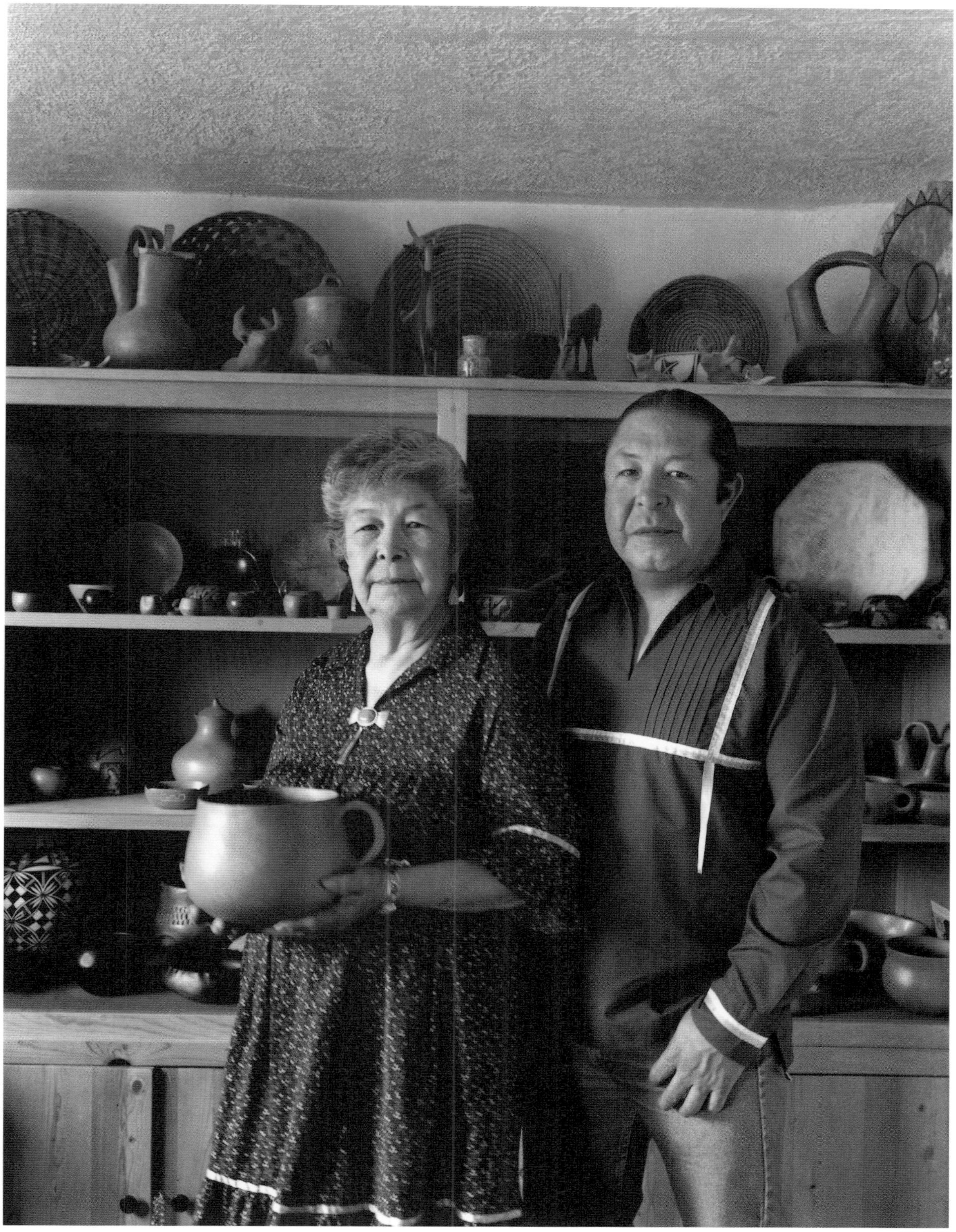

55
CORDI GOMEZ, Pojoaque,
with son GLENN L. GOMEZ, Taos/Pojoaque
Traditional and Contemporary Micaceous Pottery

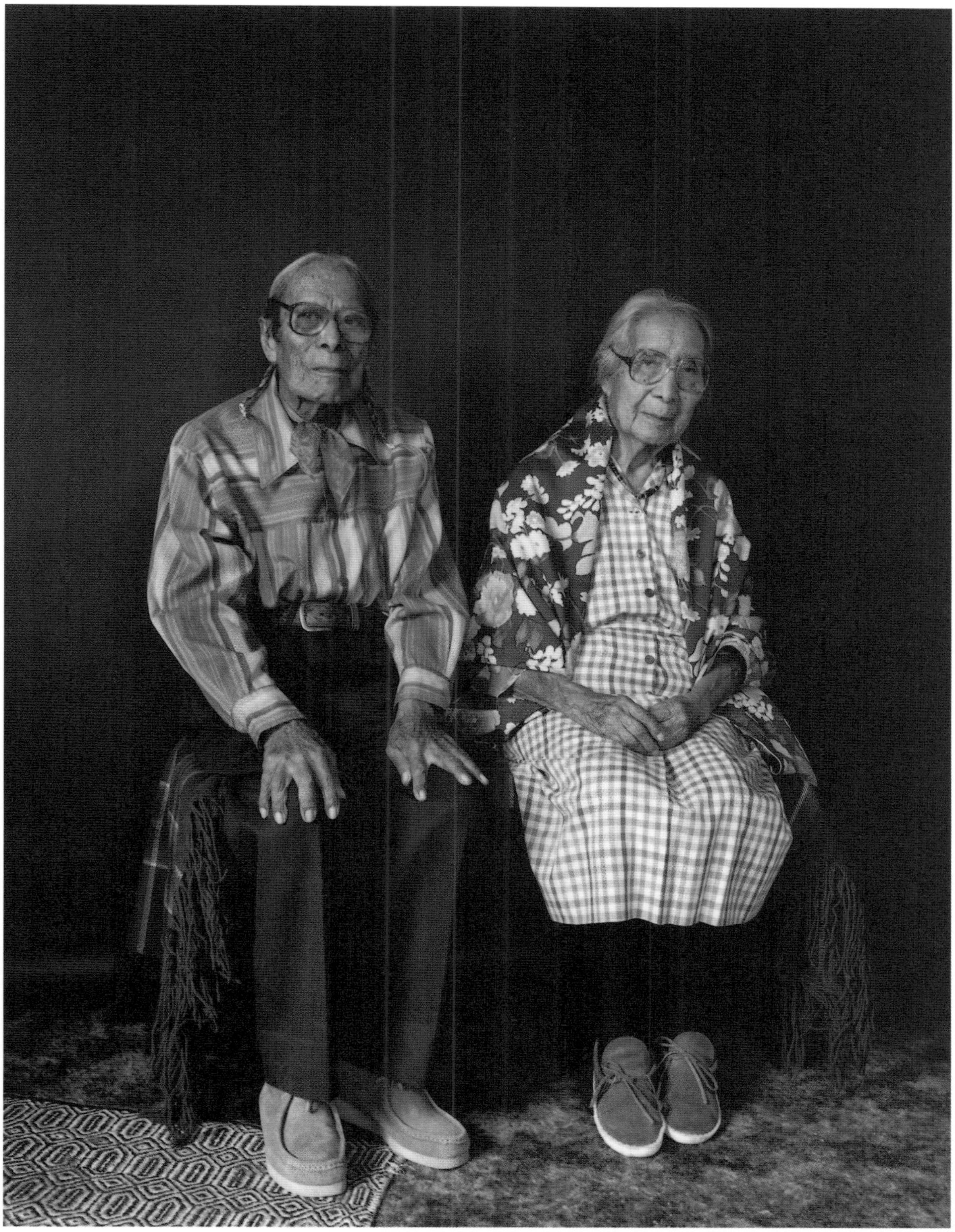

56

ADAM MARTINEZ, age ninety-four

Maria Martinez's son

with wife SANTANA MARTINEZ

Traditional Potters

San Ildefonso Pueblo

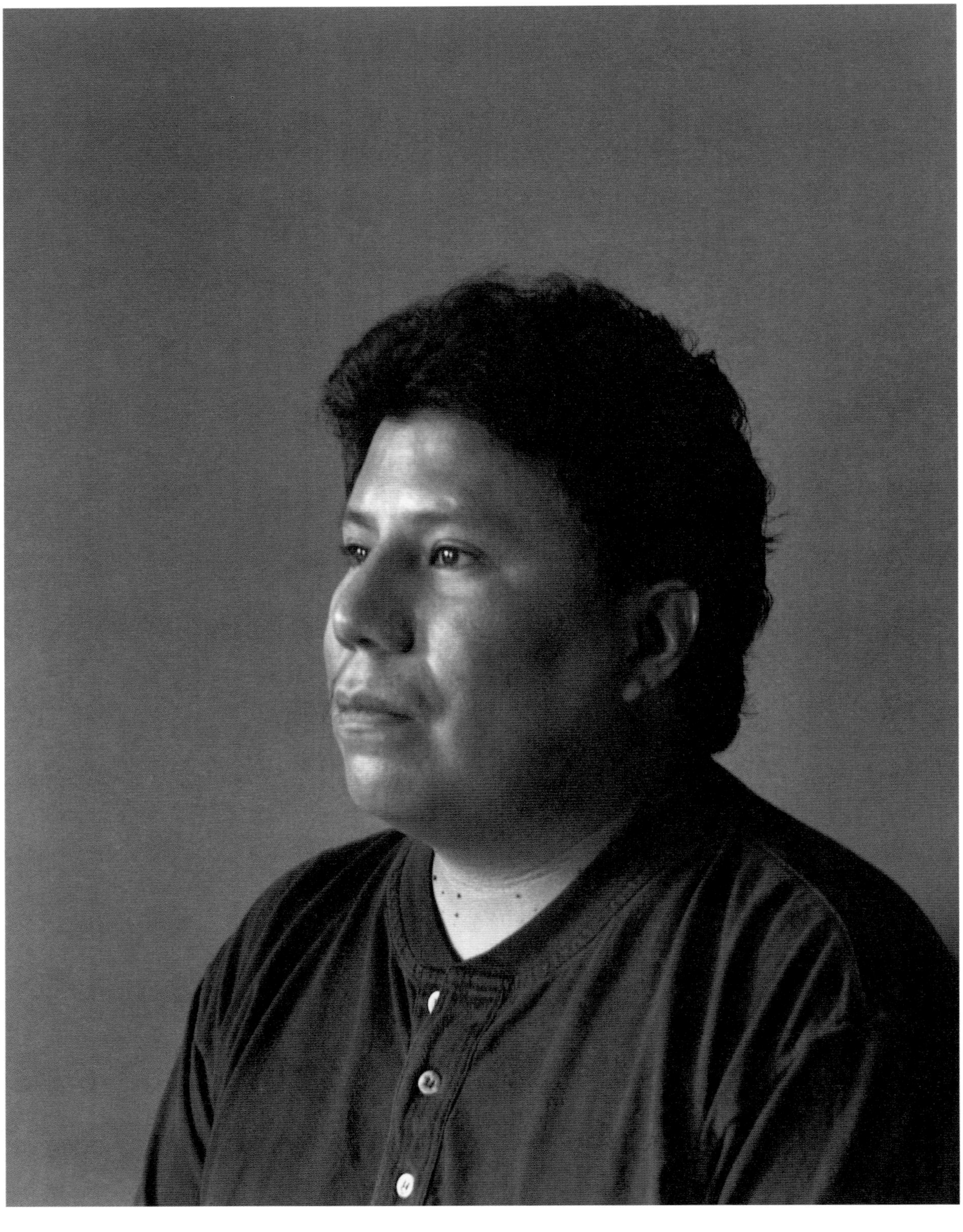

57

MARVIN MARTINEZ

Maria Martinez's great-grandson

Traditional Potter

San Ildefonso Pueblo

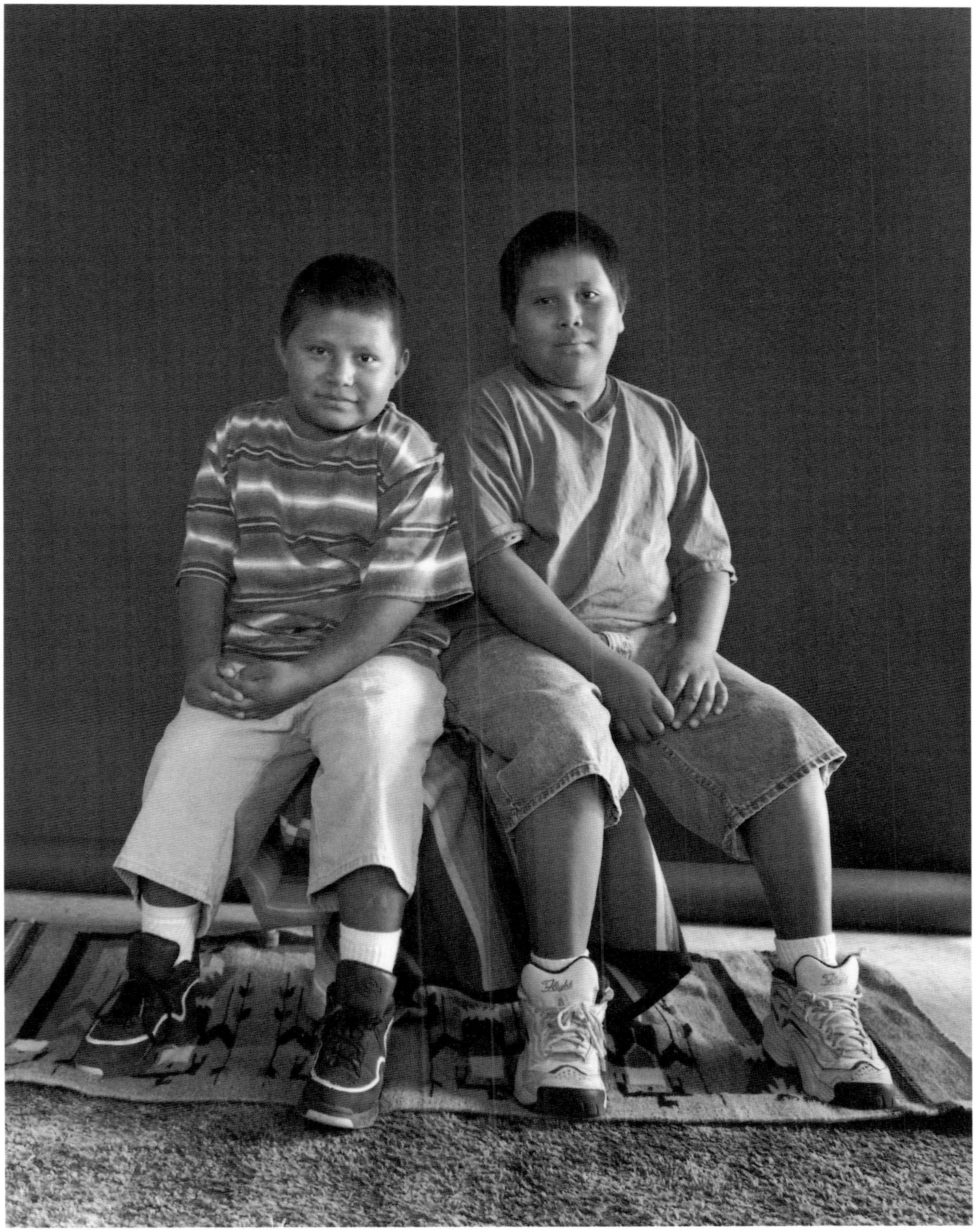

58
MANUEL ERIC MARTINEZ and MARVIN LEE MARTINEZ
Marvin Martinez's sons
Traditional Potters
San Ildefonso Pueblo

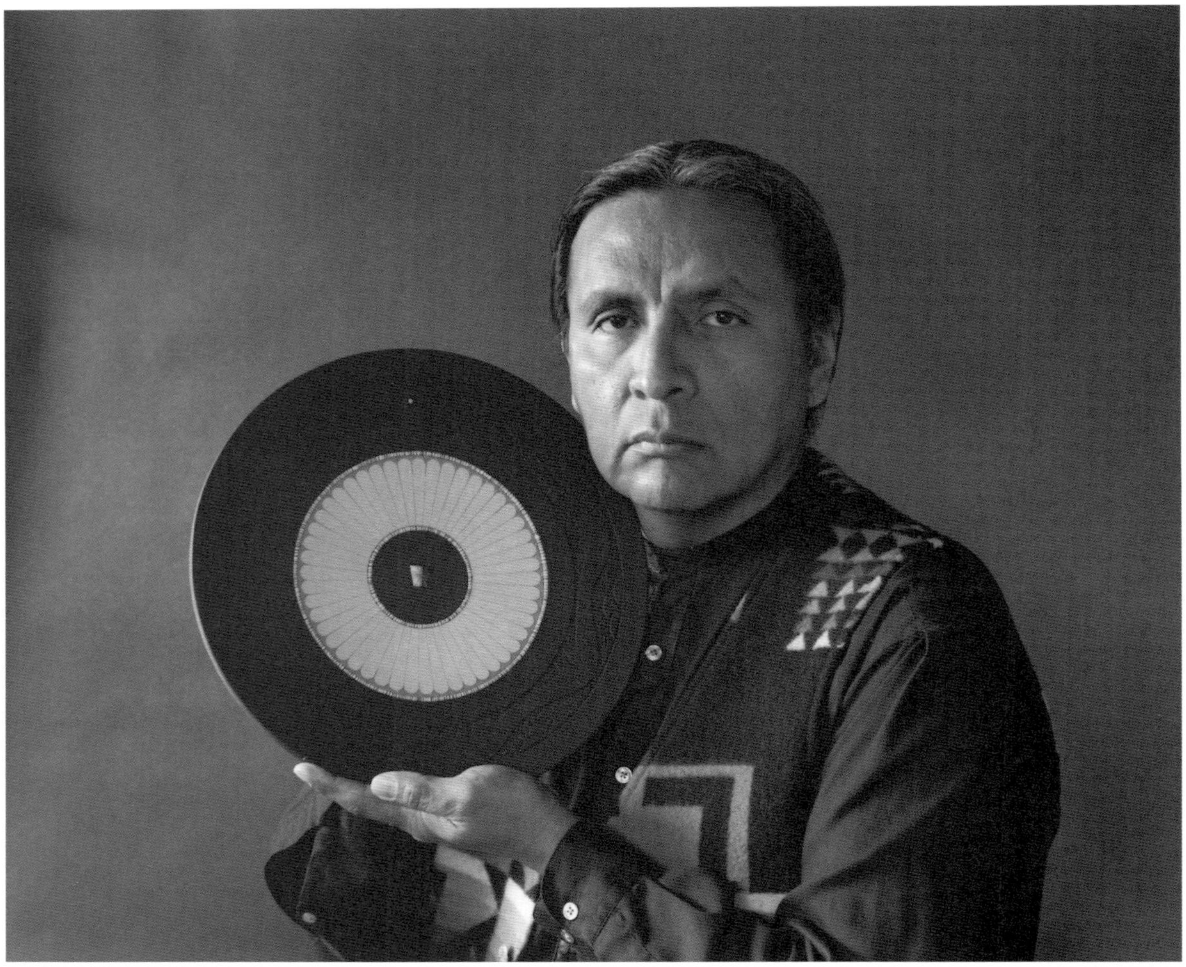

59

JOHN F. GONZALES

Cavan Gonzales's uncle

Potter—Contemporary representation of traditional designs

San Ildefonso Pueblo

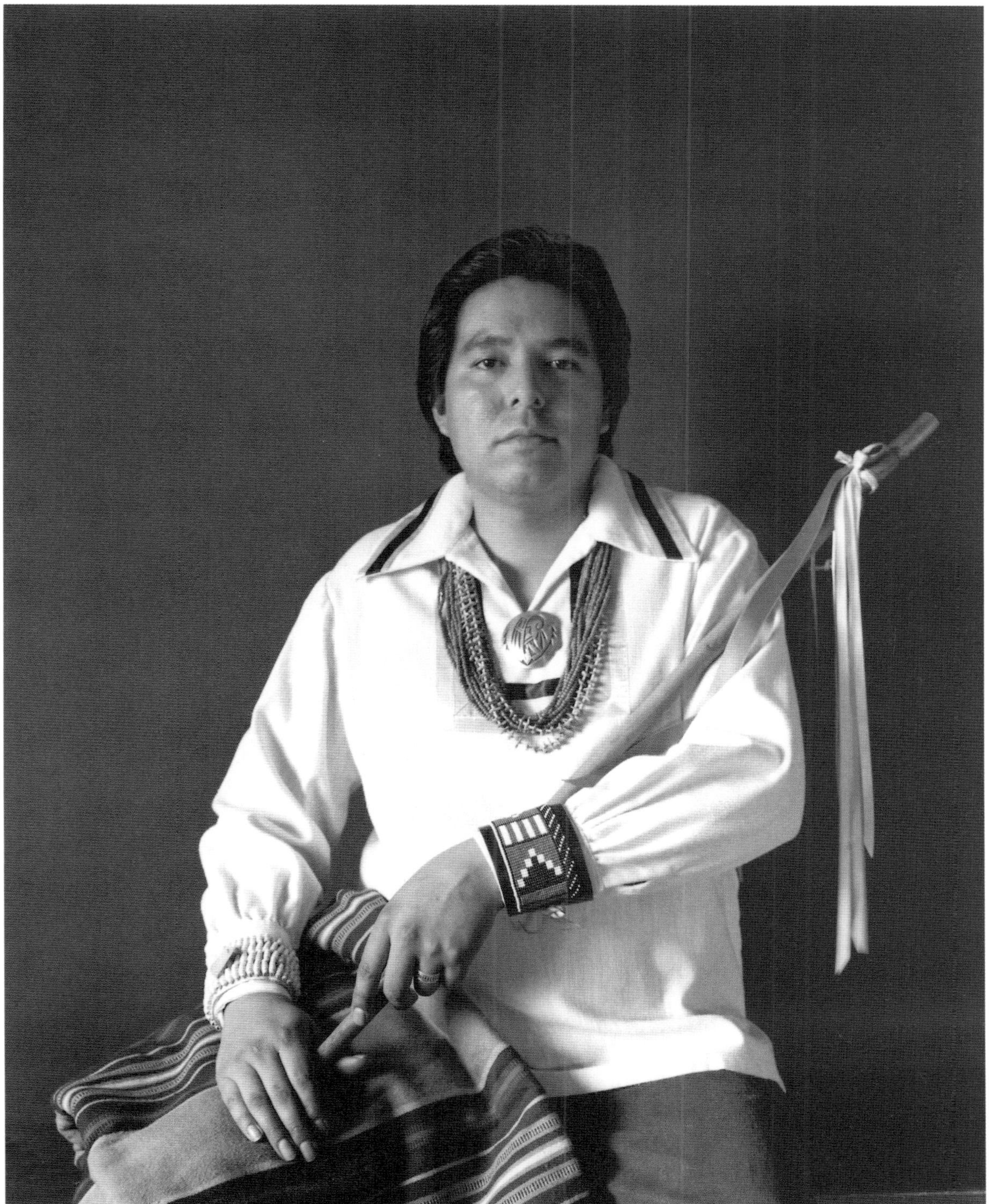

60

1st LT. GOVERNOR CAVAN (Tse-Whang) GONZALES

Maria Martinez's great-grandson

Holding Lt. Governor's cane given to the elected officials of the Pueblos by President Abraham Lincoln

Traditional Polychrome Potter

San Ildefonso Pueblo

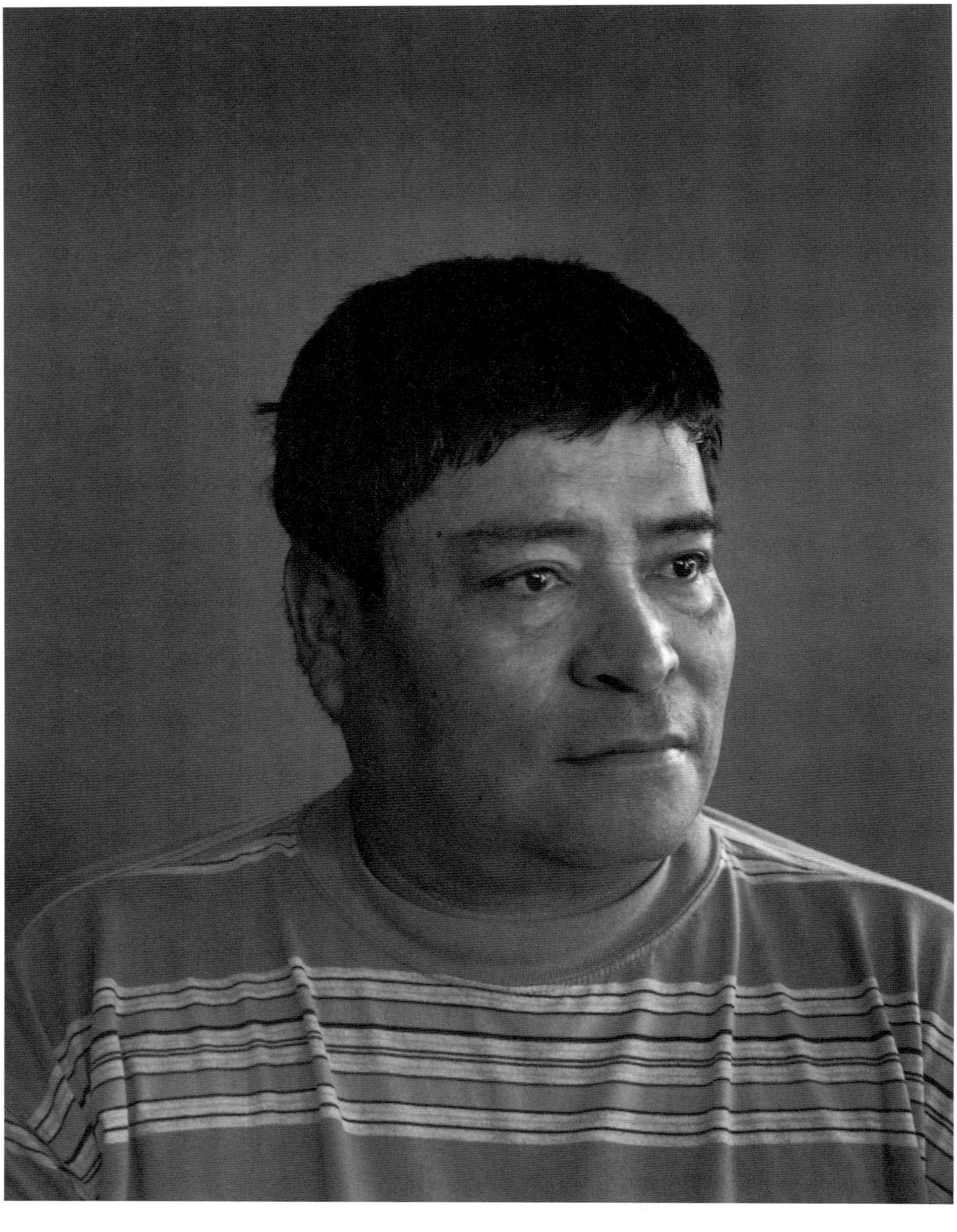

61

ANDY LEE KIRK

Contemporary Jeweler

Isleta/Navajo

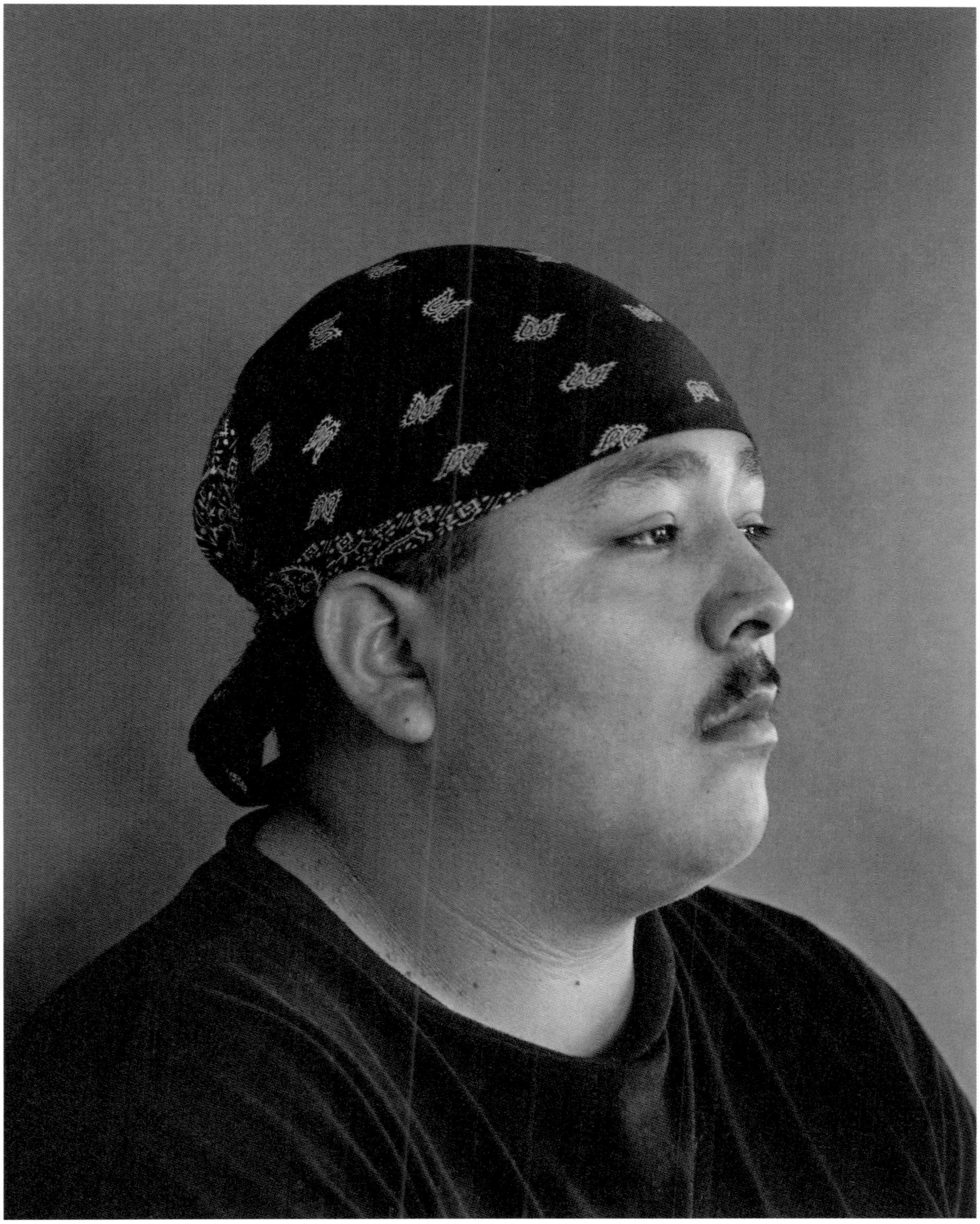

62

LAURENCE (Thurshan) KIRK

Andy Lee Kirk's nephew

Contemporary Jeweler

Isleta Pueblo

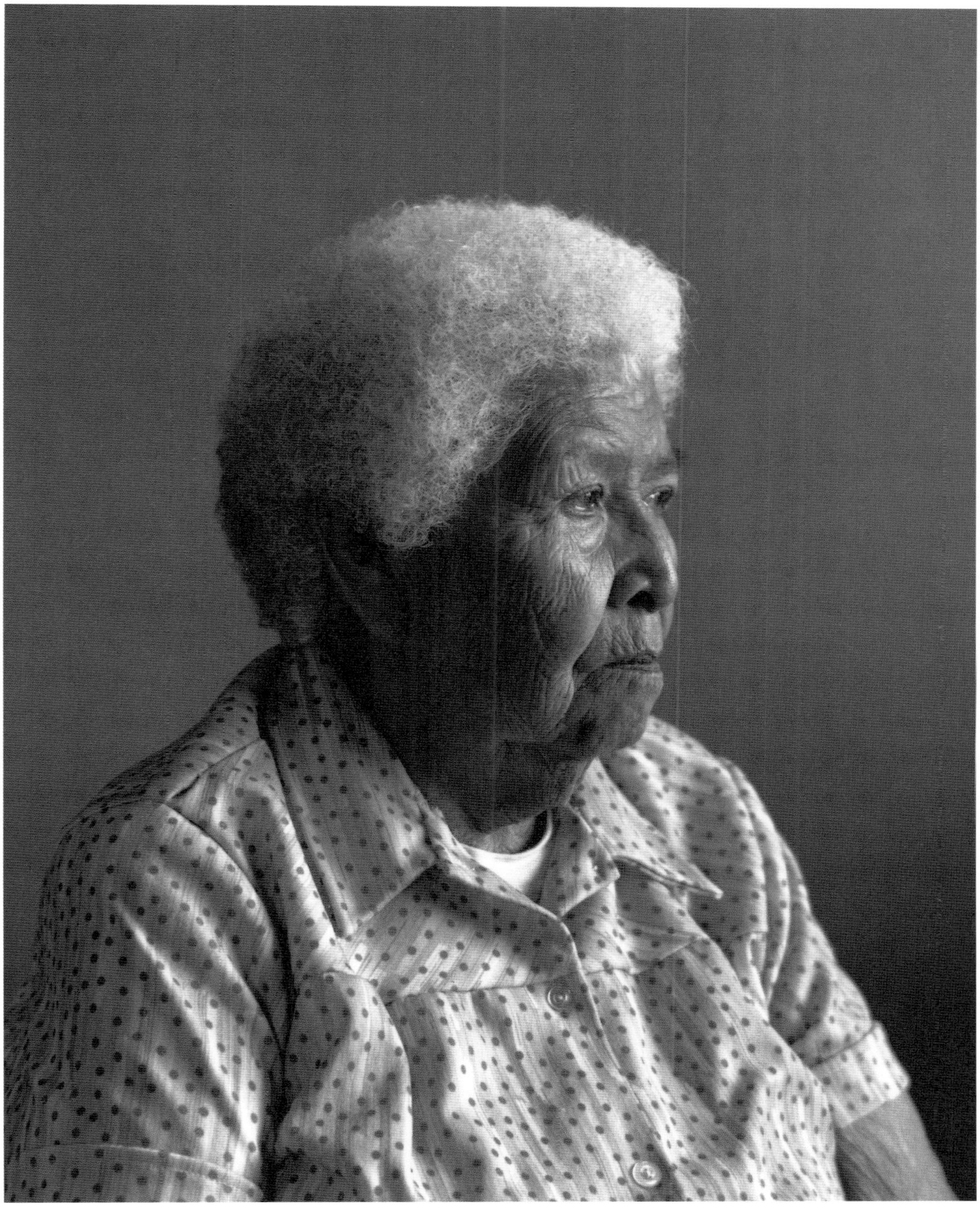

63
MOLLIE NARANJO
Traditional Potter
Santa Clara Pueblo

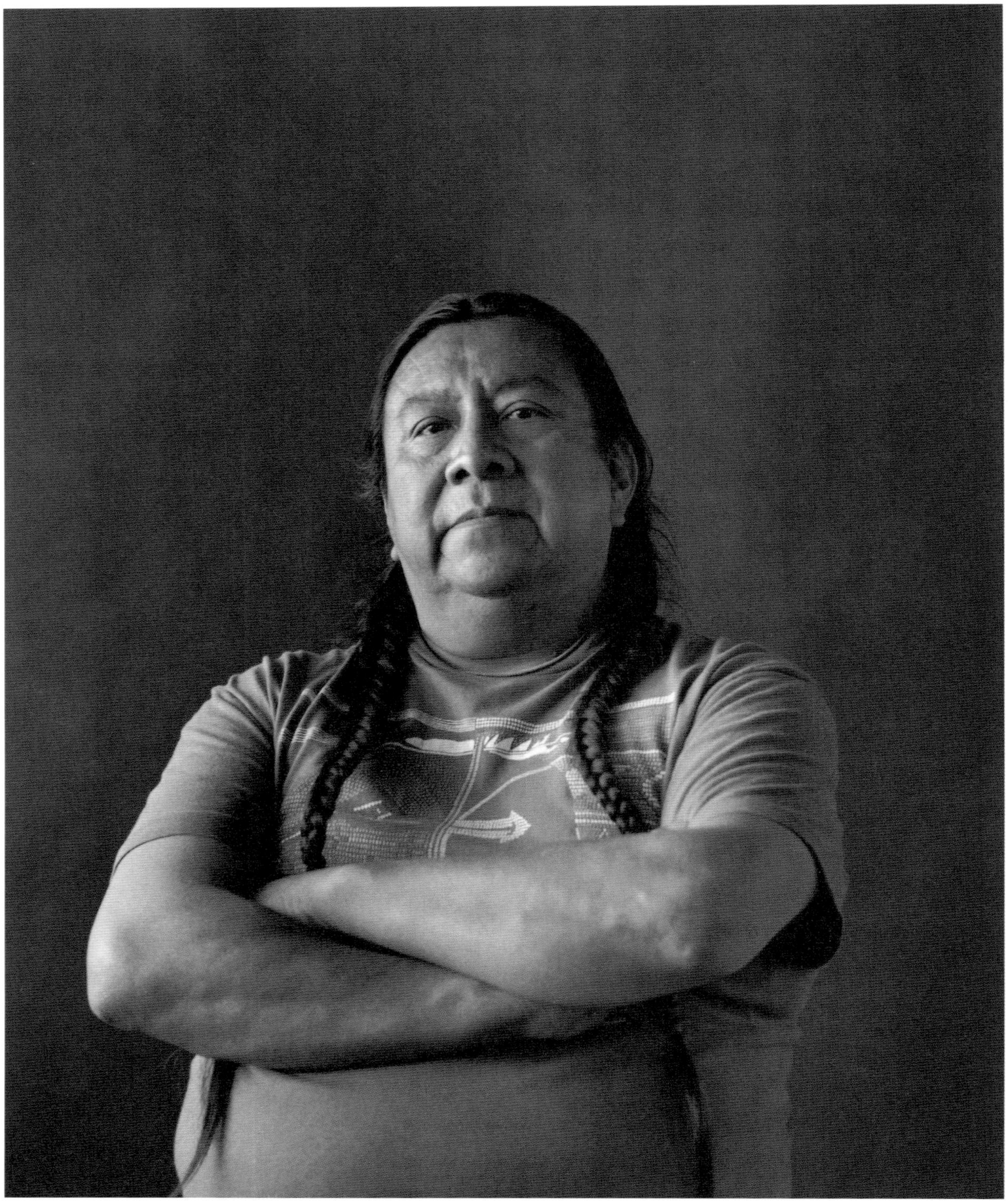

64

ROBERT NARANJO

Mollie Naranjo's son

Traditional Potter

Santa Clara Pueblo

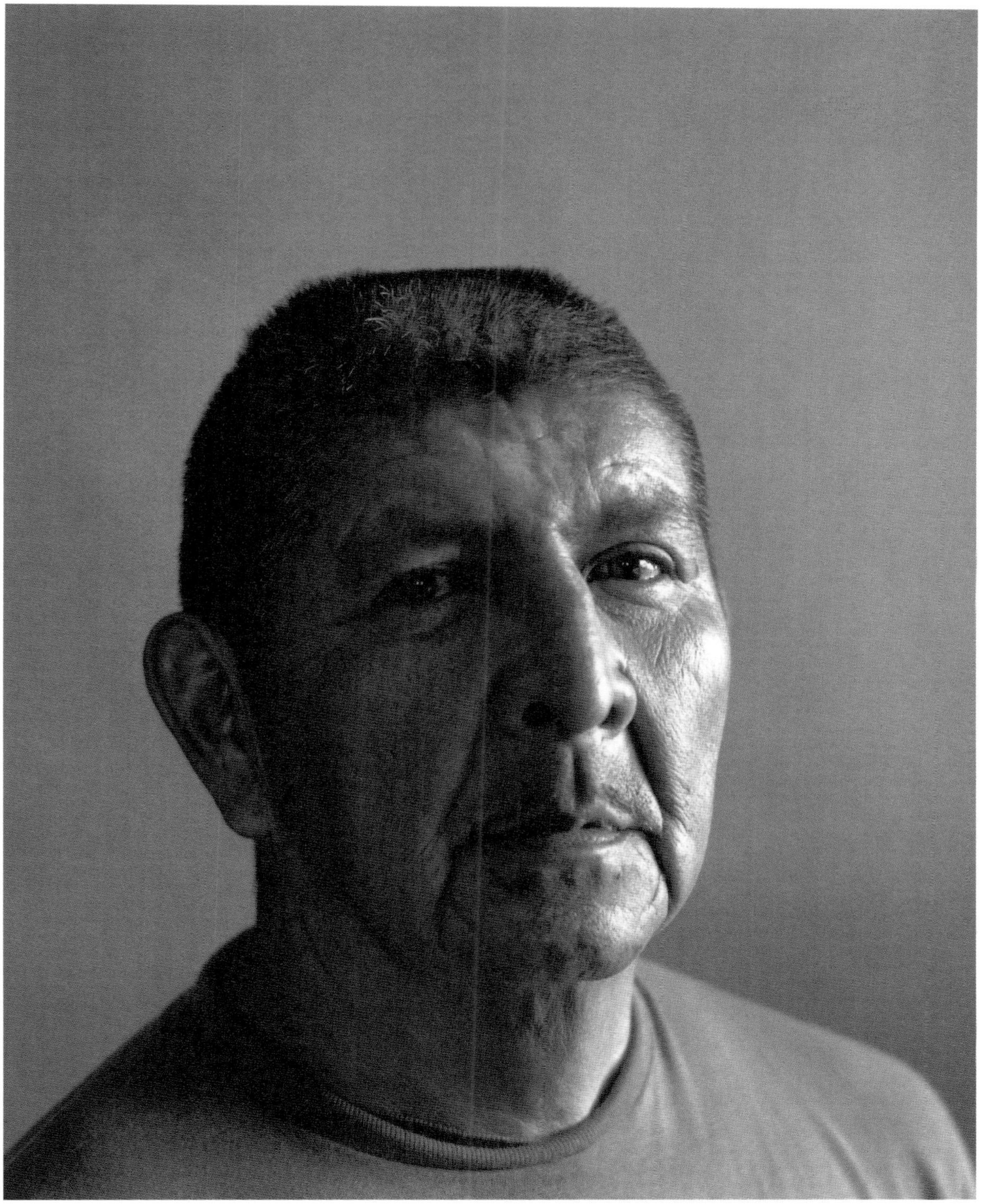

65

JOE NARANJO

Mollie Naranjo's son

Traditional Potter

Santa Clara Pueblo

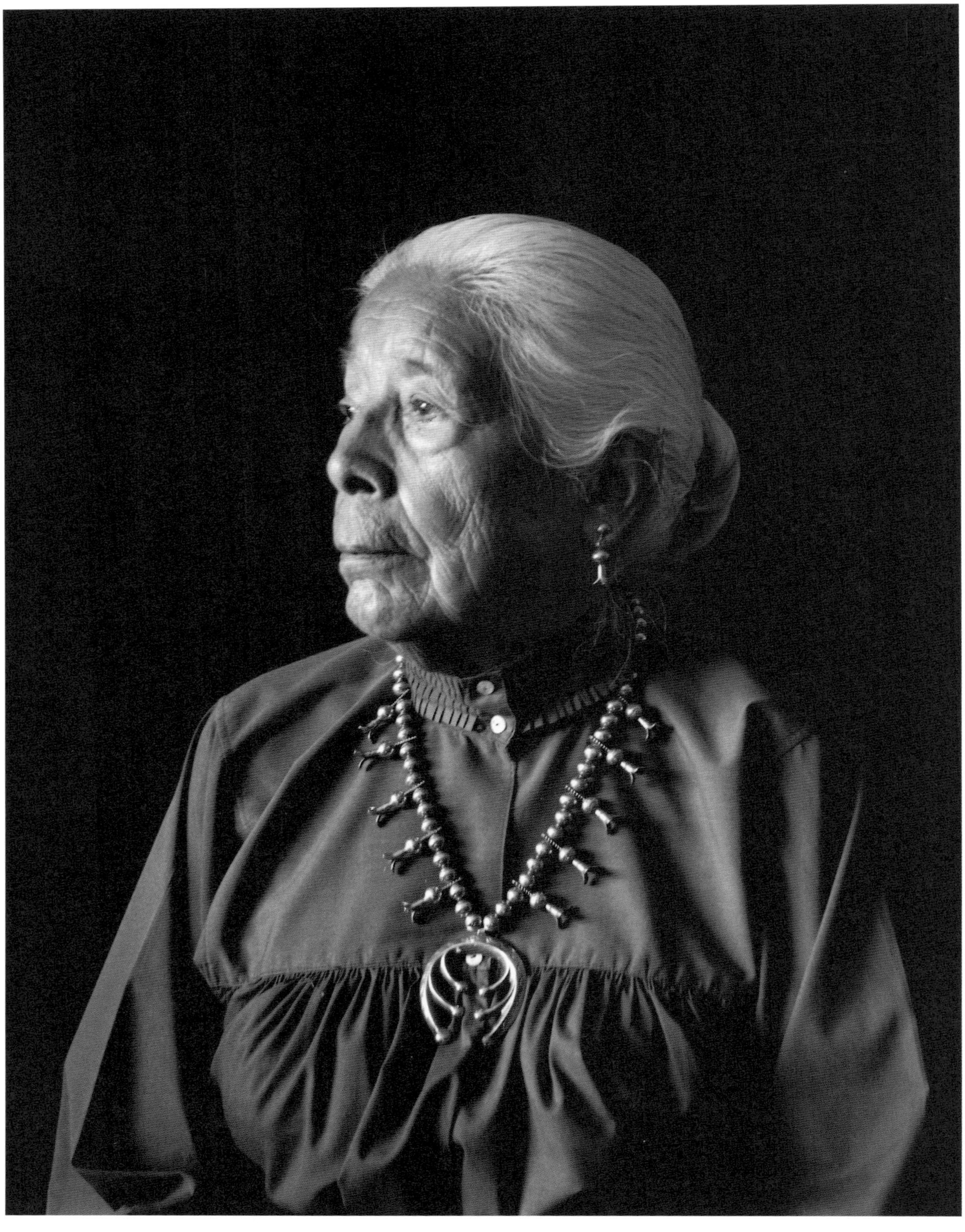

66

GERONIMA CRUZ MONTOYA

Painter, Dorothy Dunn School of Southwest Indian Painting

San Juan Pueblo

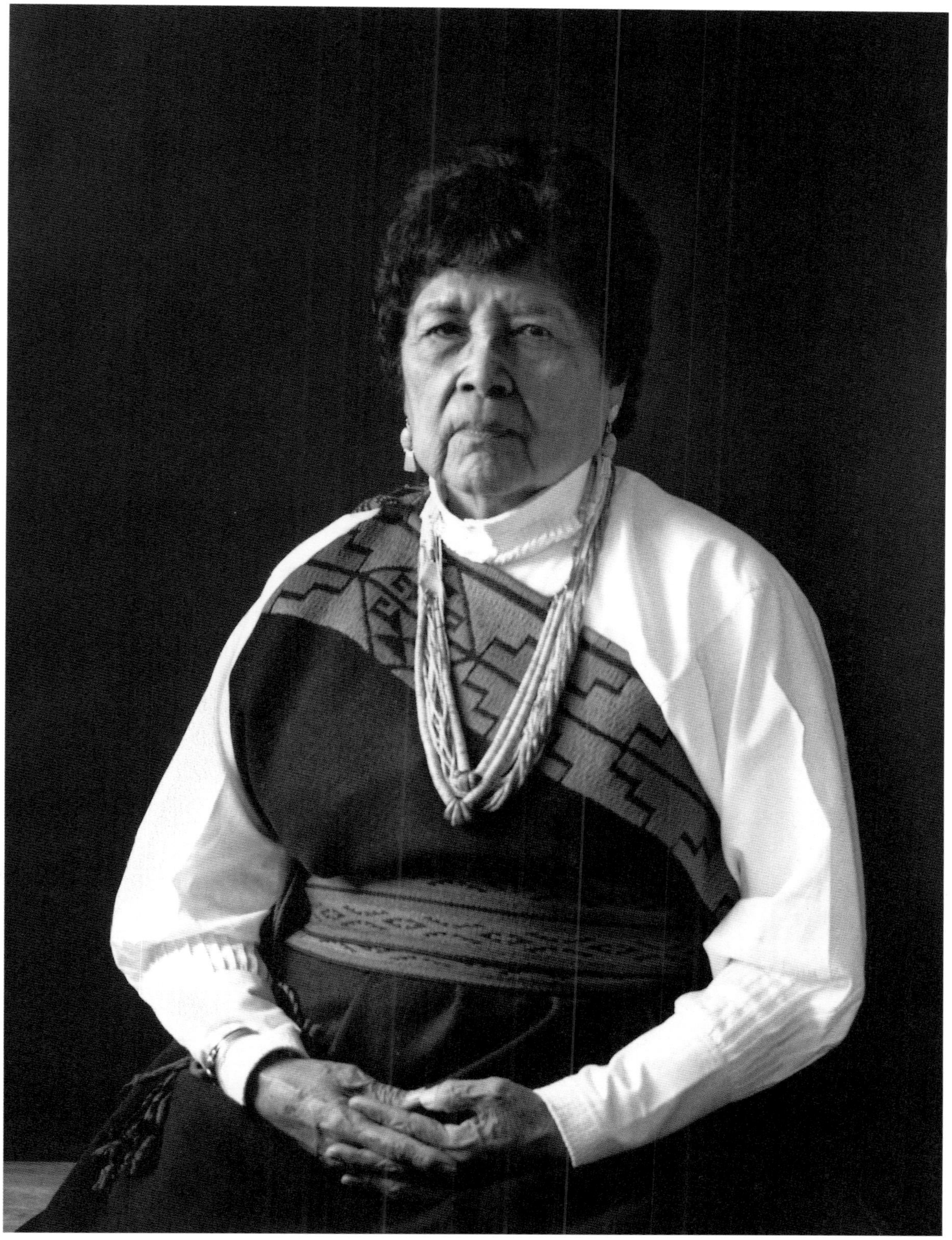

67

ROMANCITA SANDOVAL

Geronima Cruz Montoya's sister

Traditional Pueblo Embroidery and Sewing

San Juan Pueblo

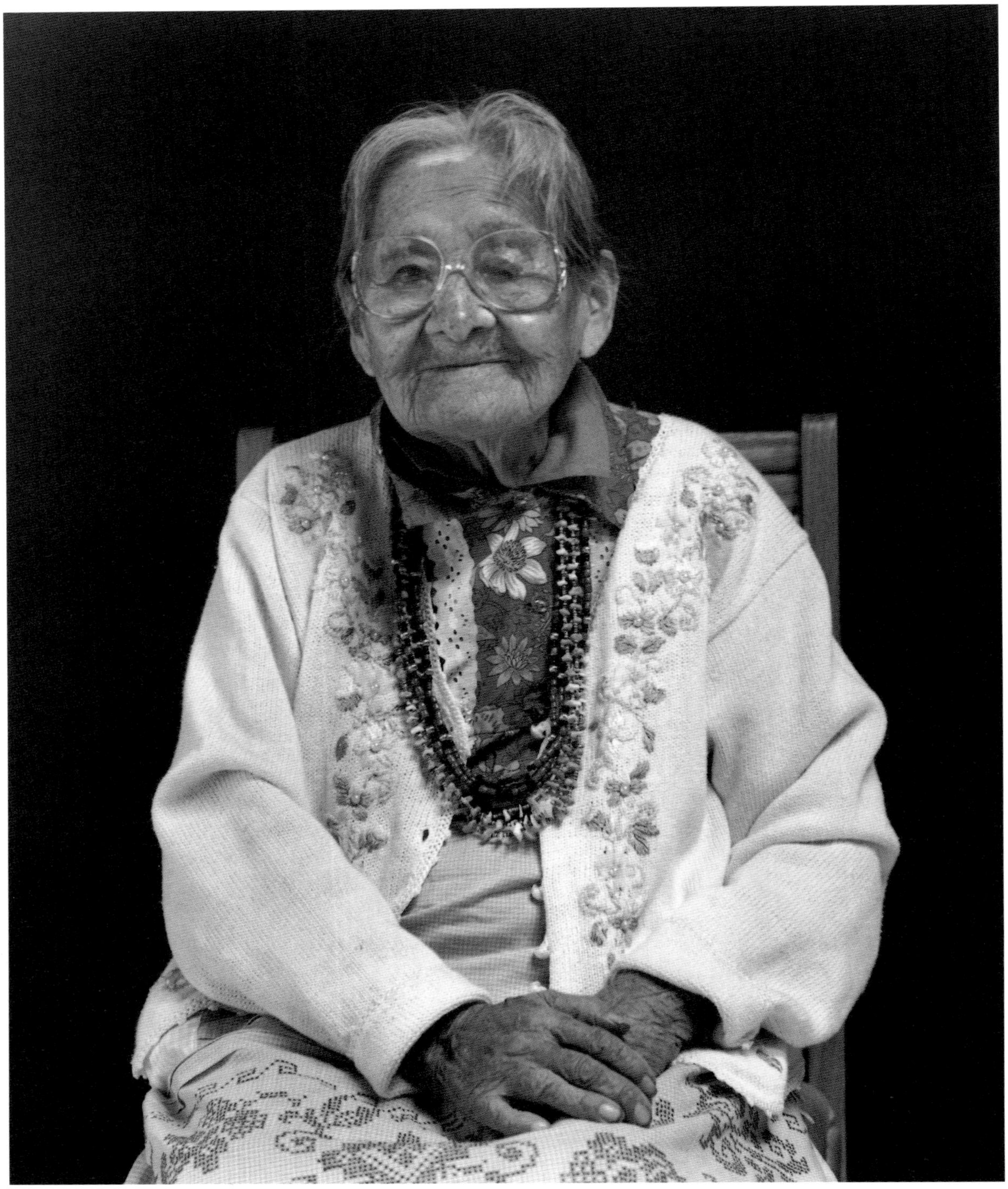

68

MARIE LUPE ROMERO, age ninety-four

Traditional Potter

Jémez Pueblo

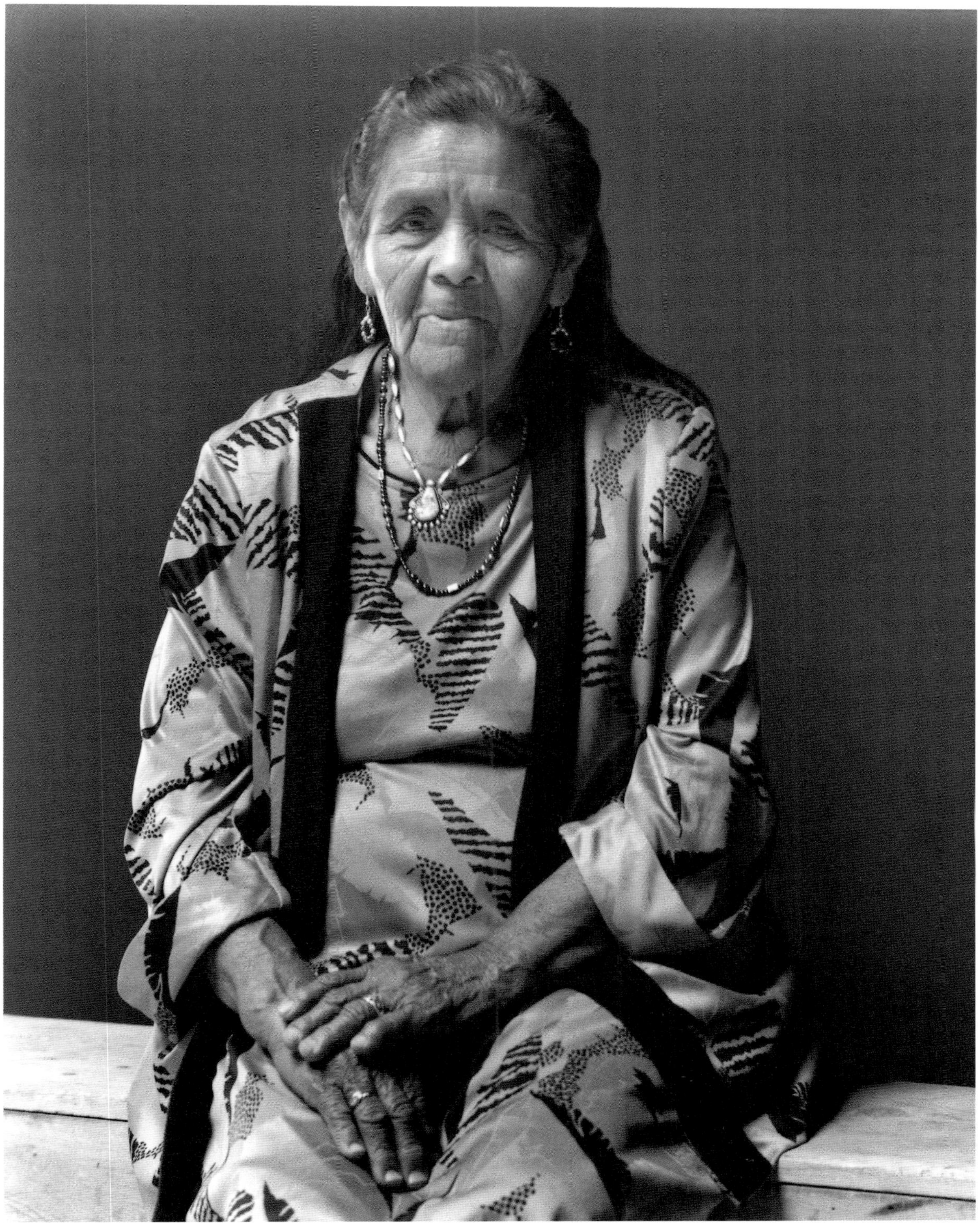

69

GERONIMA SHENDO

Marie Lupe Romero's niece

Traditional Potter

Jémez Pueblo

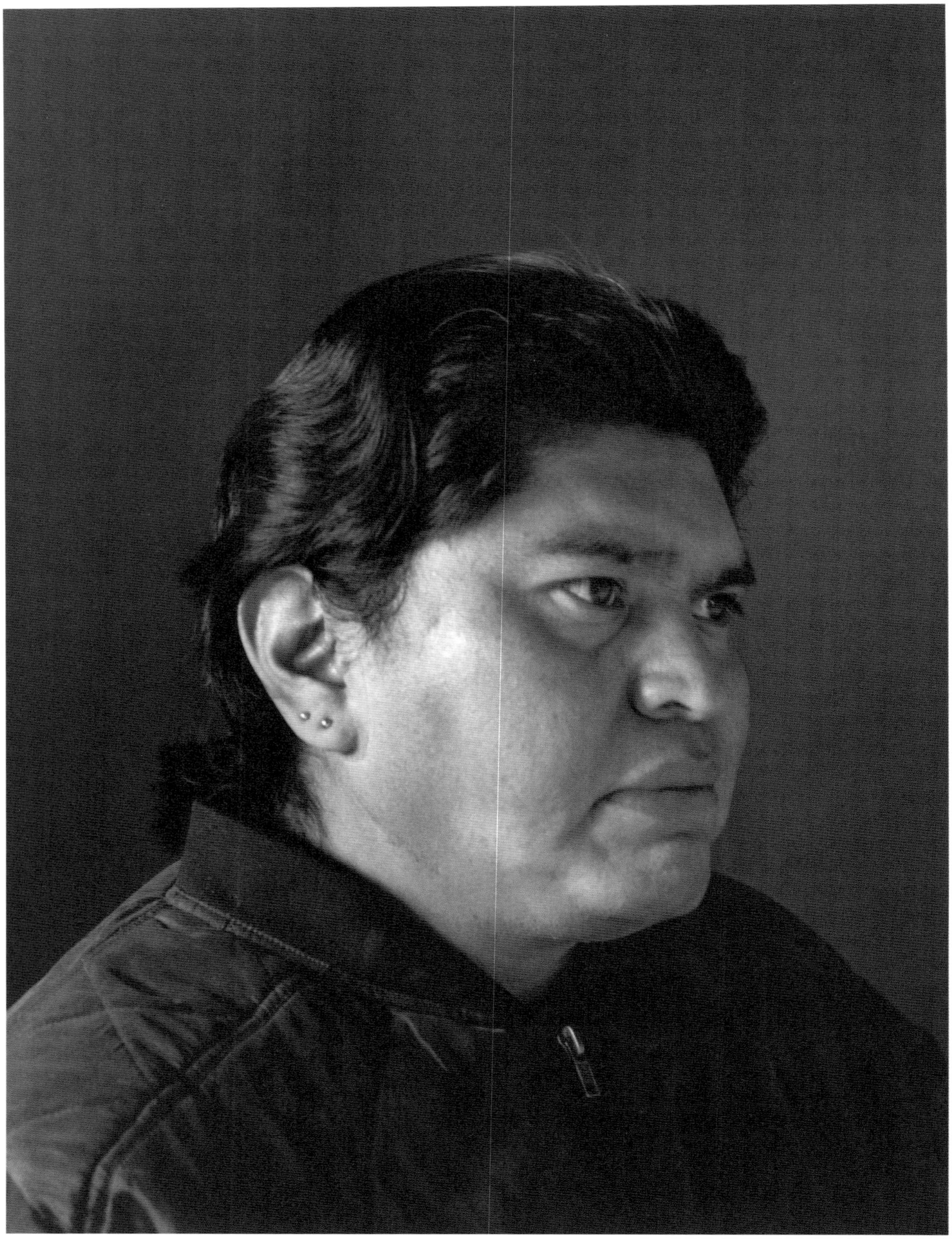

70
CLIFF FRAGUA
Juanita Fragua's son
Stone Sculptor
Jémez Pueblo

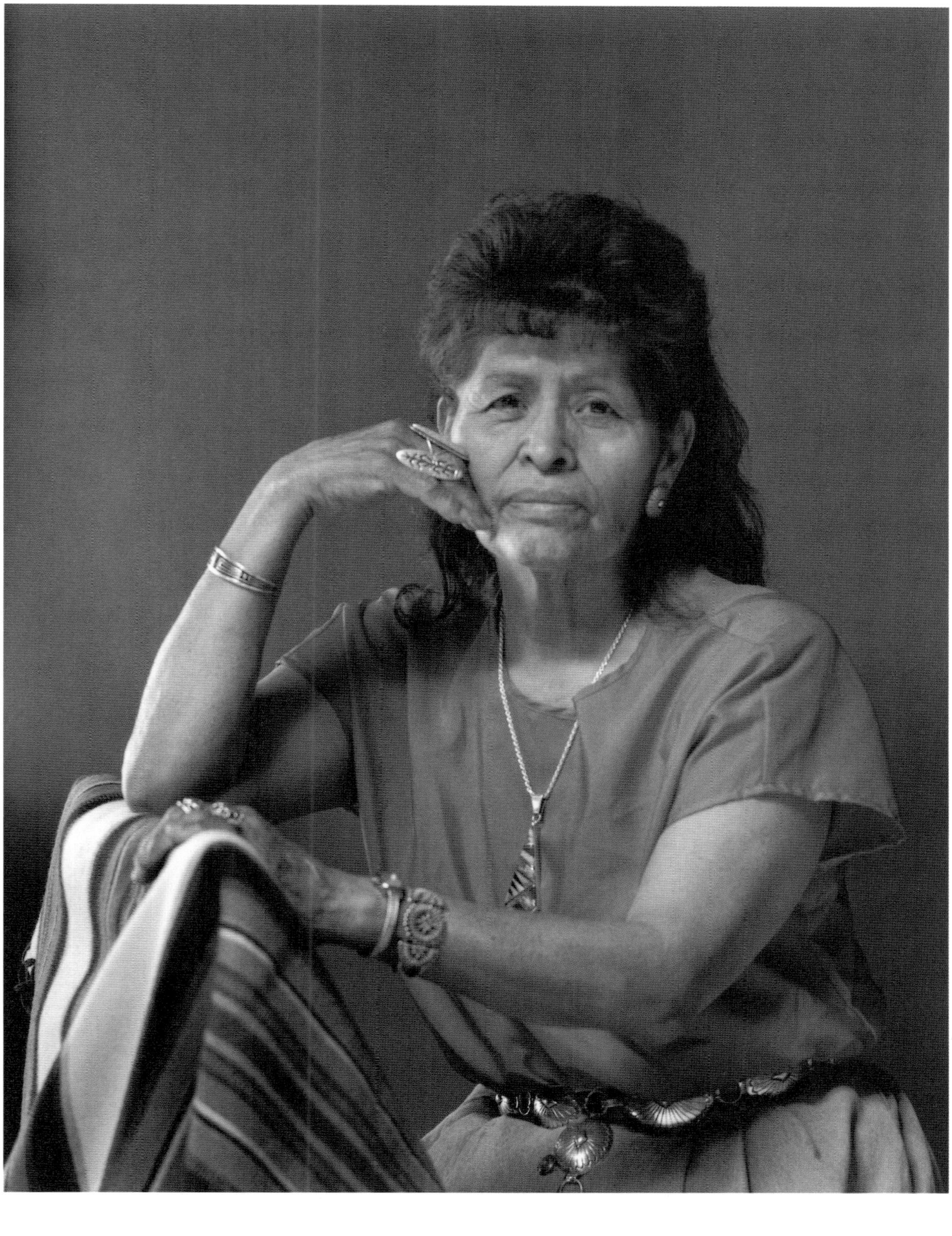

71

JUANITA FRAGUA

Marie Lupe Romero's niece

Traditional Potter

Jémez Pueblo

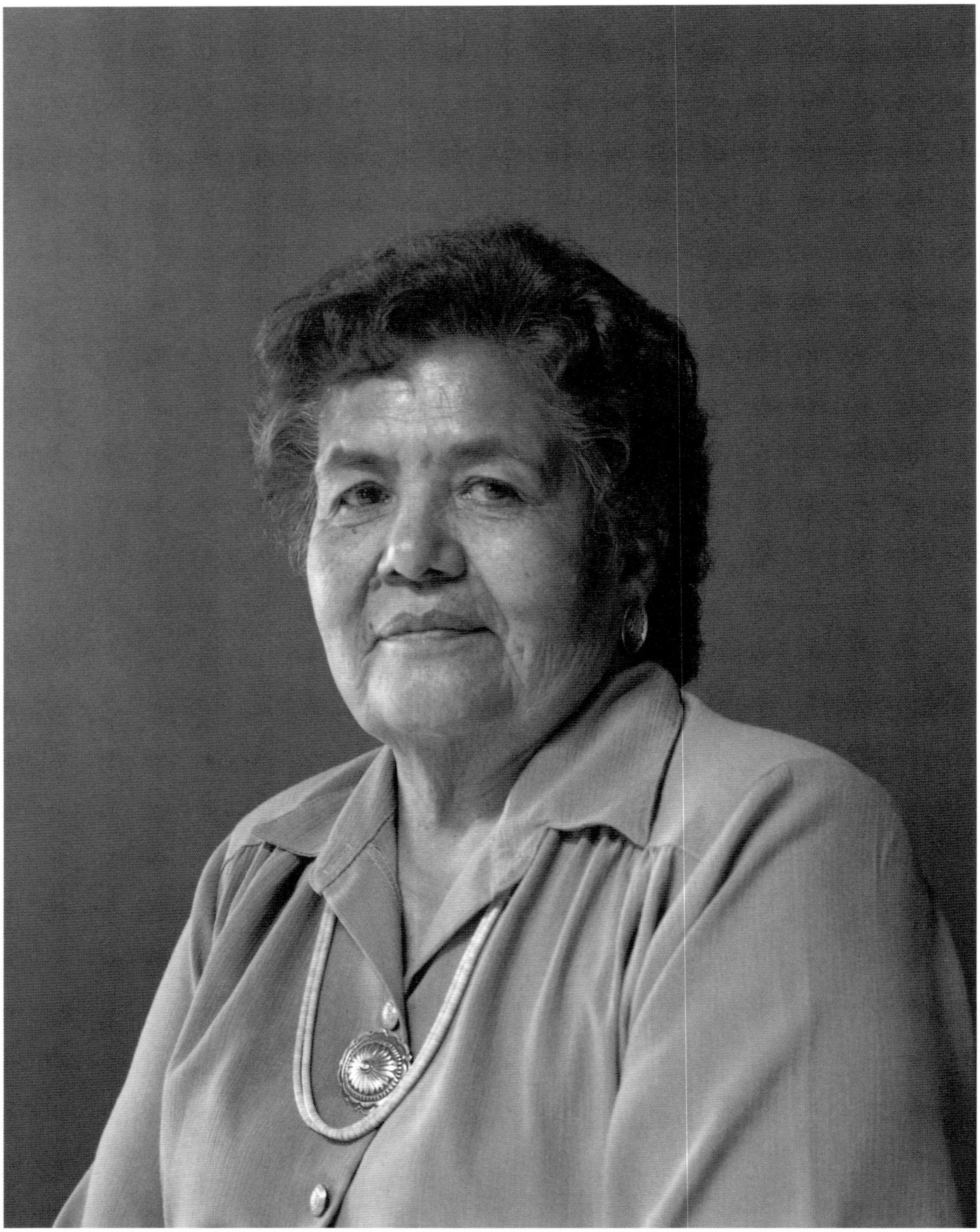

72

MARIE ROMERO

Marie Lupe Romero's niece

Traditional Potter

Jémez Pueblo

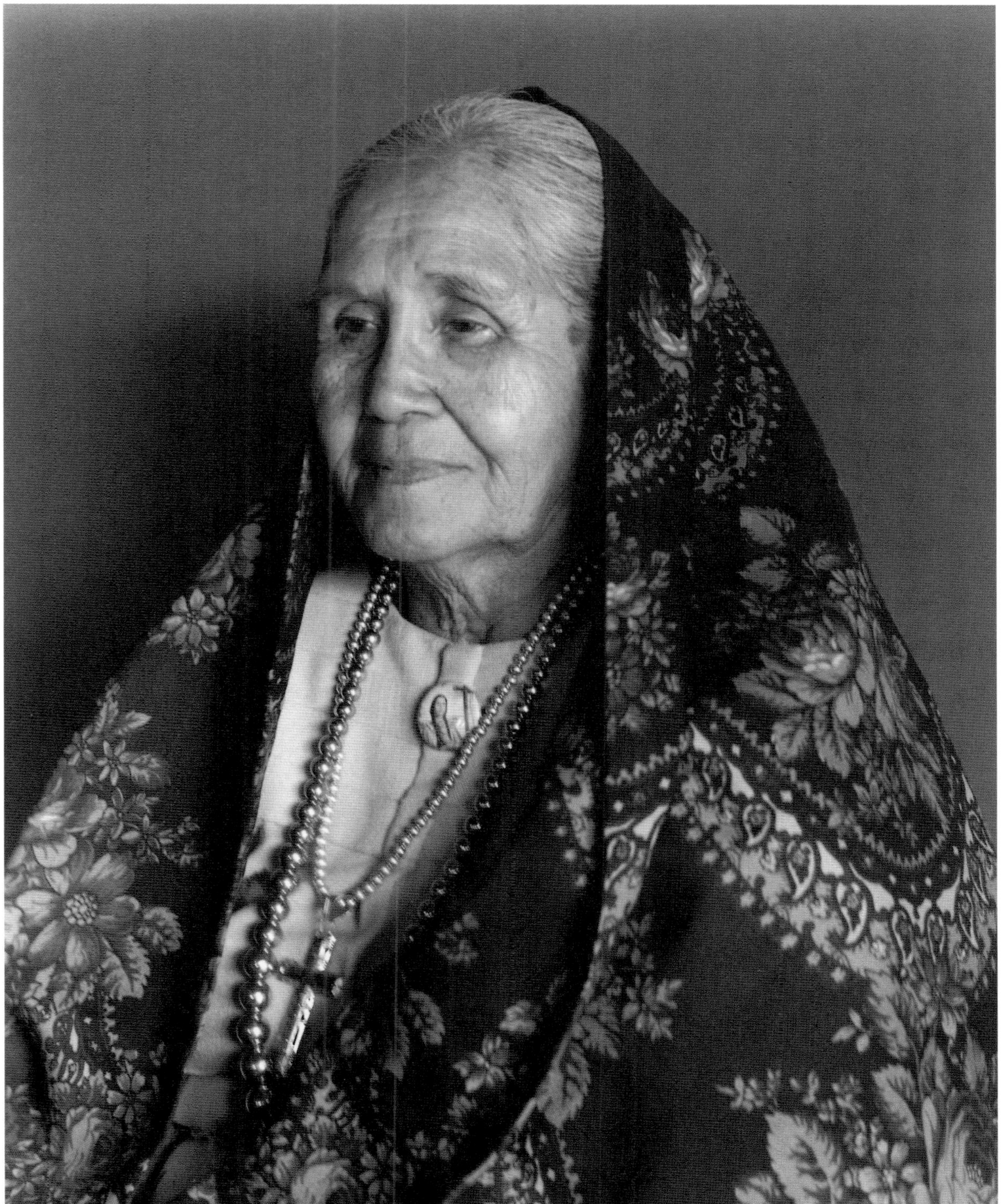

73
JUANA MARIA PECOS
Traditional Pueblo Embroidery
Jémez Pueblo

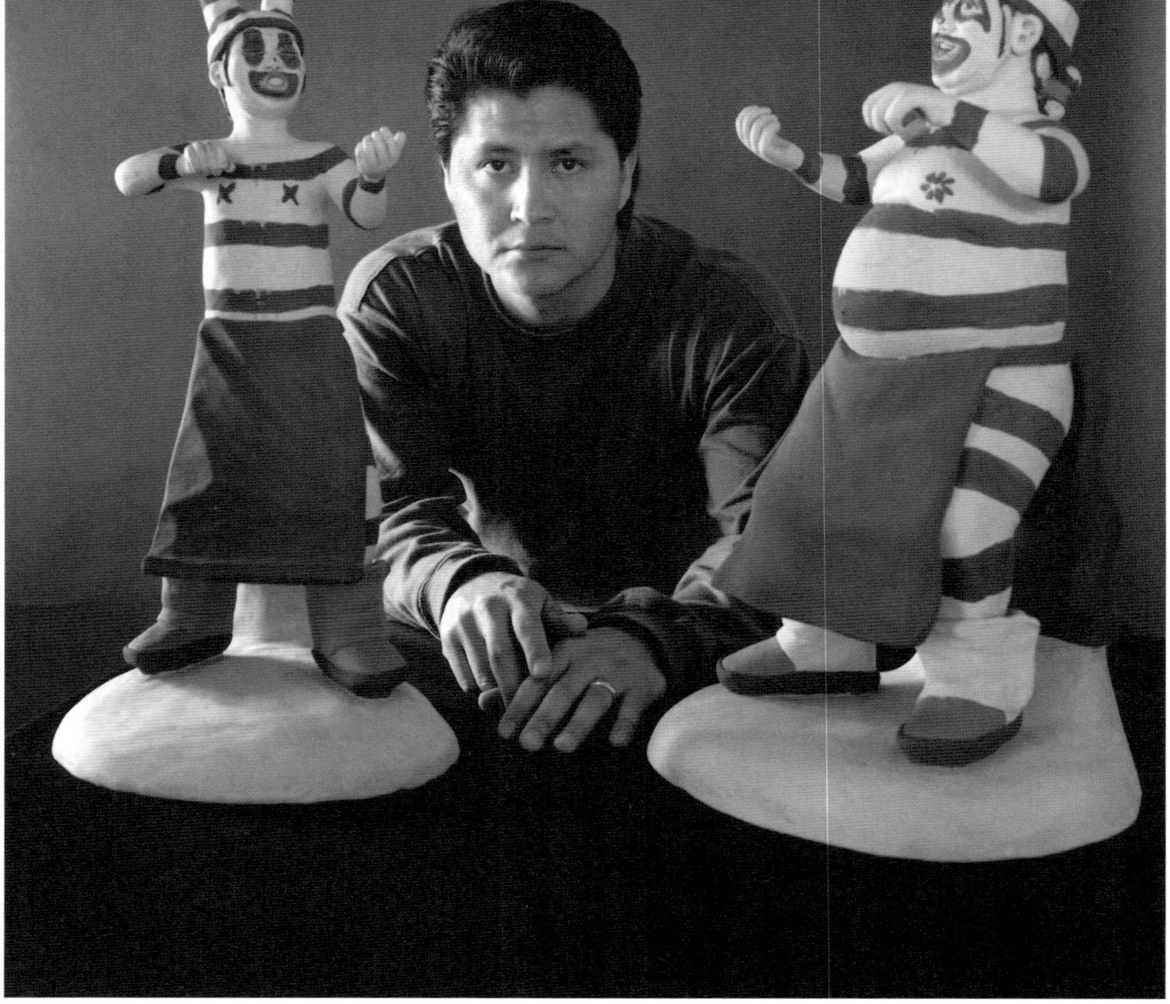

74

JOE CAJERO, Jr.

Esther H. Cajero's son

Juana Maria Pecos's grandson

Clay Sculptor

Jémez Pueblo

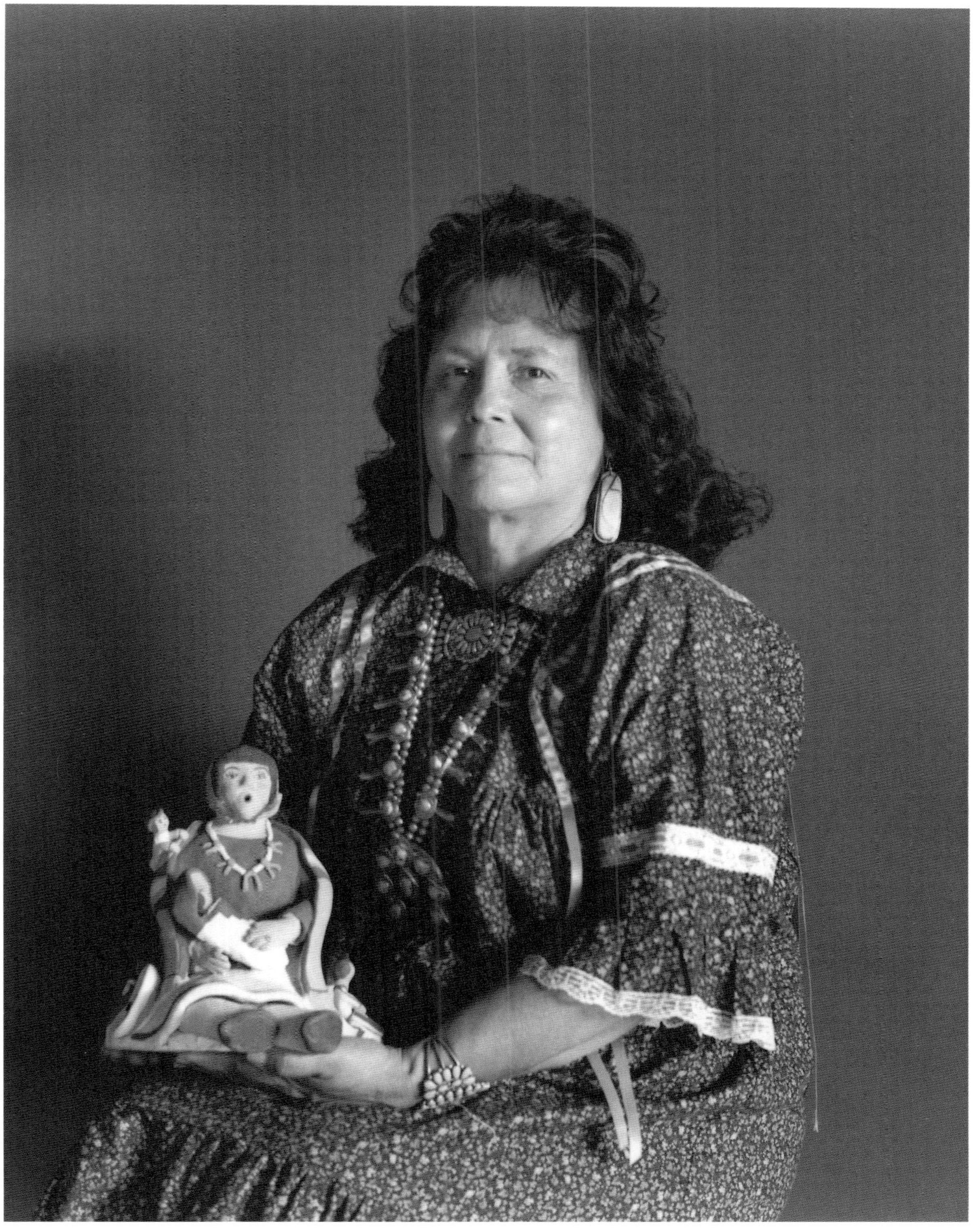

75
ESTHER H. CAJERO
Juana Maria Pecos's daughter
Traditional Potter
Jémez Pueblo

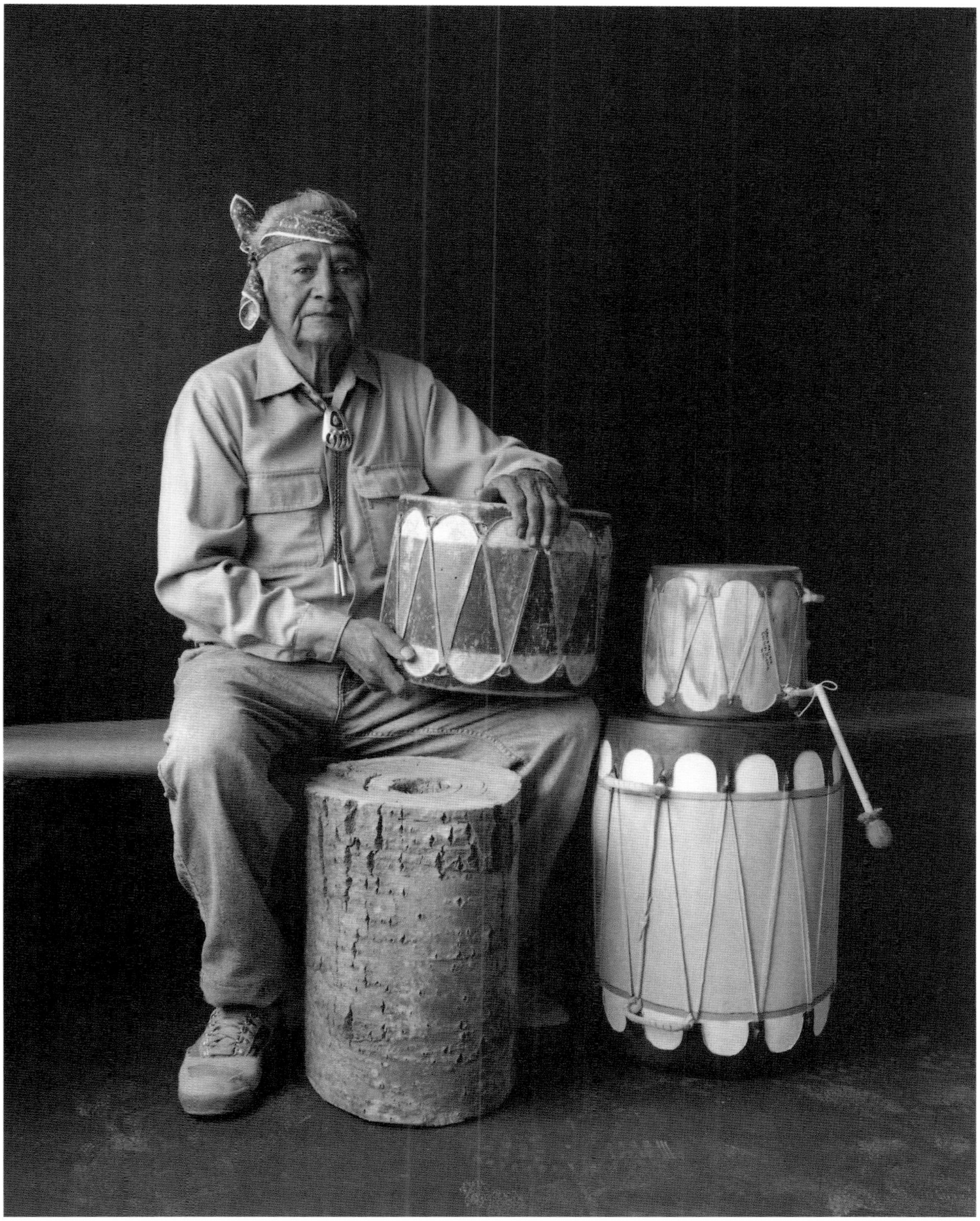

76

STEVEN HERRERA

with drum his father made one hundred years ago

Traditional Drum Maker

Cochiti Pueblo

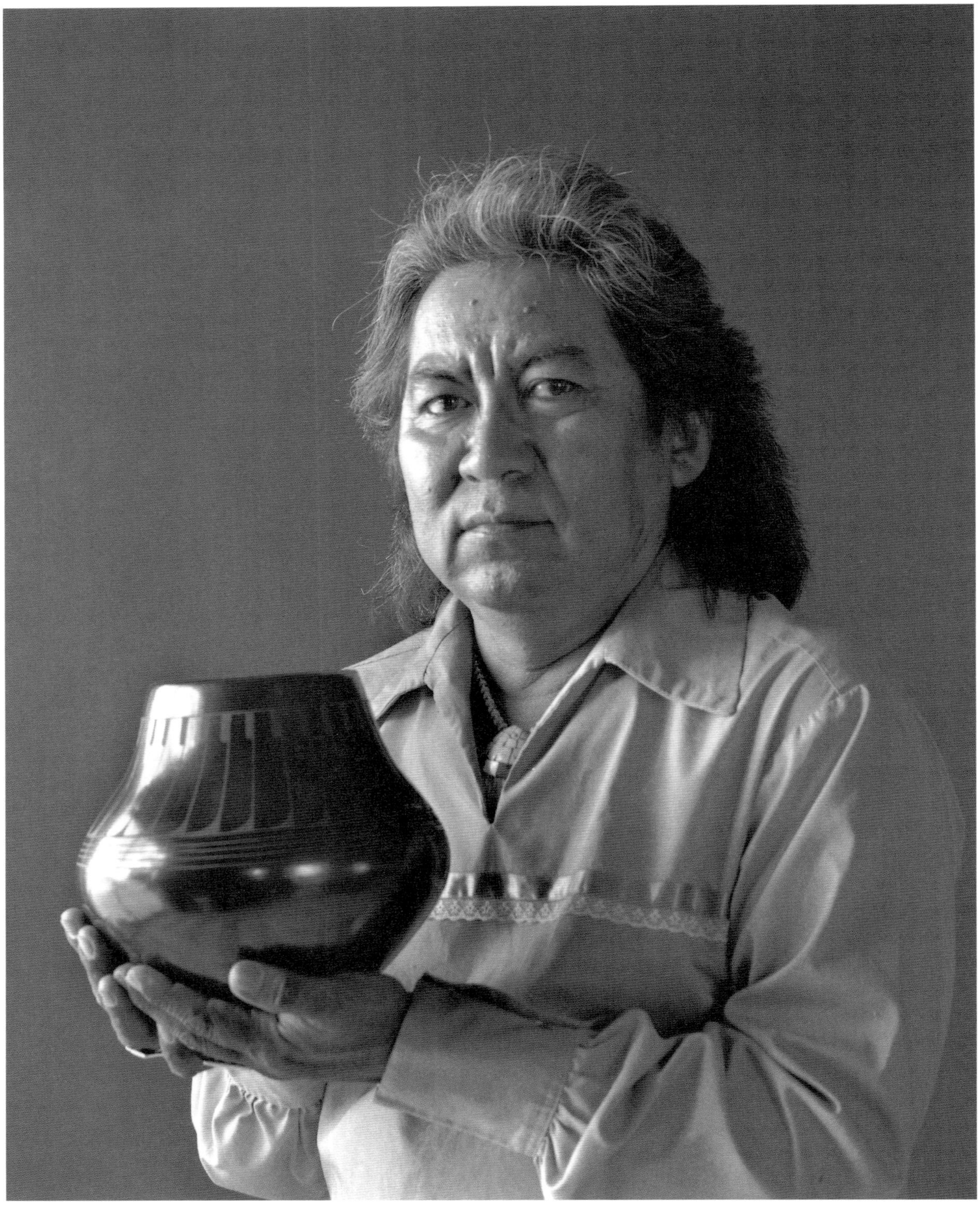

77
JUAN TAFOYA
Traditional Potter
San Ildefonso/San Juan

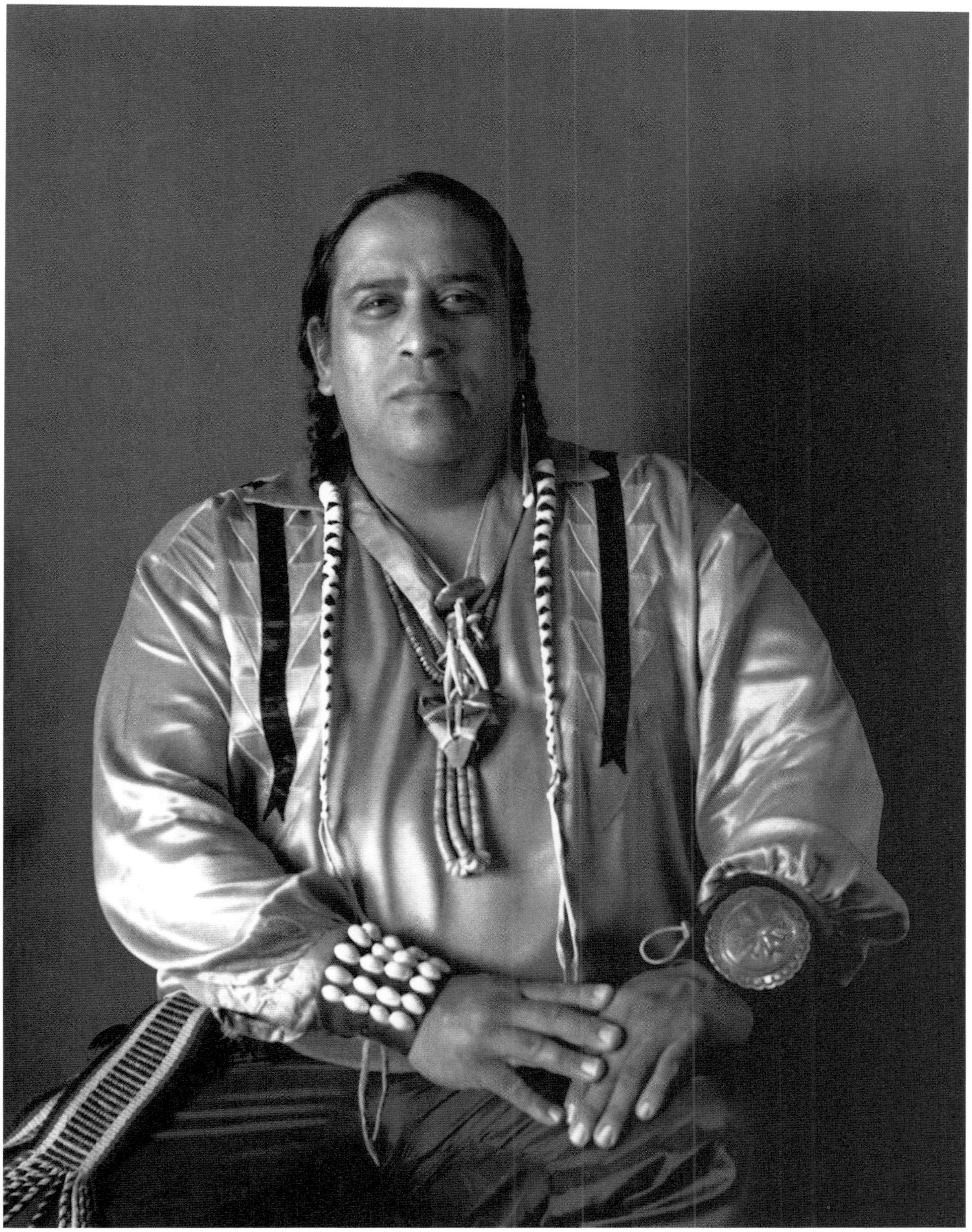

78
CLOUD EAGLE
Sculptor, Painter, Mixed-Media Artist
Nambé Pueblo

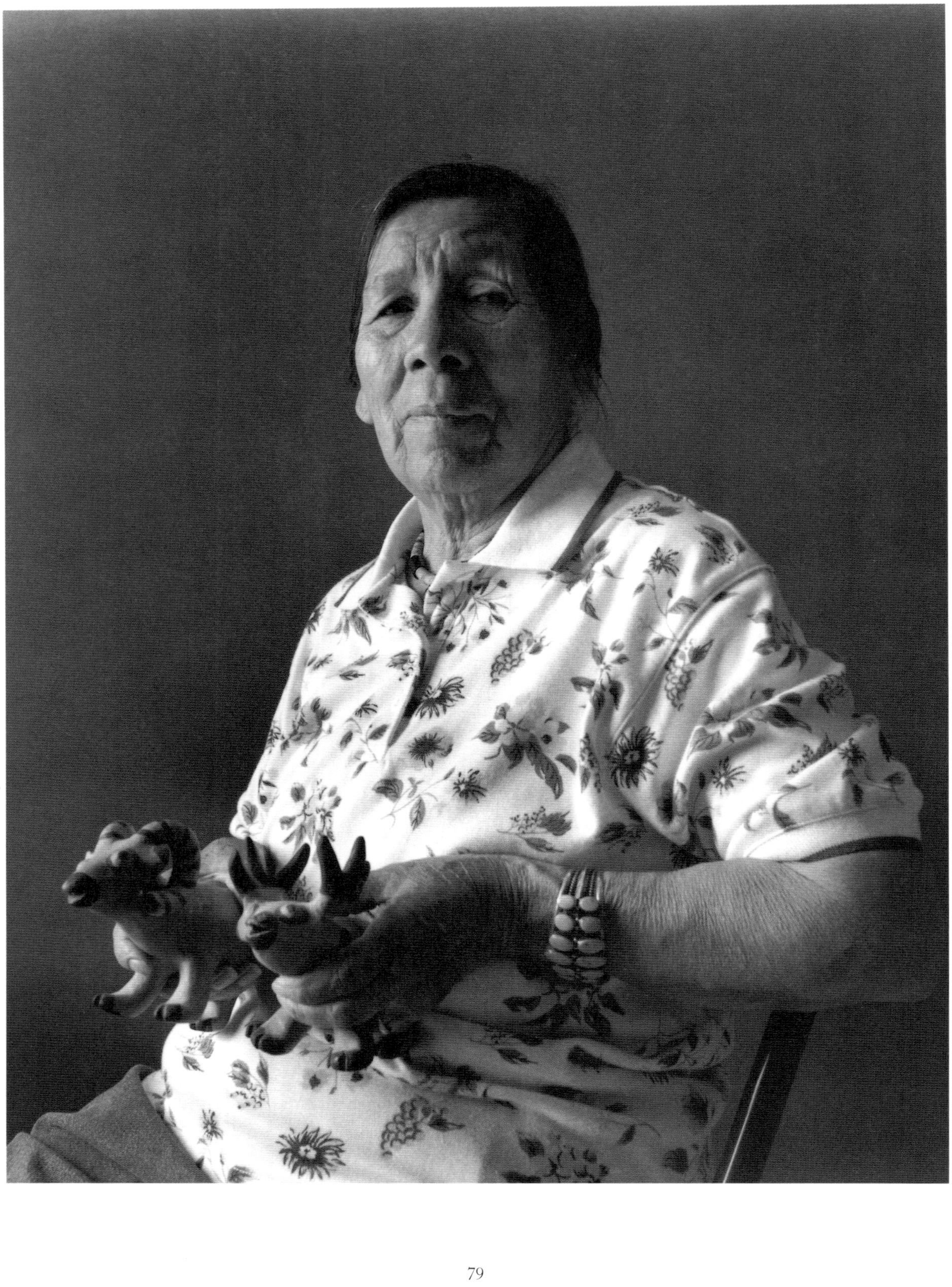

79
JOSEPHINE ARQUERO
Traditional Potter
Cochiti Pueblo

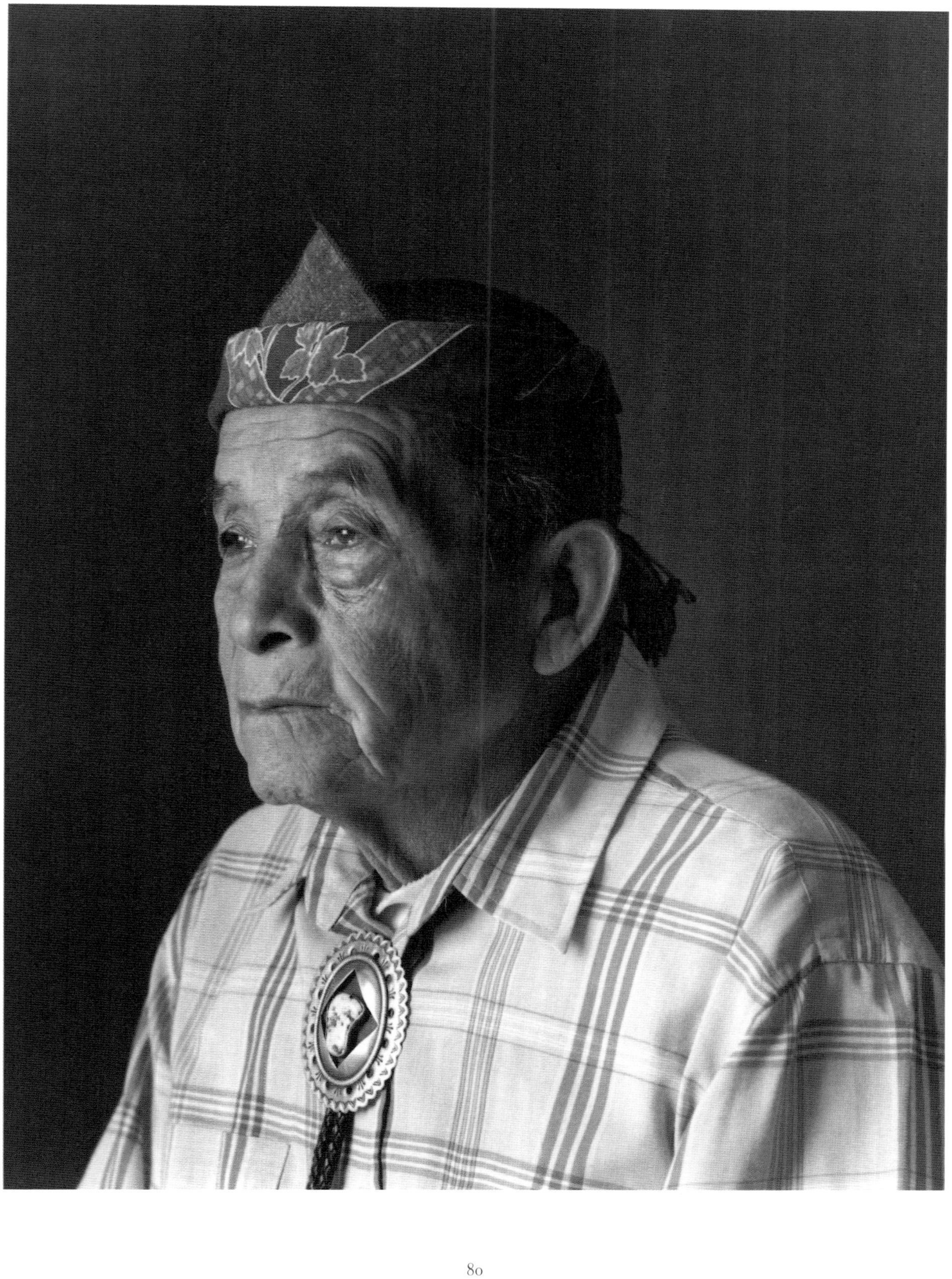

80

JOHNNIE ARQUERO

Josephine Arquero's husband

Traditional Drum Maker

Cochiti Pueblo

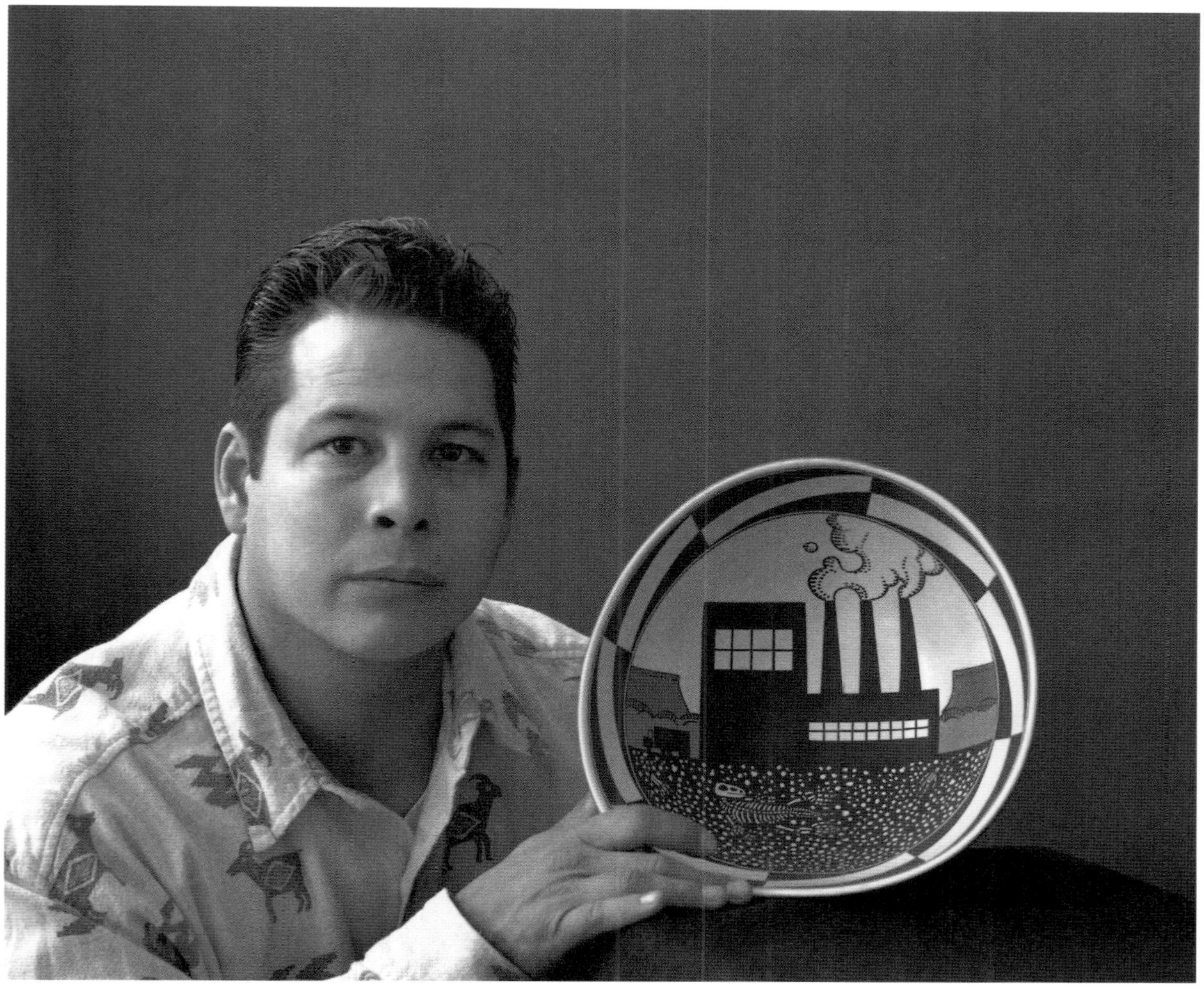

81

DIEGO ROMERO

Mateo Romero's brother

Contemporary Potter

Cochiti Pueblo

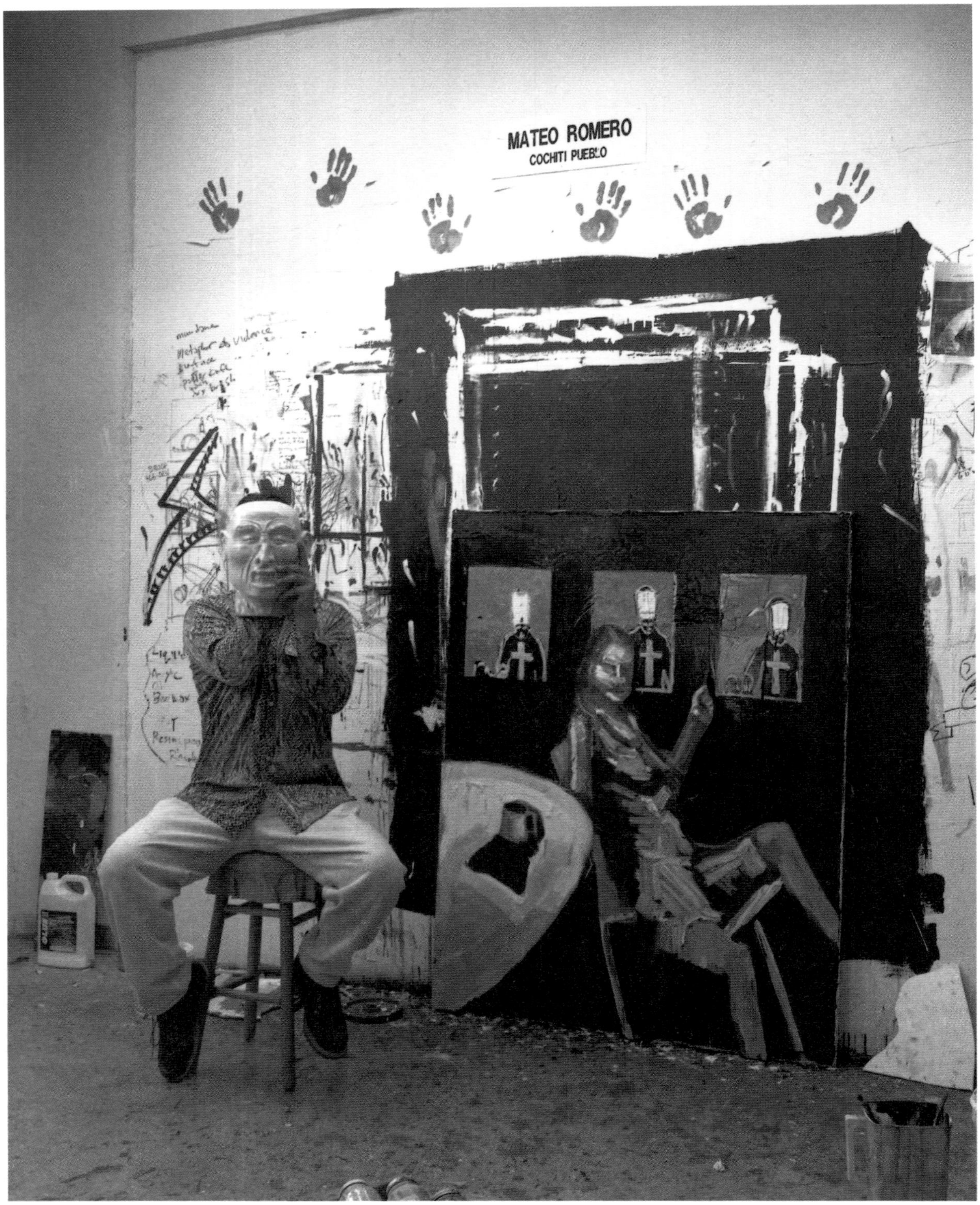

82
MATEO ROMERO
in studio with painting, wearing mask
Contemporary Painter
Cochiti Pueblo

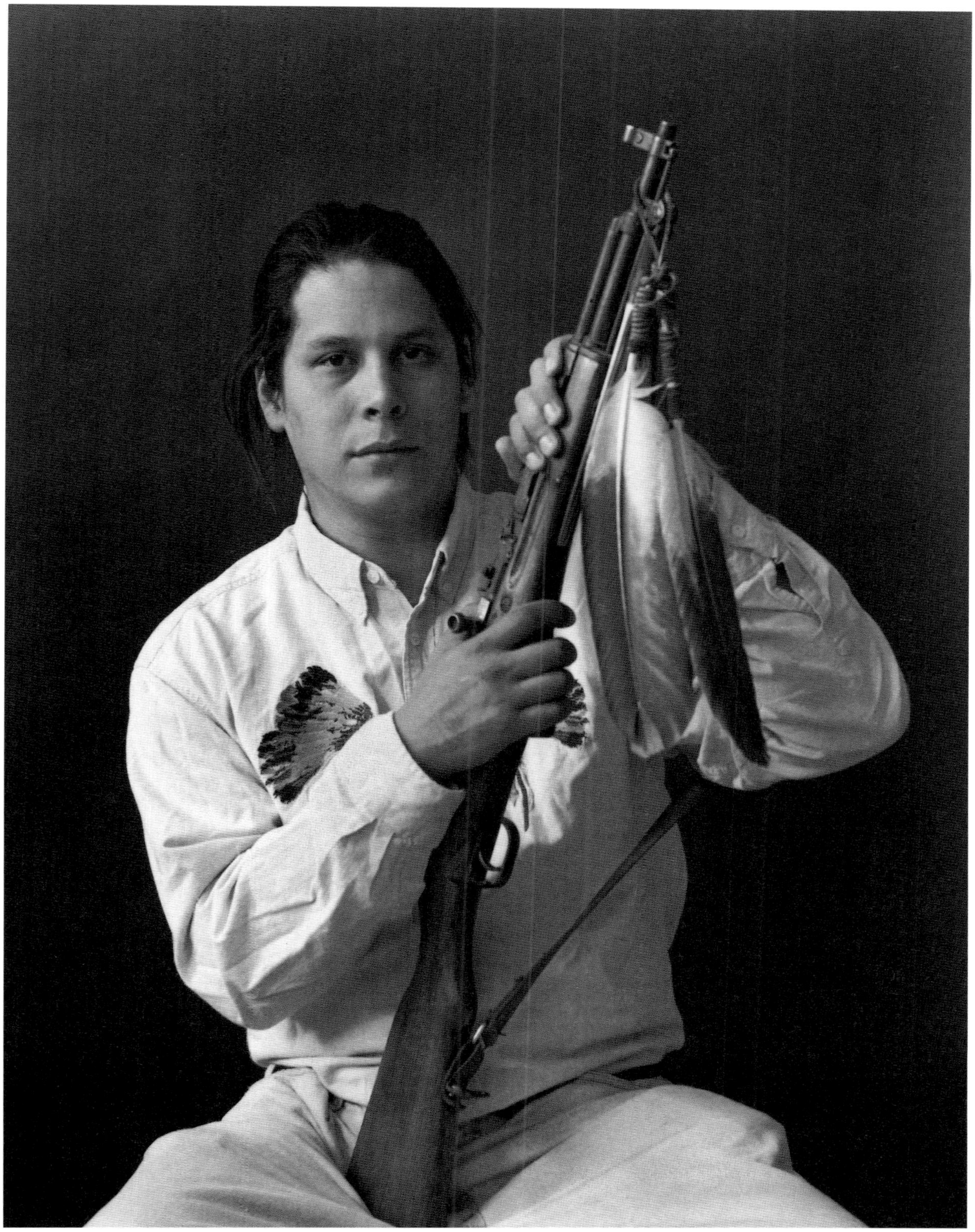

83
MATEO ROMERO
Diego Romero's brother
holding hunting rifle
Contemporary Painter
Cochiti Pueblo

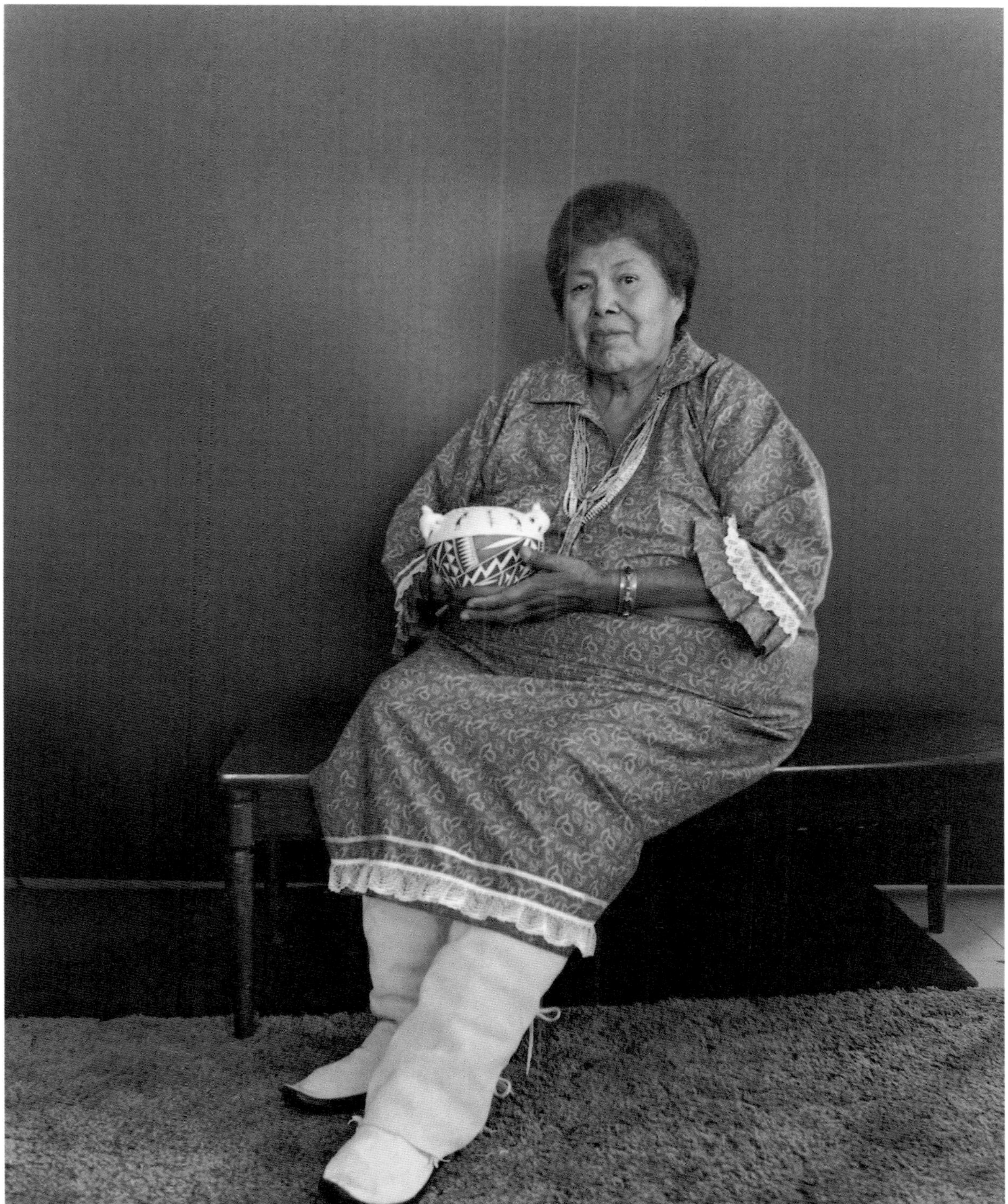

84
MYRNA CHINO
Traditional Potter
Acoma Pueblo

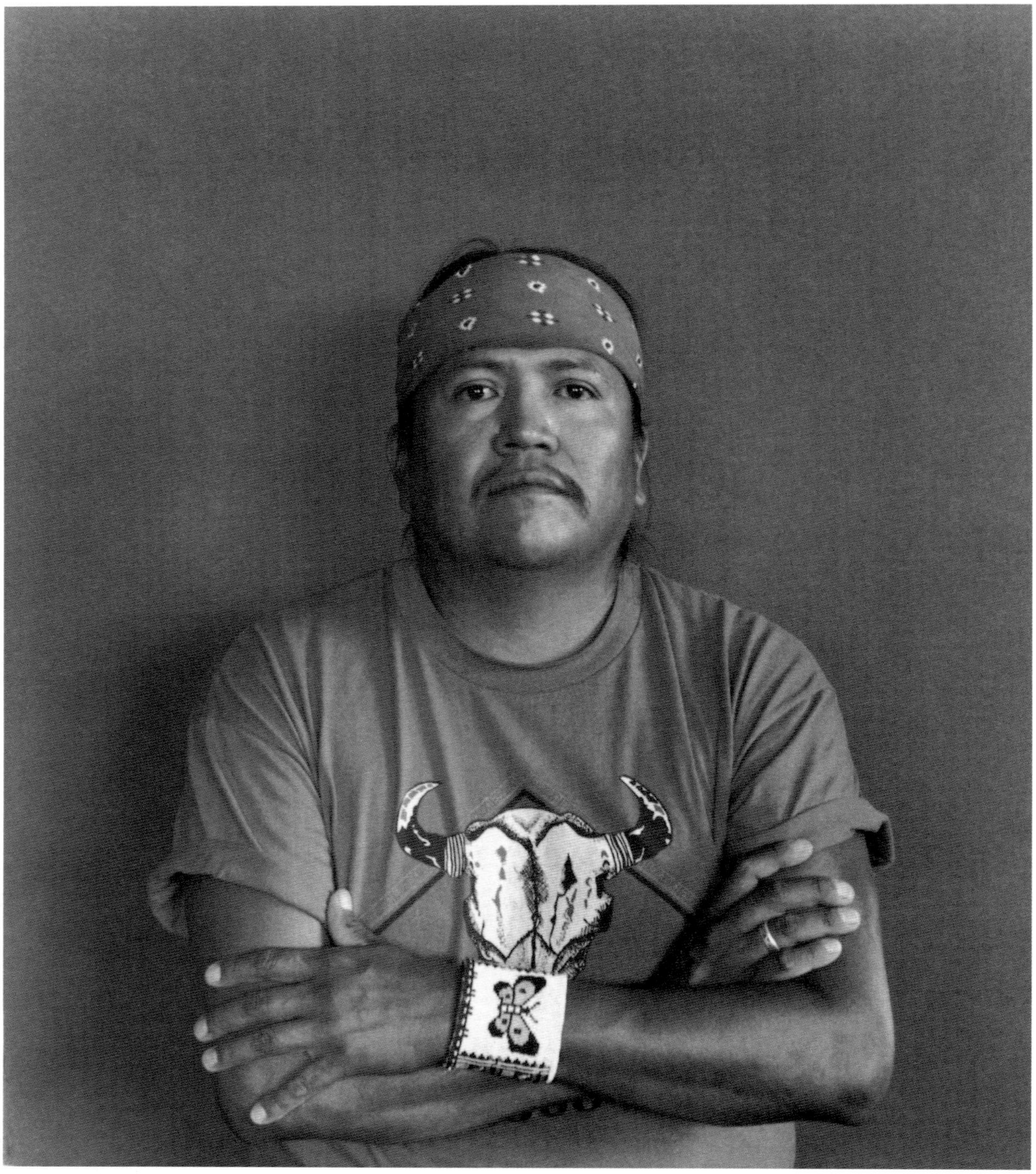

85

LARRY A. CHINO

Myrna Chino's son

Traditional Potter

Acoma Pueblo

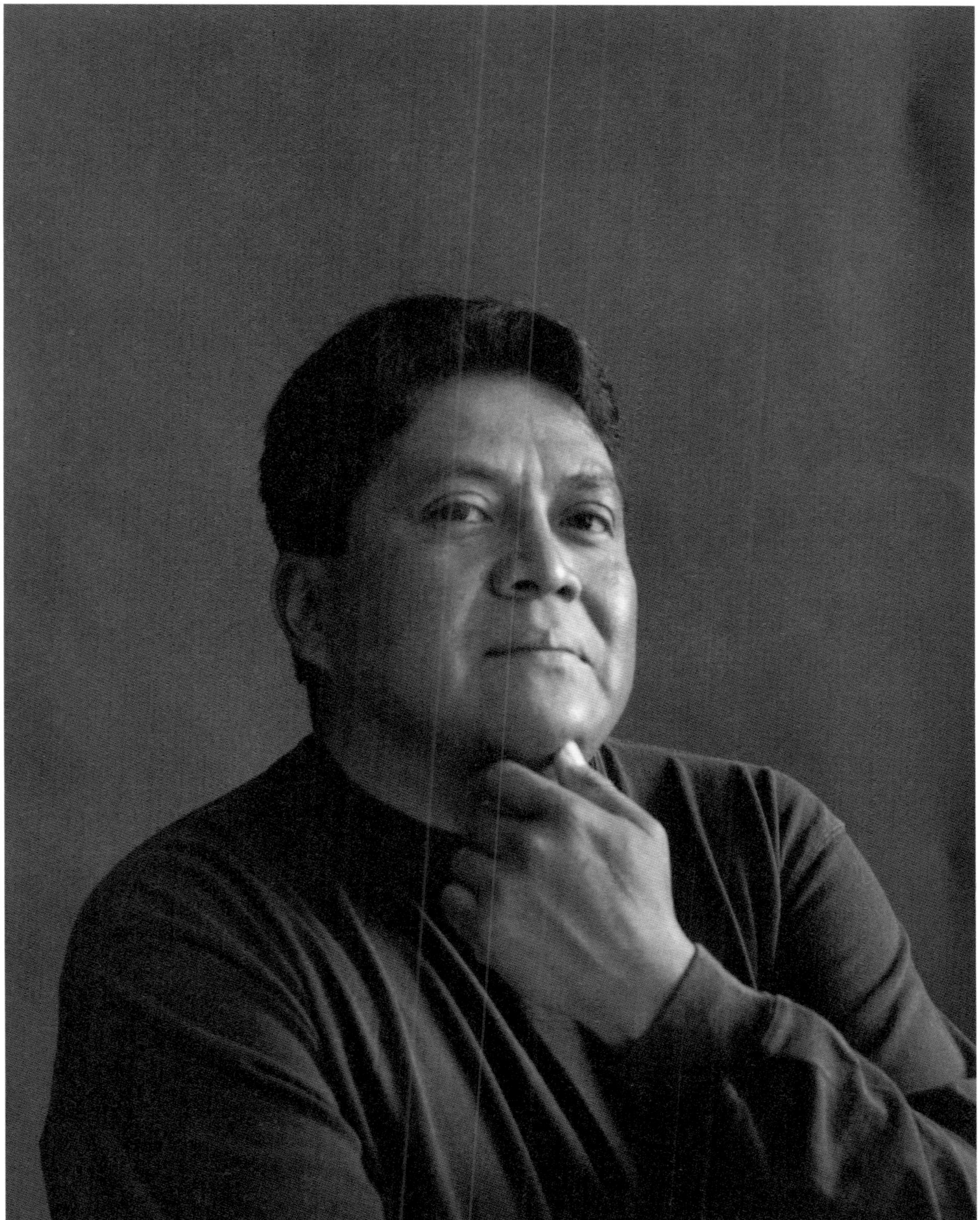

86

C. MAURUS CHINO

Myrna Chino's son

Painter, Printmaker, Potter

Acoma Pueblo

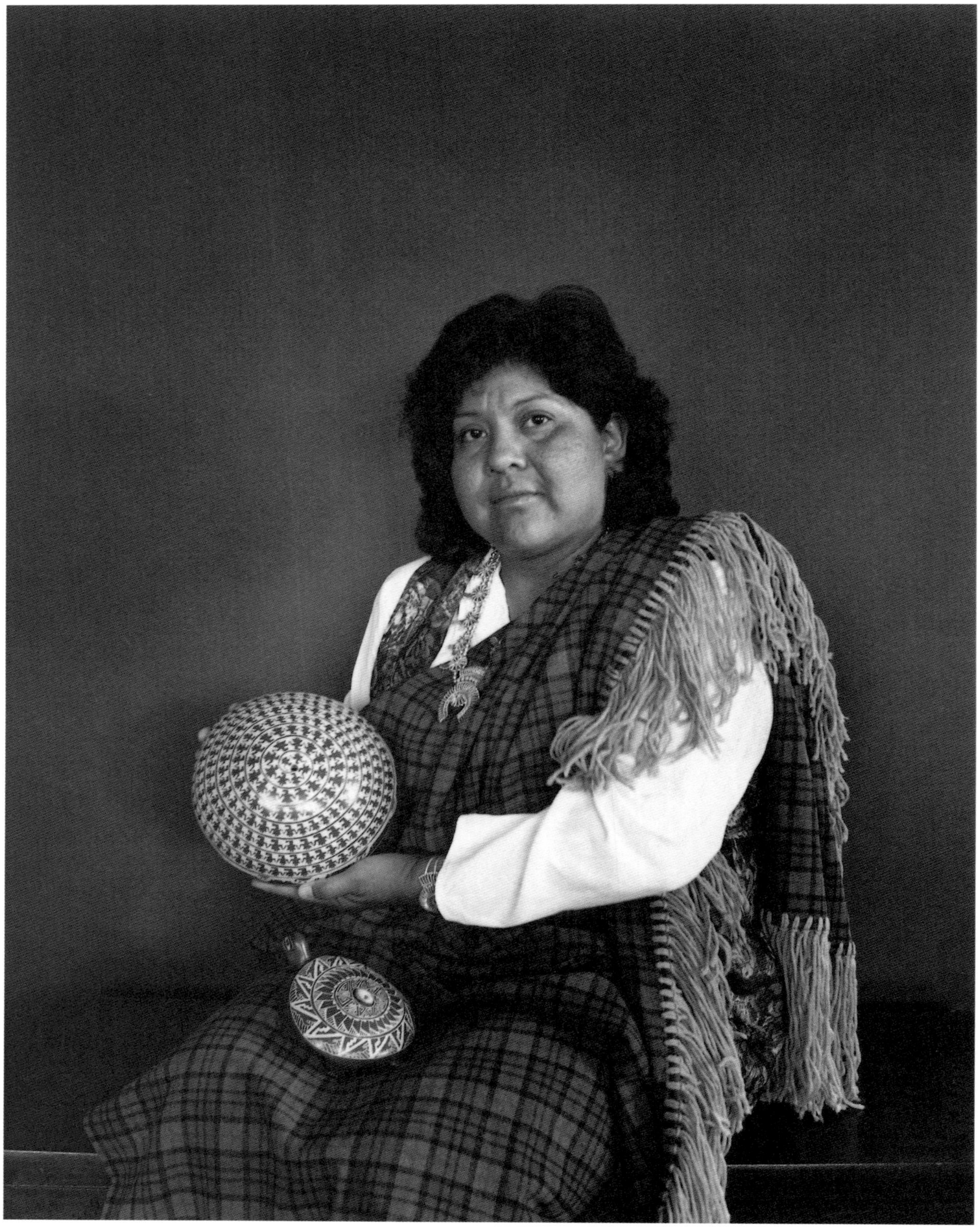

87

MELODY SIMPSON

Traditional Pottery Sculpture

Acoma Pueblo

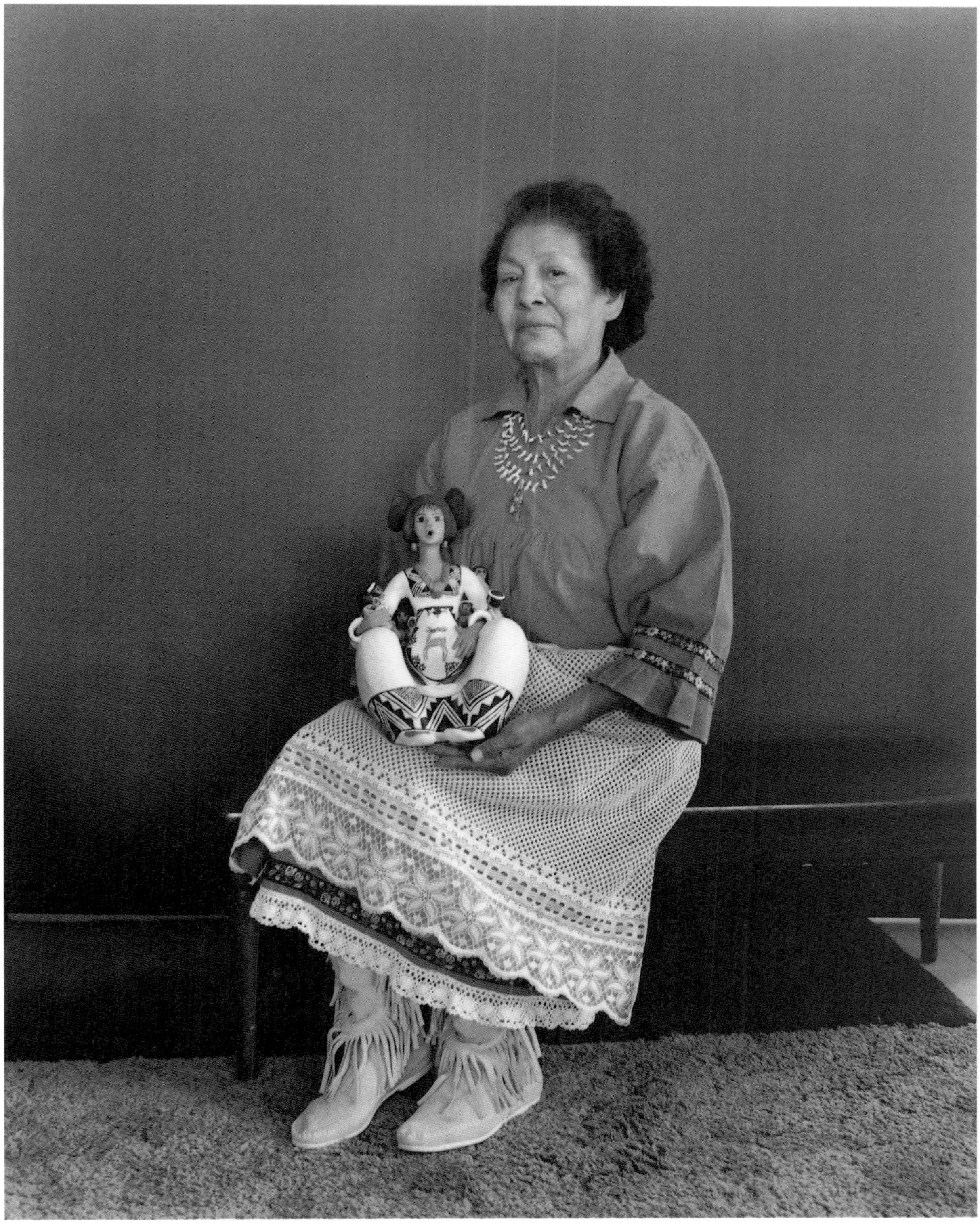

88

RACHEL ARNOLD

Melody Simpson's mother

Myrna Chino's sister

Traditional Pottery Sculpture

Acoma Pueblo

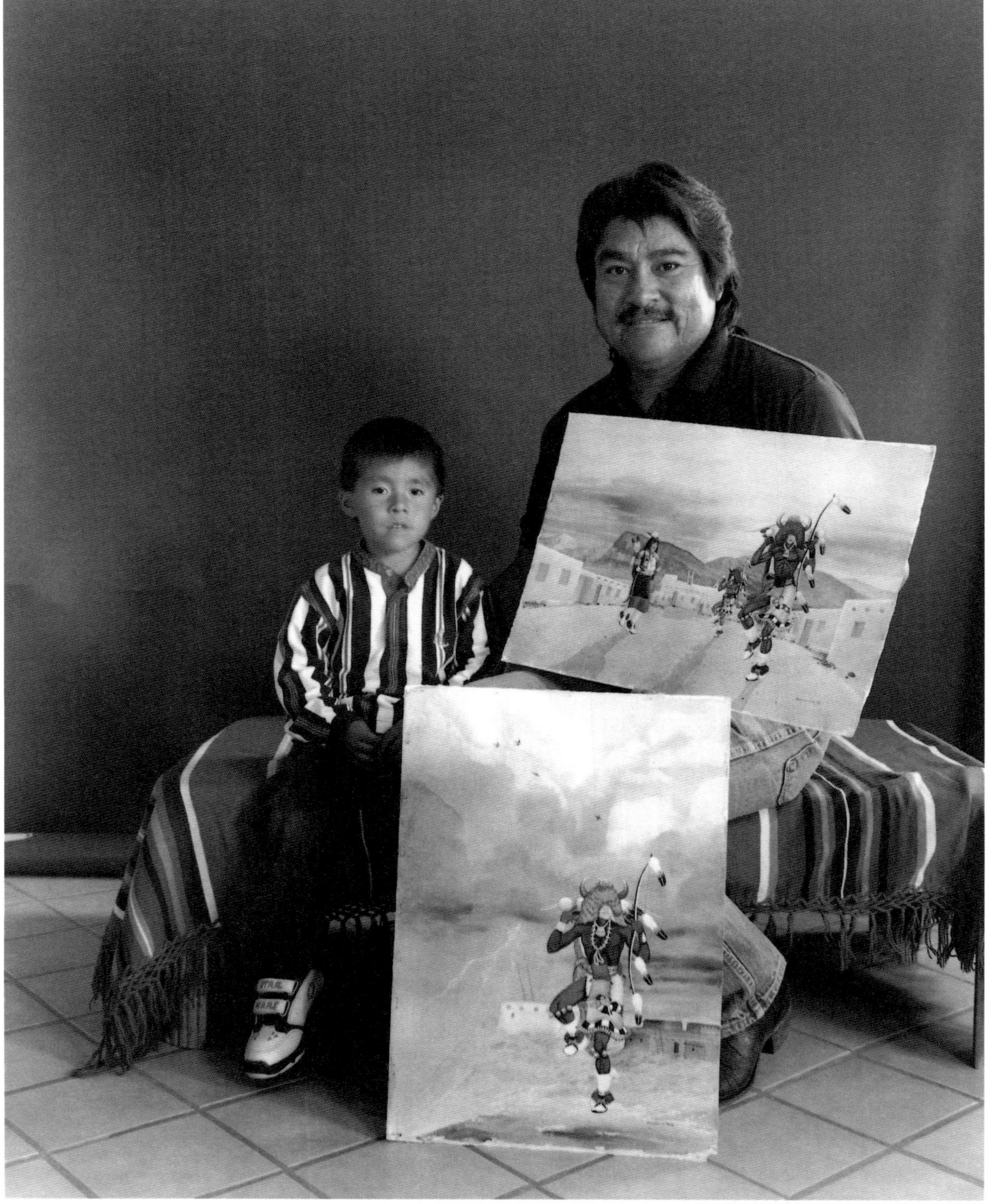

89

MARCELLUS MEDINA

with grandson Gavin Medina

Painter, Watercolors

Zia Pueblo

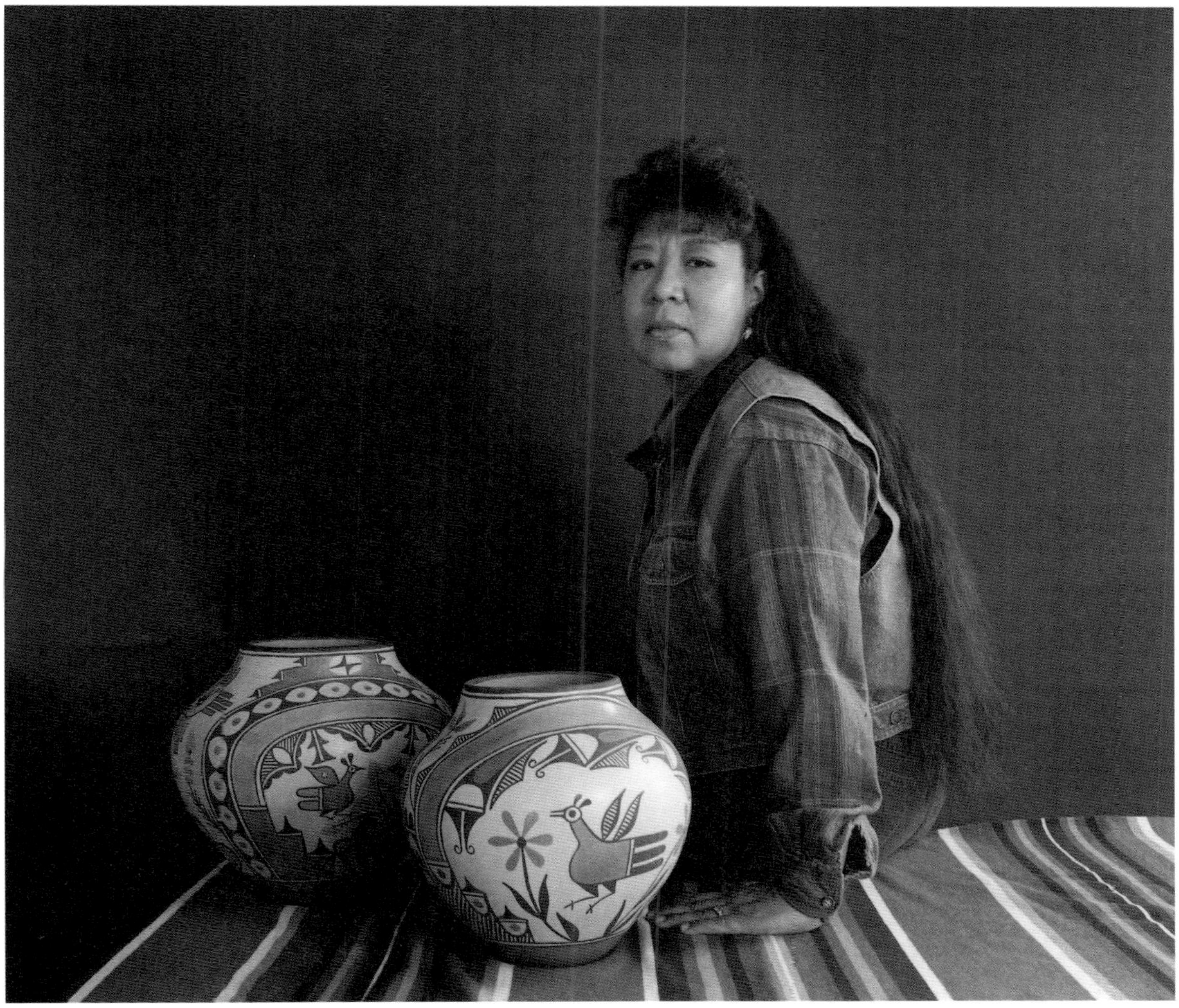

90

ELIZABETH MEDINA

Marcellus Medina's wife

Traditional Pottery

Zia Pueblo

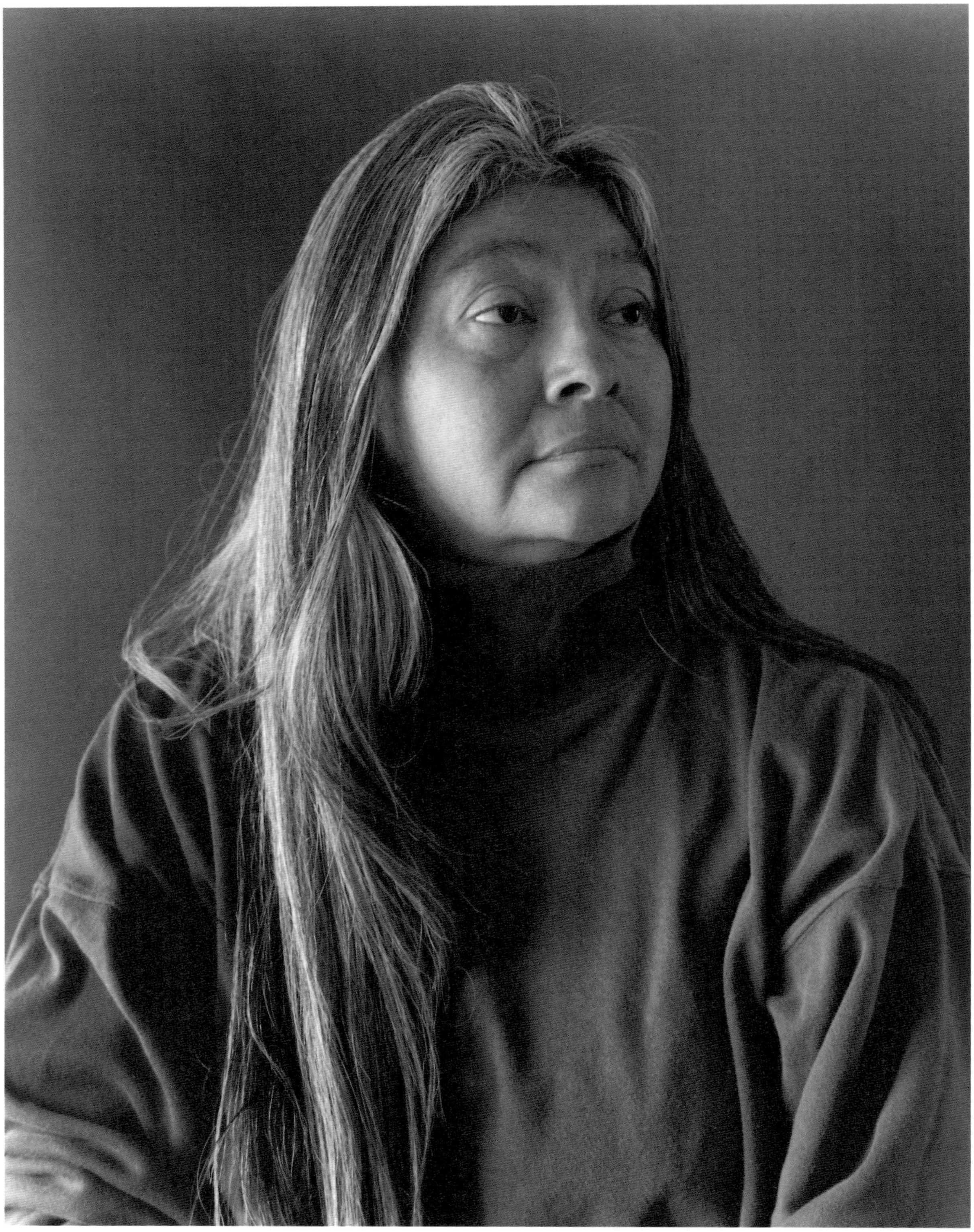

91

GAIL BIRD

Jeweler

Santo Domingo/Laguna

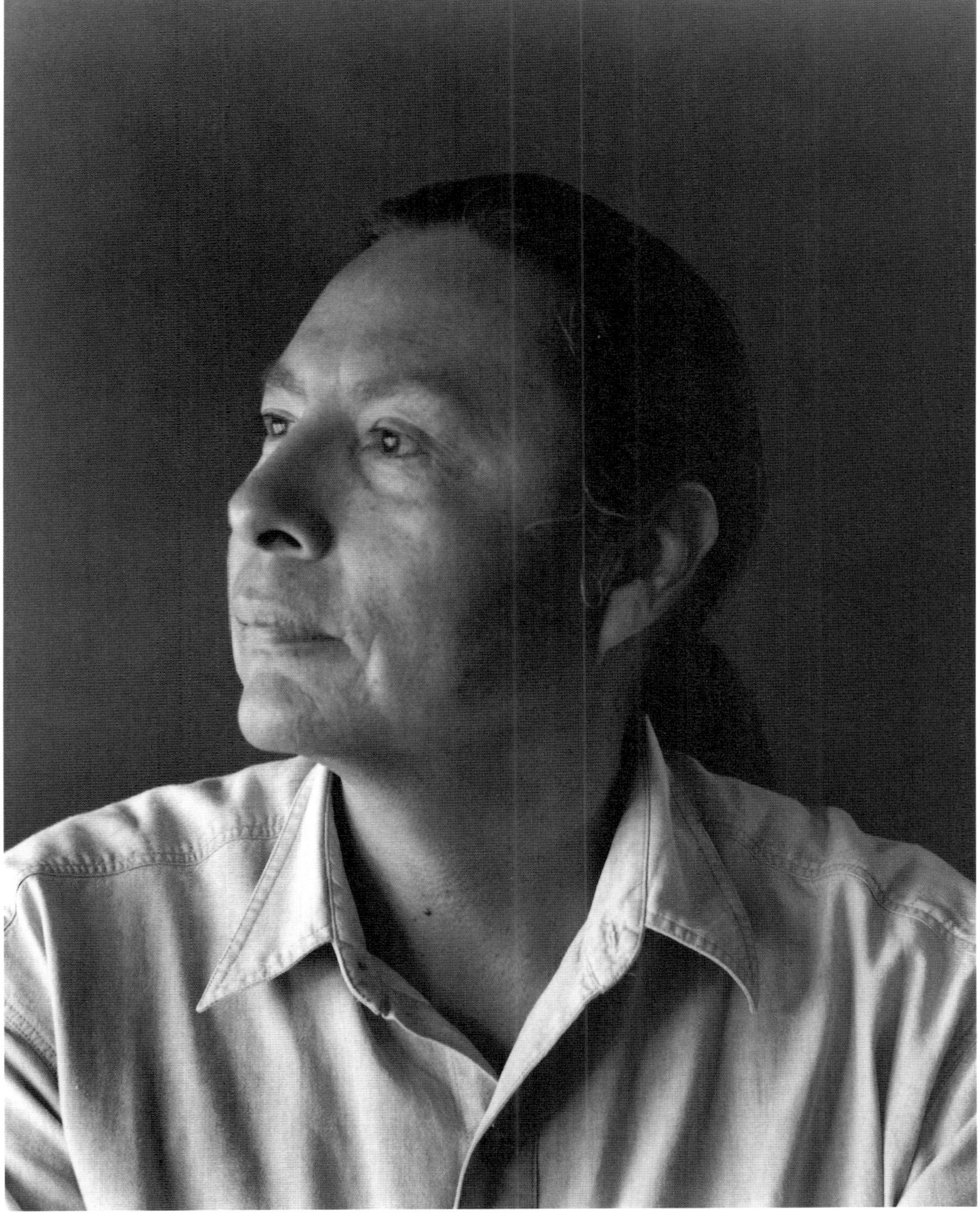

92
YAZZIE JOHNSON
Gail Bird's partner
Jeweler
Navajo

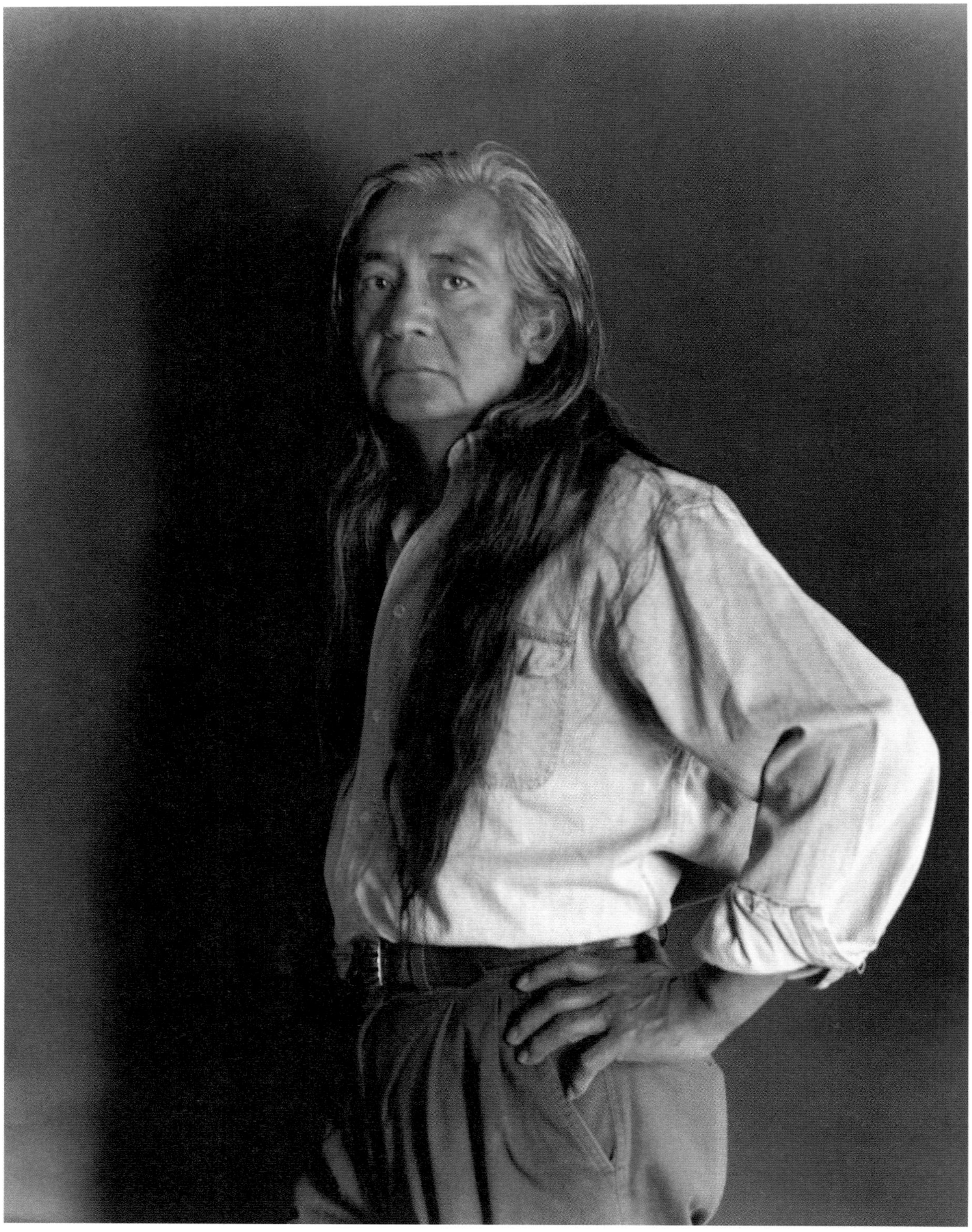

93

CHARLIE BIRD

Gail Bird's brother

Mosaic Jeweler

Santo Domingo/Laguna

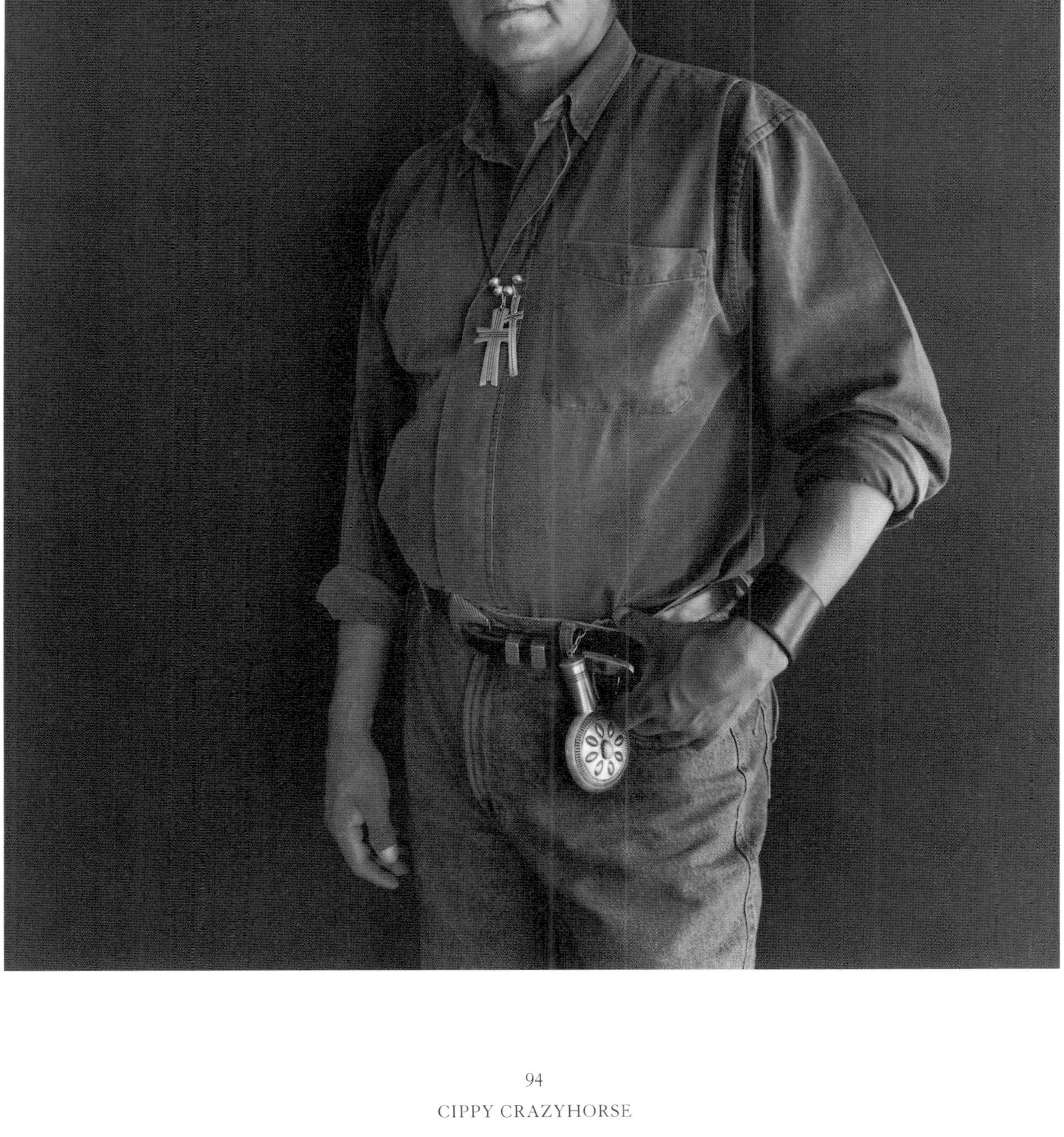

94
CIPPY CRAZYHORSE
Silversmith
Cochiti Pueblo

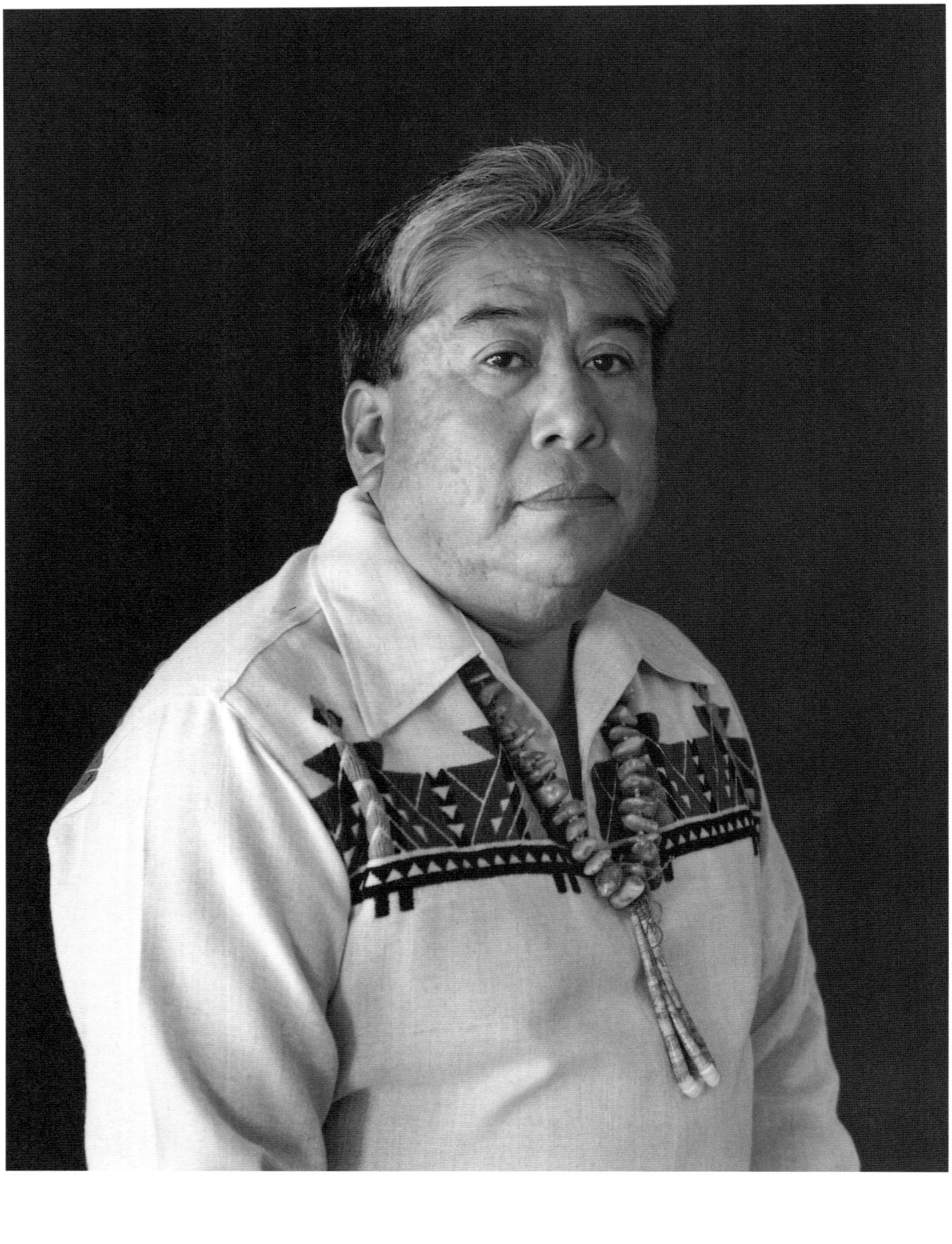

95

BENNETT G. HISTIA

Contemporary Potter

Acoma Pueblo

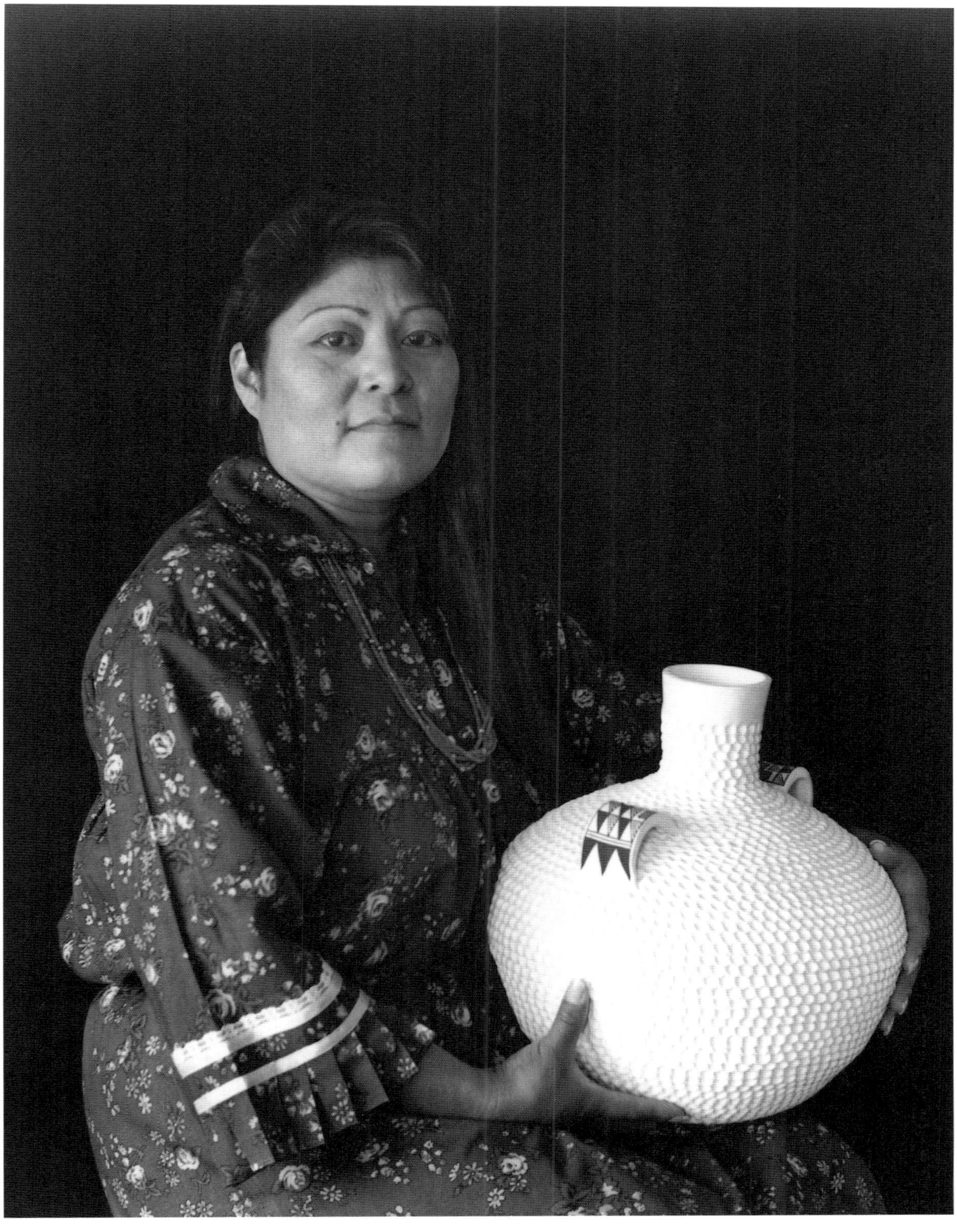

96

JACKIE SHUTIVA HISTIA

Bennett G. Histia's wife

Traditional Corrugated Pottery

Acoma Pueblo

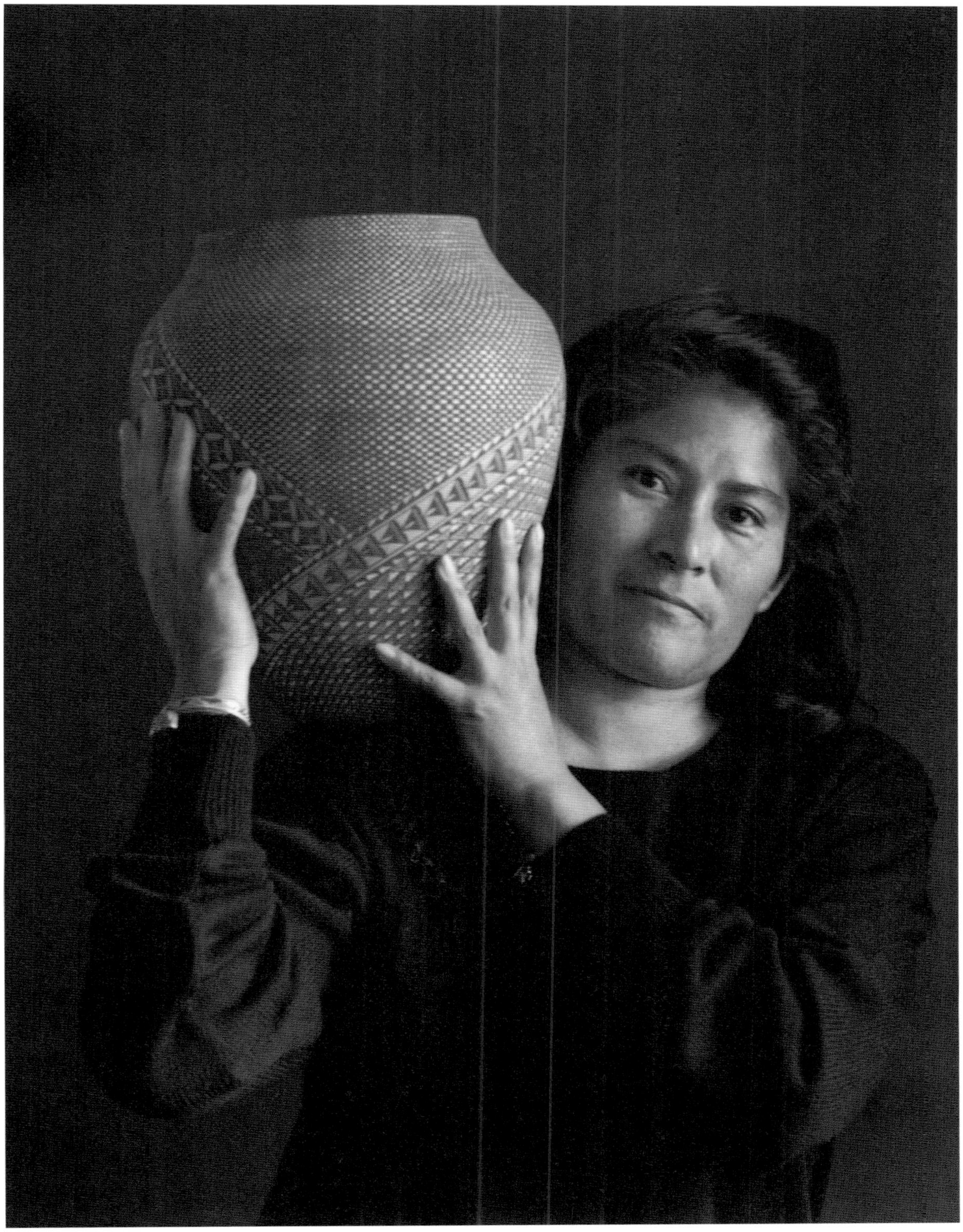

97
SANDRA VICTORINO
Traditional Potter
Acoma Pueblo

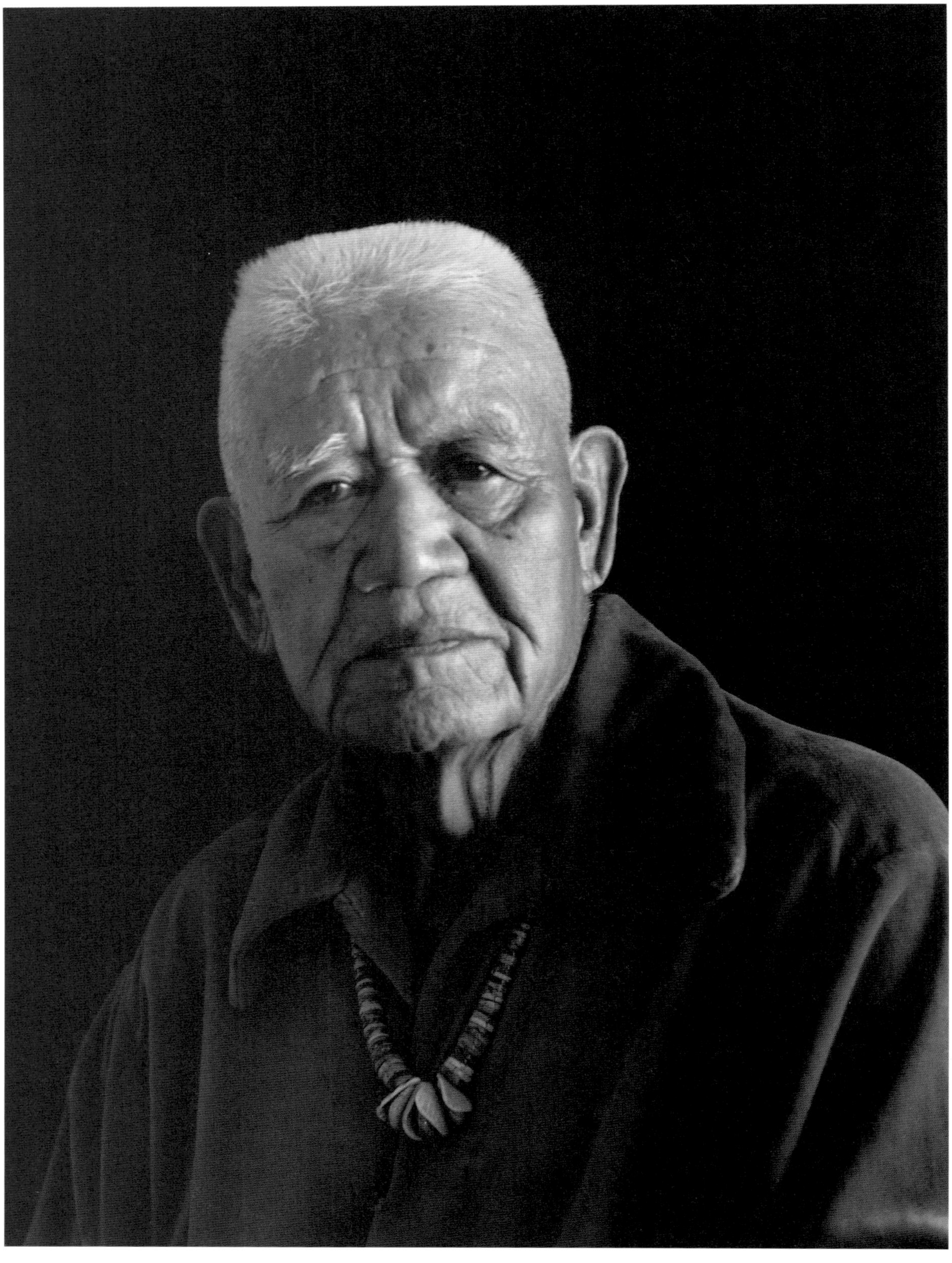

98

AUGUSTINE LOVATO

Traditional Pueblo Necklace Maker

Santo Domingo Pueblo

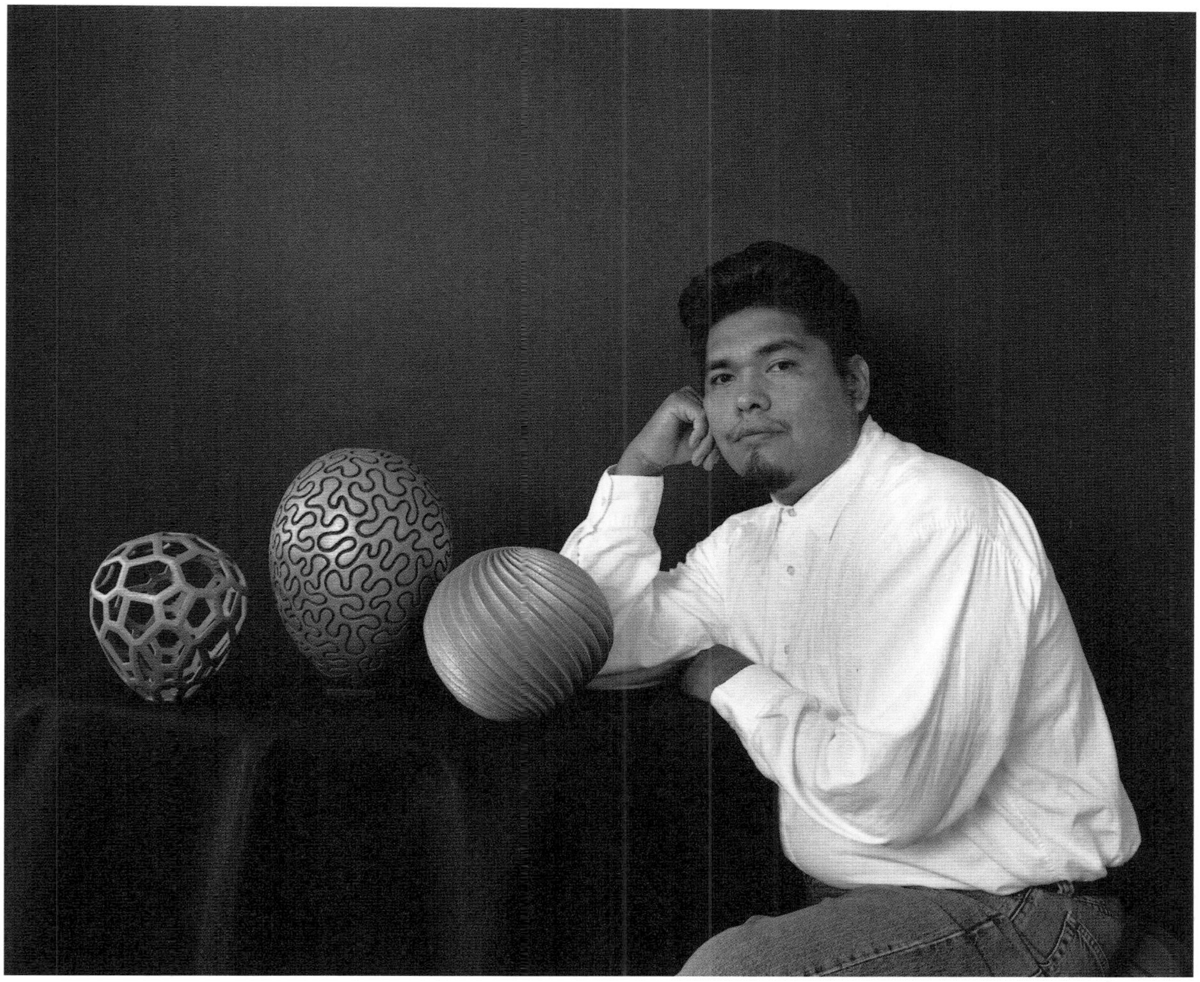

99
HUBERT CANDELARIO
Contemporary Micaceous Potter
San Felipe Pueblo

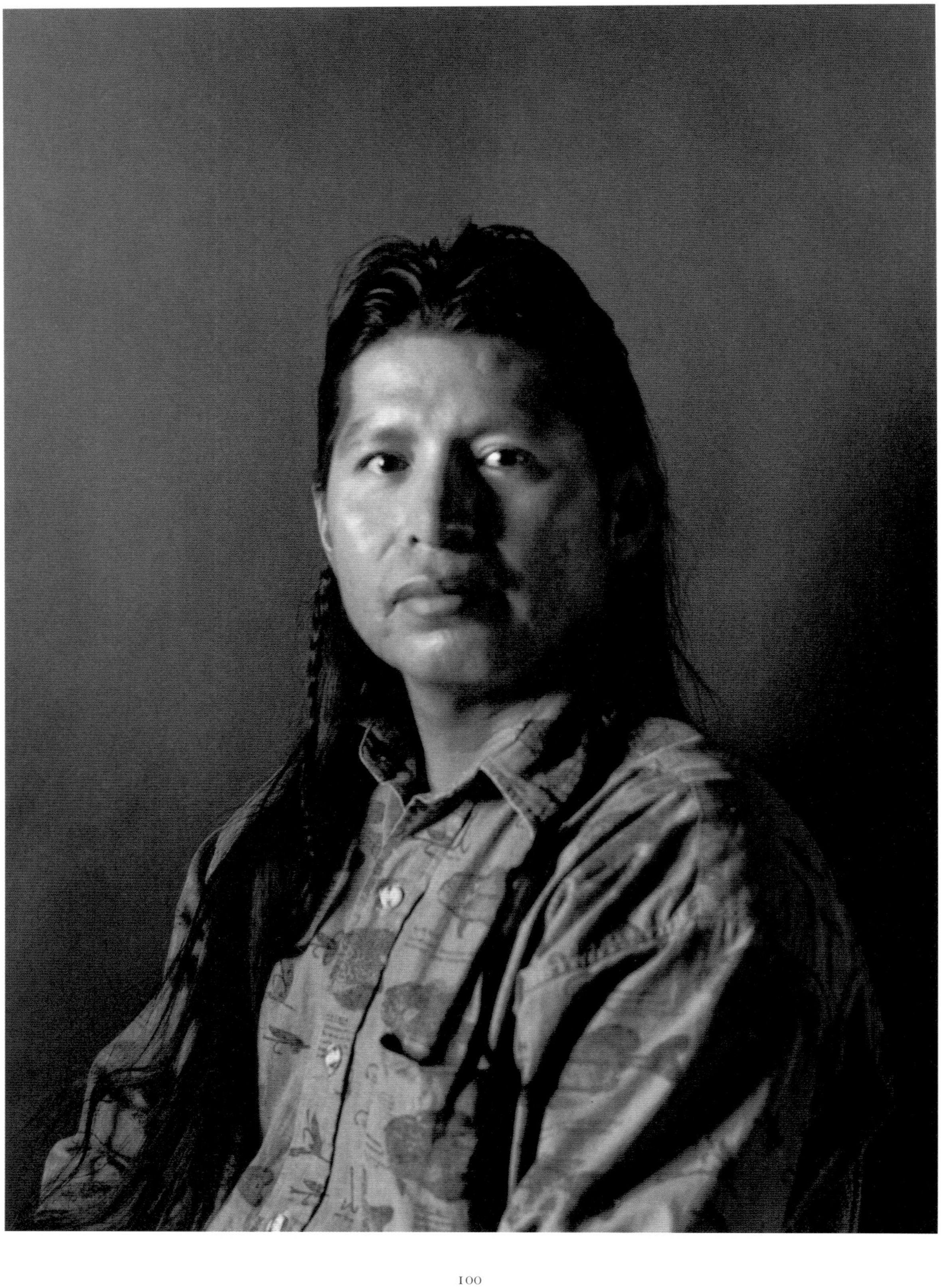

100

MICHAEL KANTEENA

Potter—Contemporary interpretations of ancient pottery forms

Laguna Pueblo

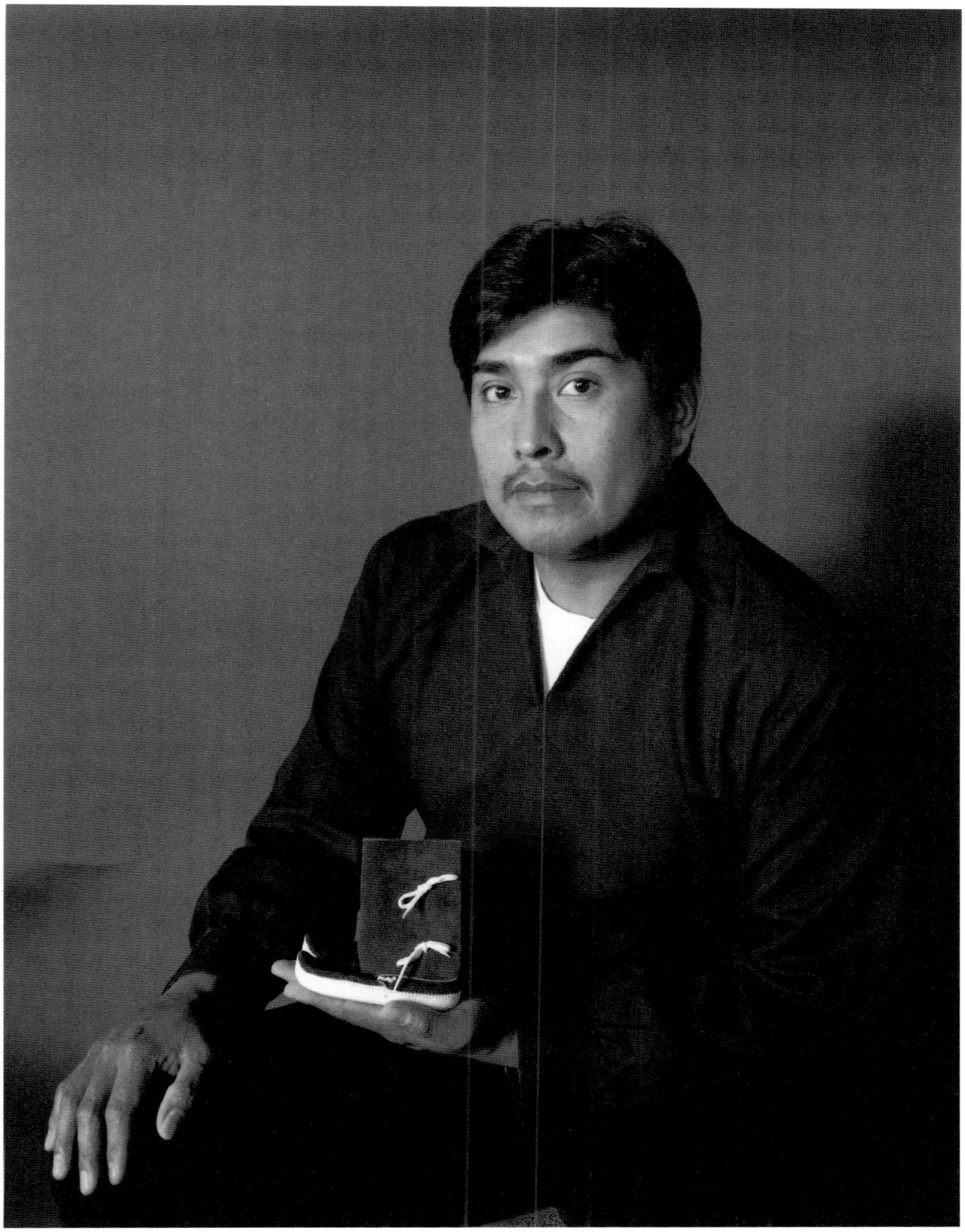

101

GARRETT J. LORENZO, Jr.

Traditional Moccasins

Laguna Pueblo

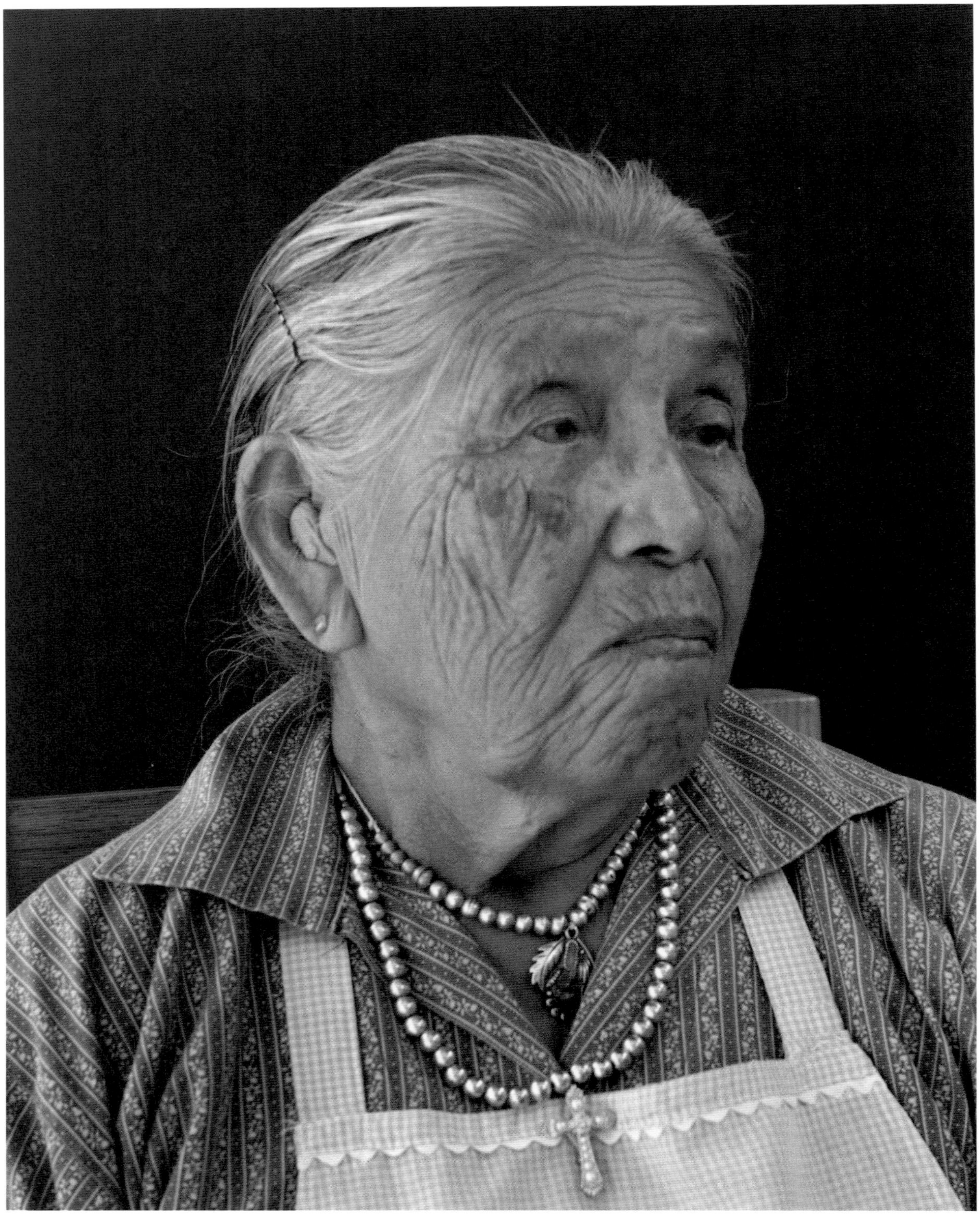

102

ELVIRA MONTOYA

Traditional Pueblo Sewing, Embroidery, Pottery

Santa Ana Pueblo

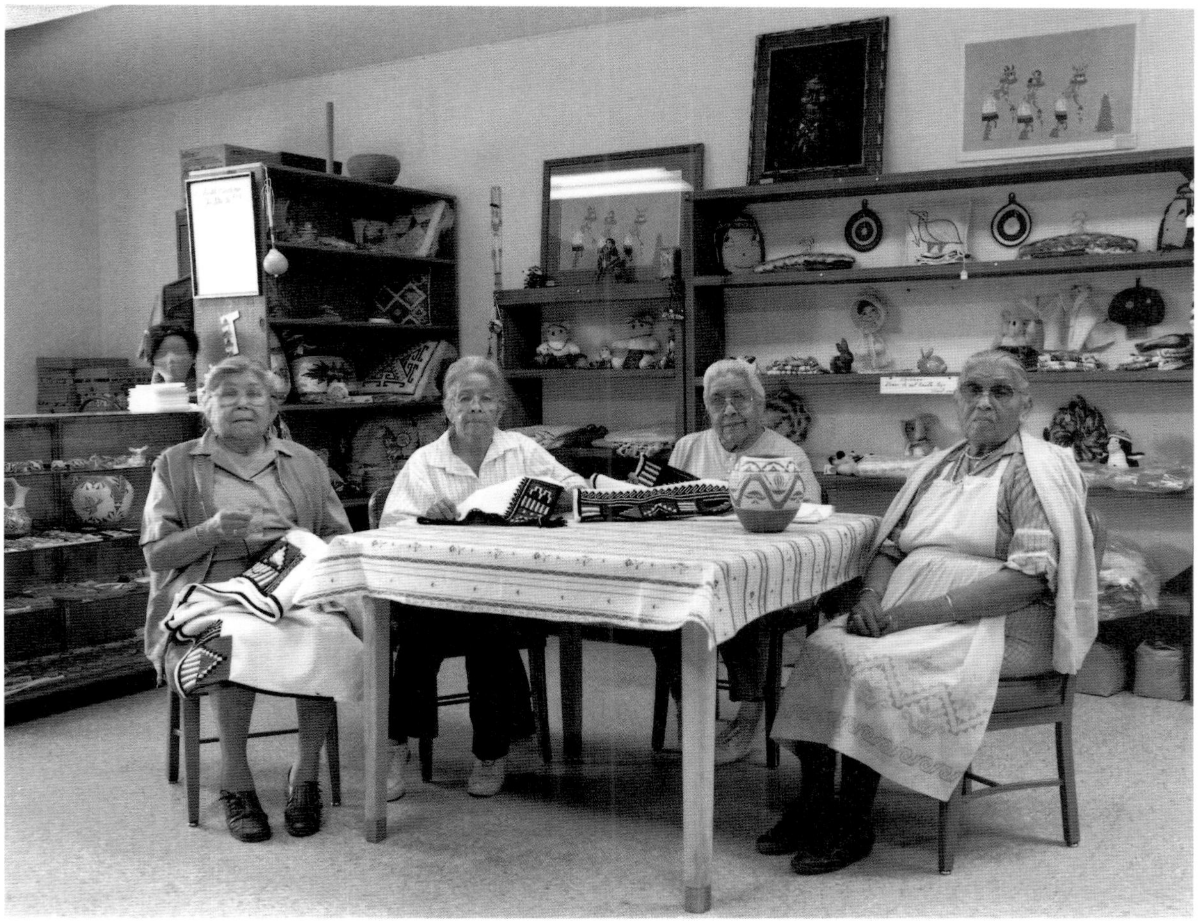

103

SANTA ANA SEWING GROUP

LENA GARCIA, BERTIE PASQUAL, CLARA PAQUIN, and ELVIRA MONTOYA

Traditional Pueblo Sewing, Embroidery, Pottery

Santa Ana Pueblo

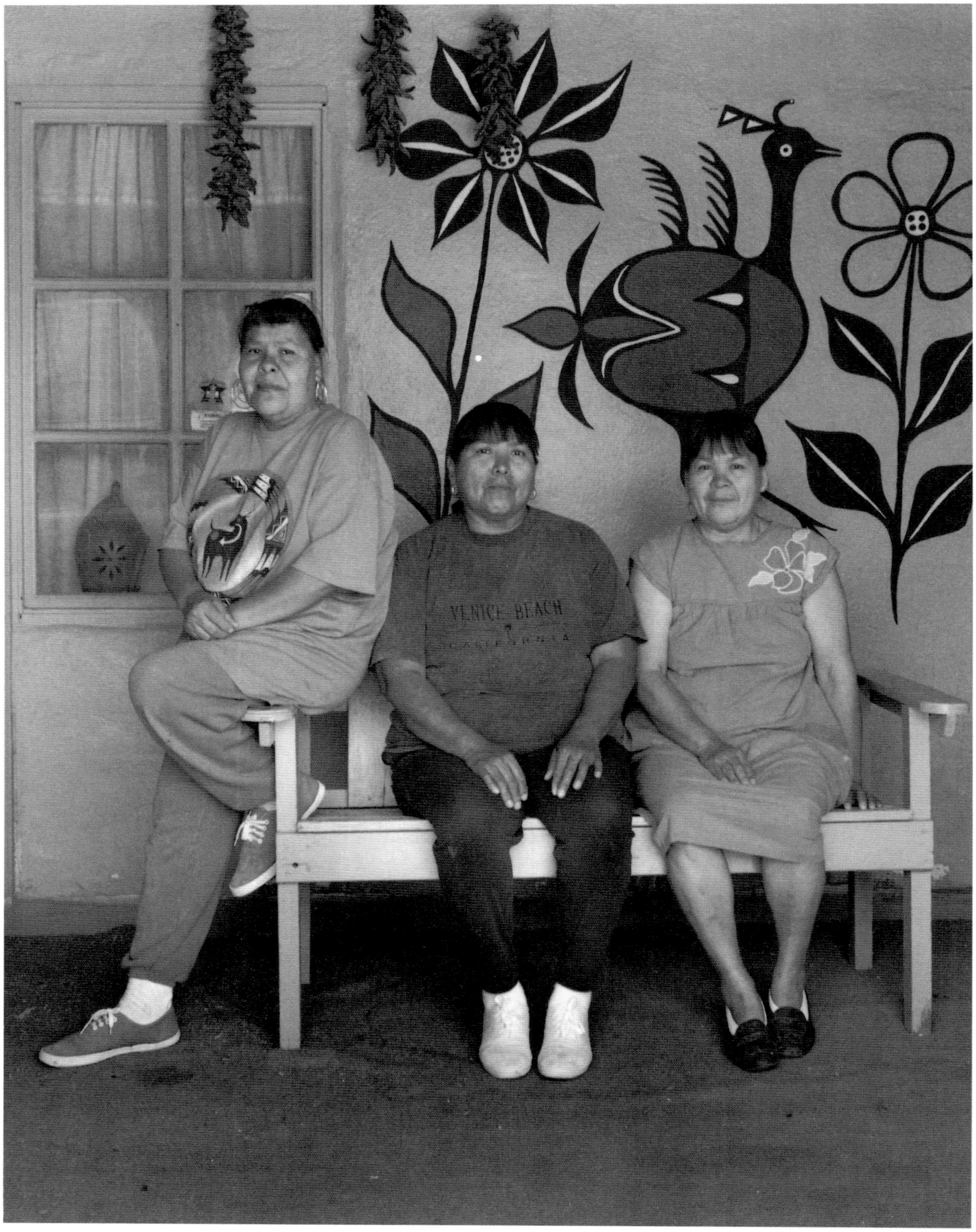

104

MARY TENORIO, PAULITA PACHECO, and HILDA CORIZ

Robert Tenorio's sisters

Traditional Polychrome Potters

Santo Domingo Pueblo

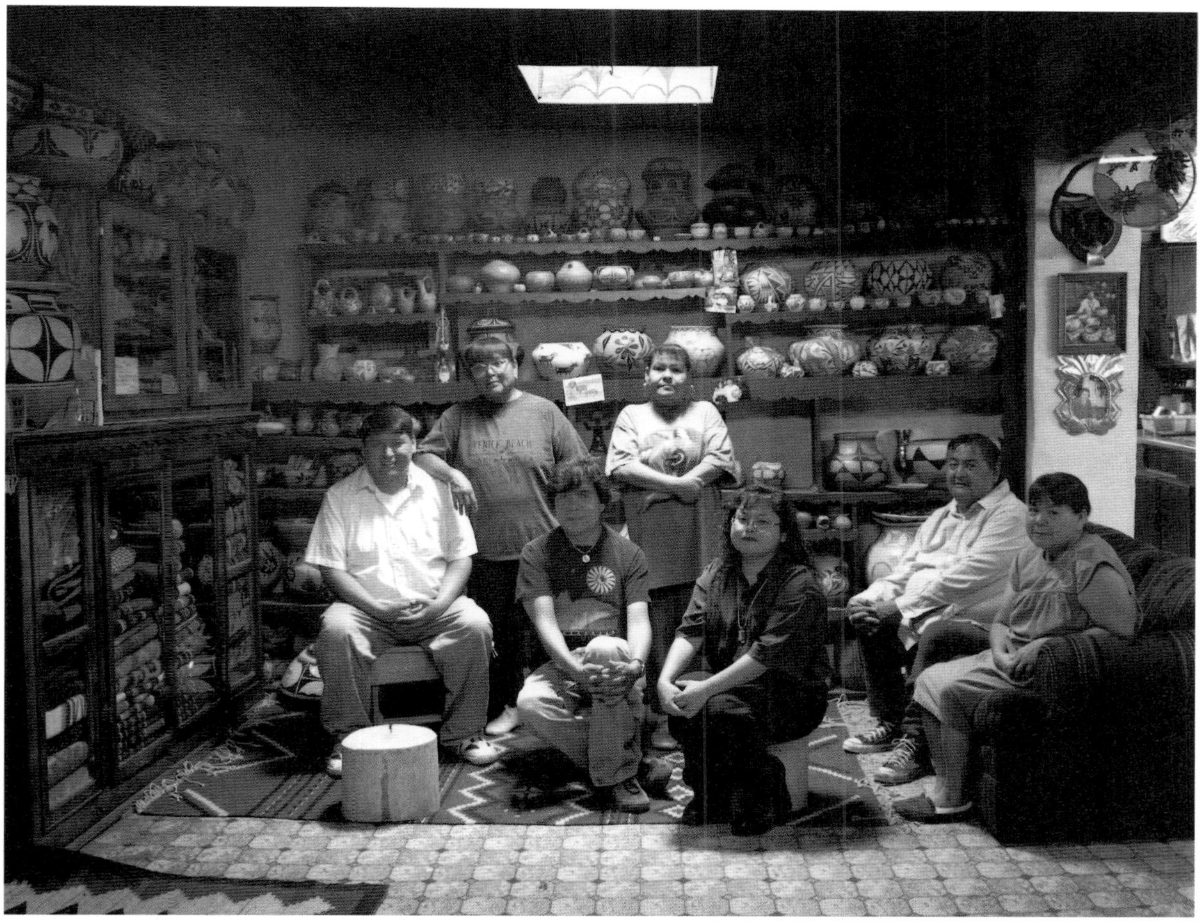

105

ROBERT TENORIO'S FAMILY

(seated) William Pacheco, Robert Tenorio,

Ione Coriz, Gilbert Pacheco, and Hilda Coriz;

(standing) Paulita Pacheco and Mary Tenorio

Traditional Polychrome Potters

Santa Domingo Pueblo

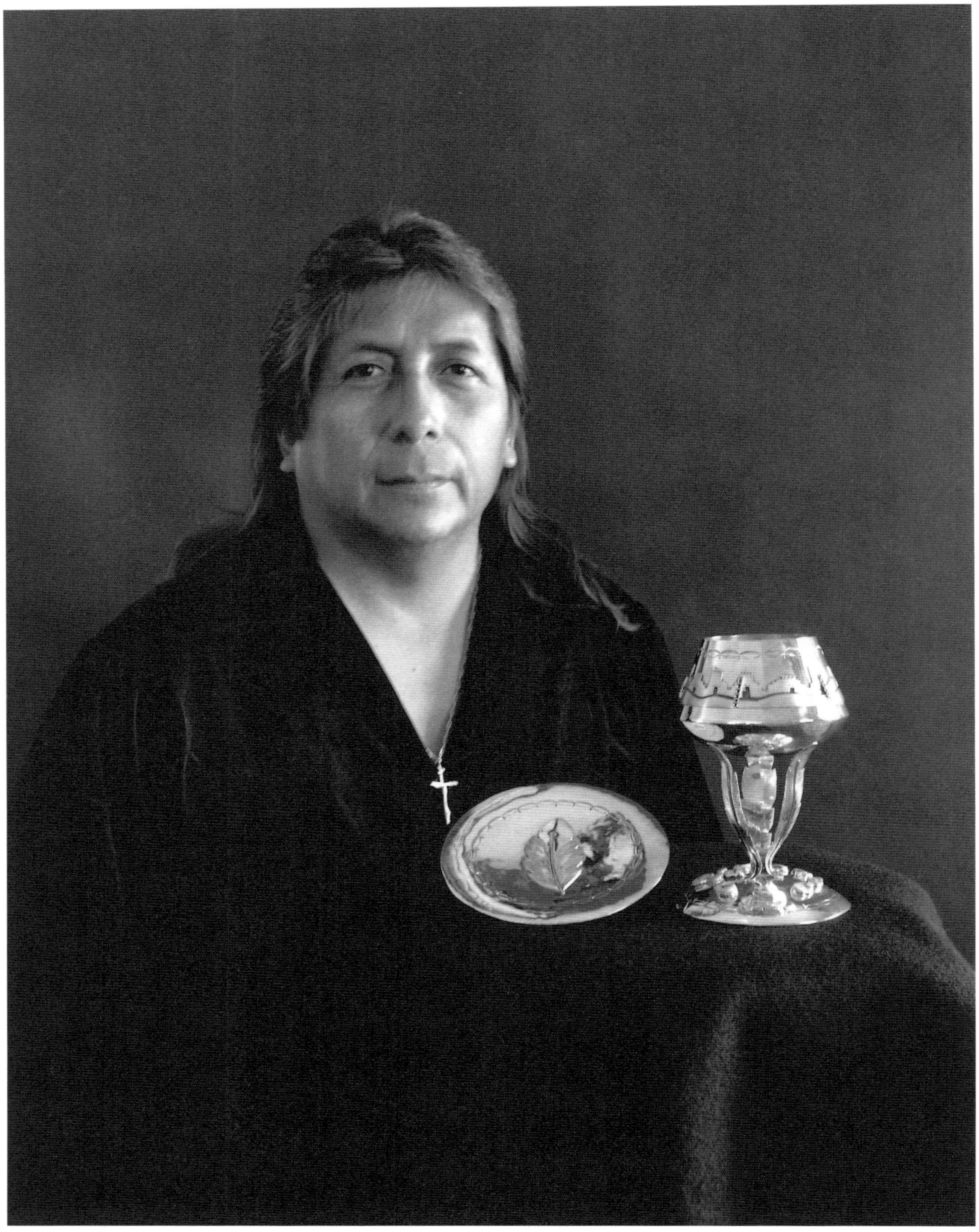

106

CHARLES SUNRISE TRUJILLO

Silversmith

Sandia Pueblo

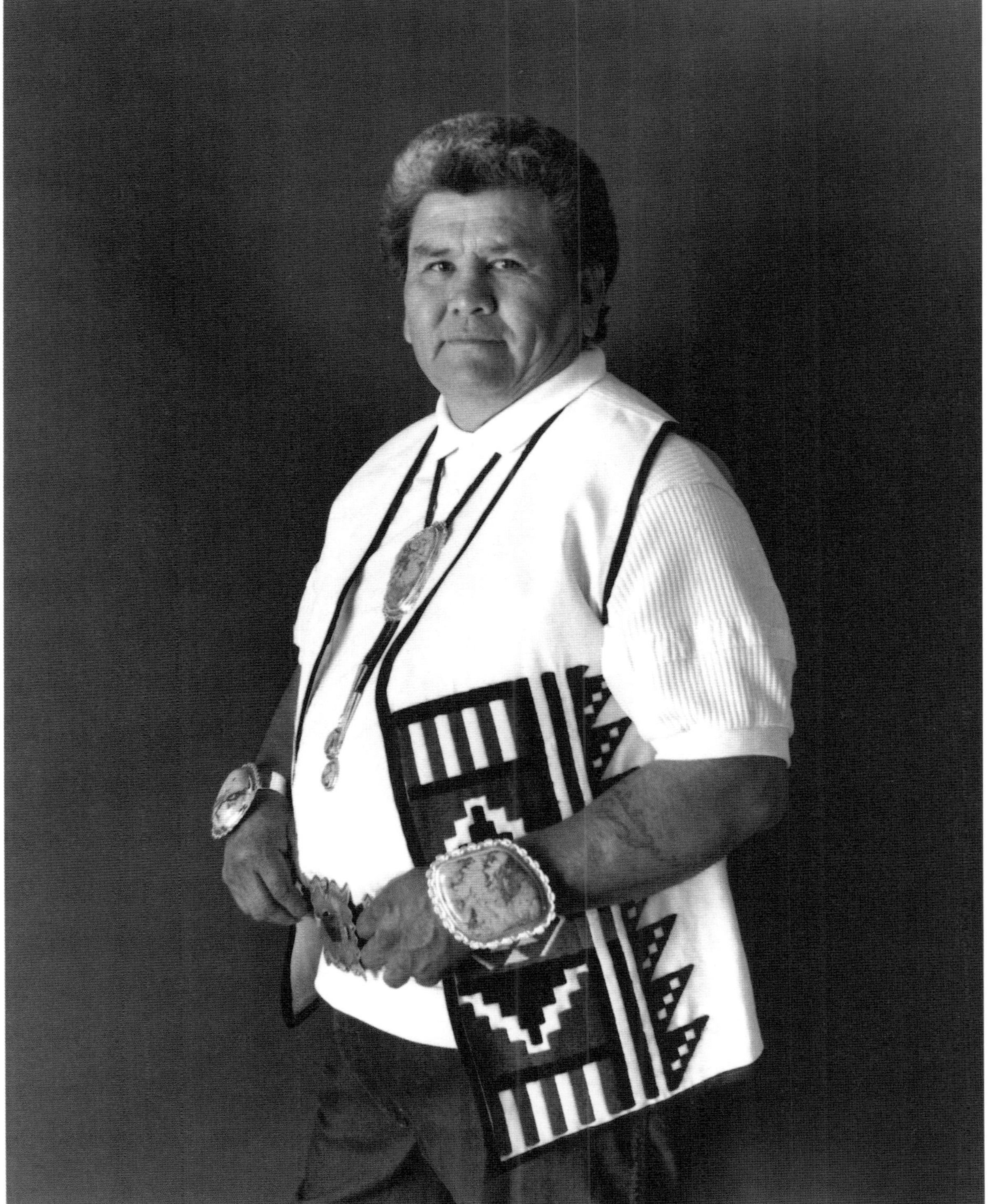

107
JIMMY F. CALABAZA
Traditional and Contemporary Jewelry
Santo Domingo Pueblo

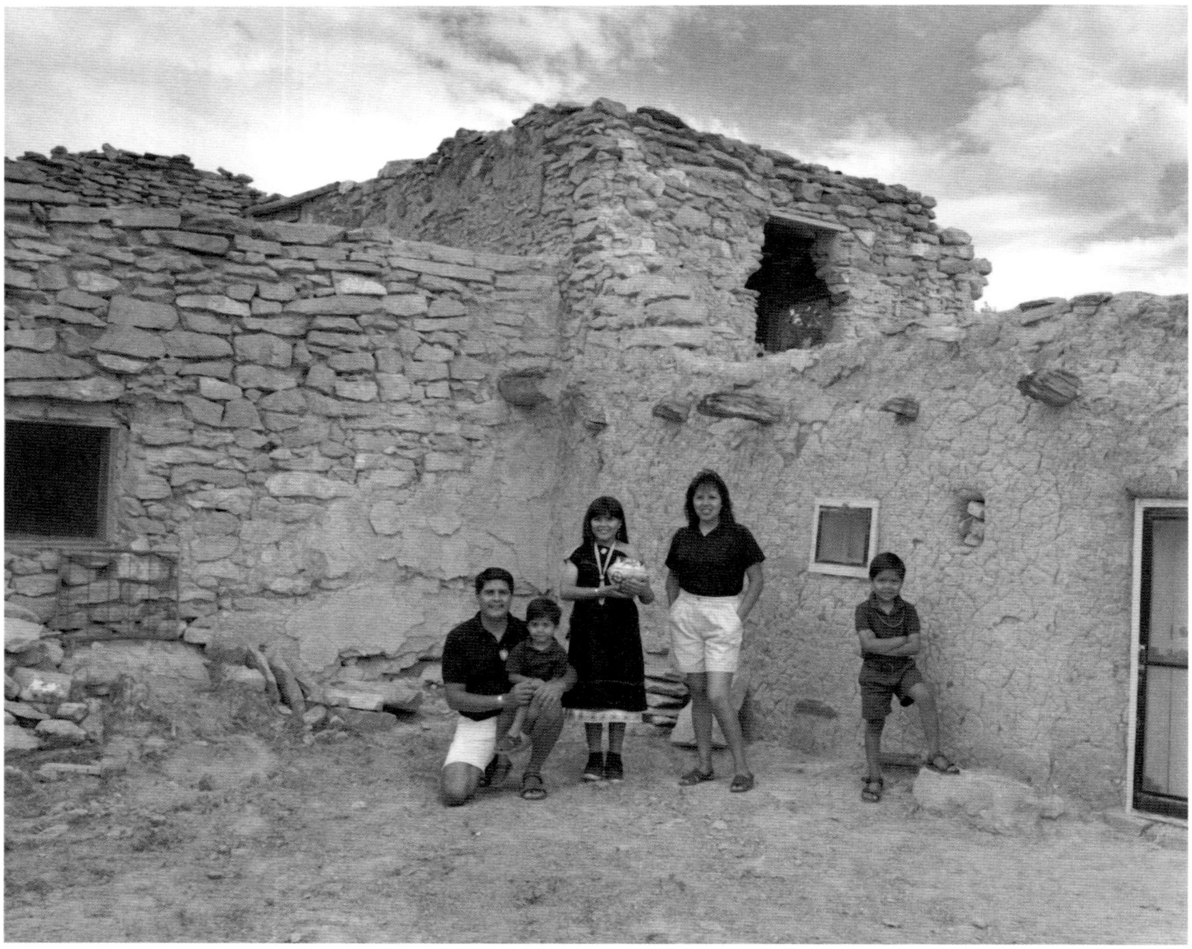

108

MAX EARLY, Laguna Pueblo, and BERTHA EARLY, Cochiti Pueblo,
with children ALAN, MARIA, and DAVID EARLY
Early family's ancestral house, Paguate Village
Laguna Pueblo

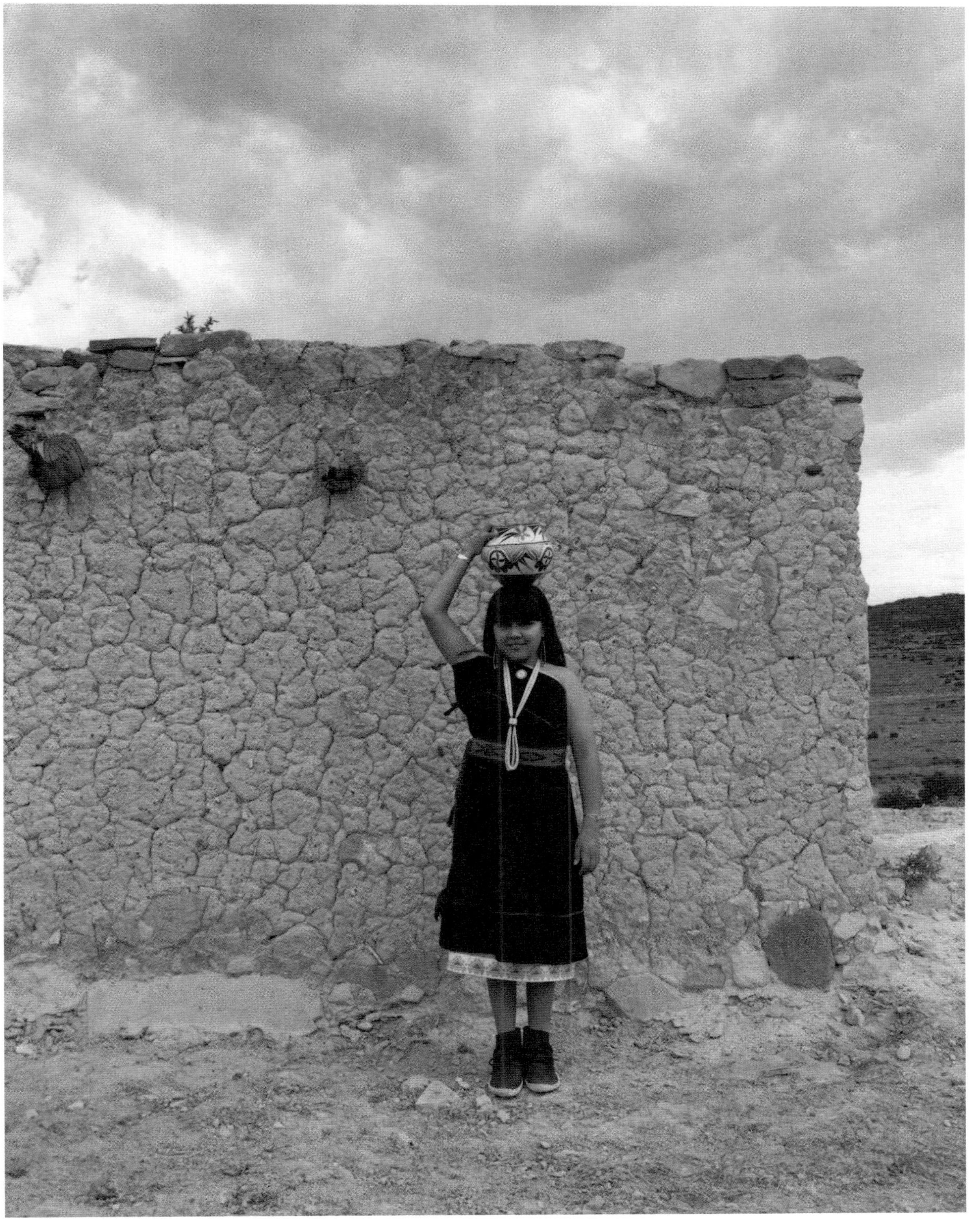

109

MARIA EARLY

Holding pot her father made for this photograph

Cochiti/Laguna

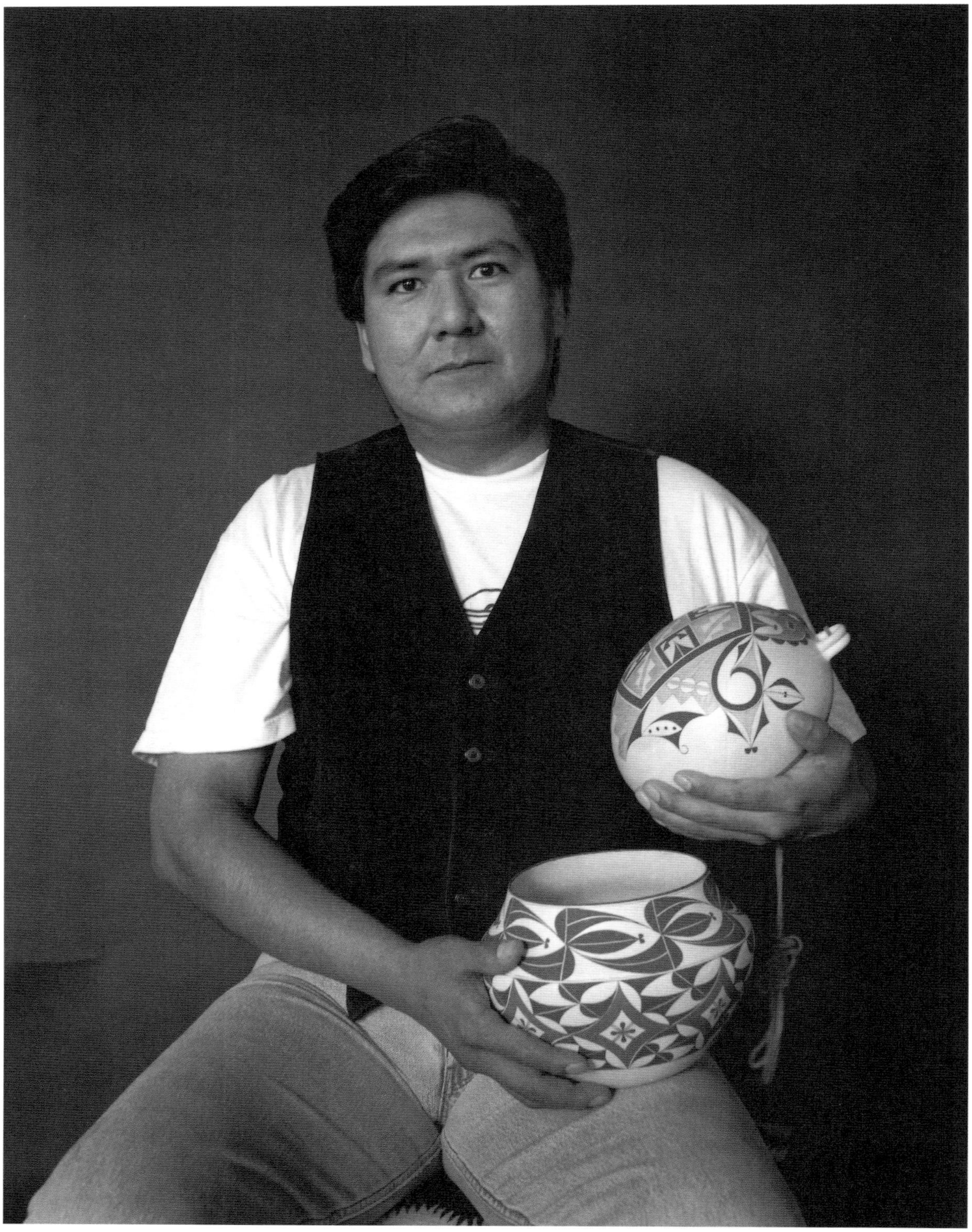

110

CALVIN ANALLA, Jr.

Traditional Potter

Laguna Pueblo

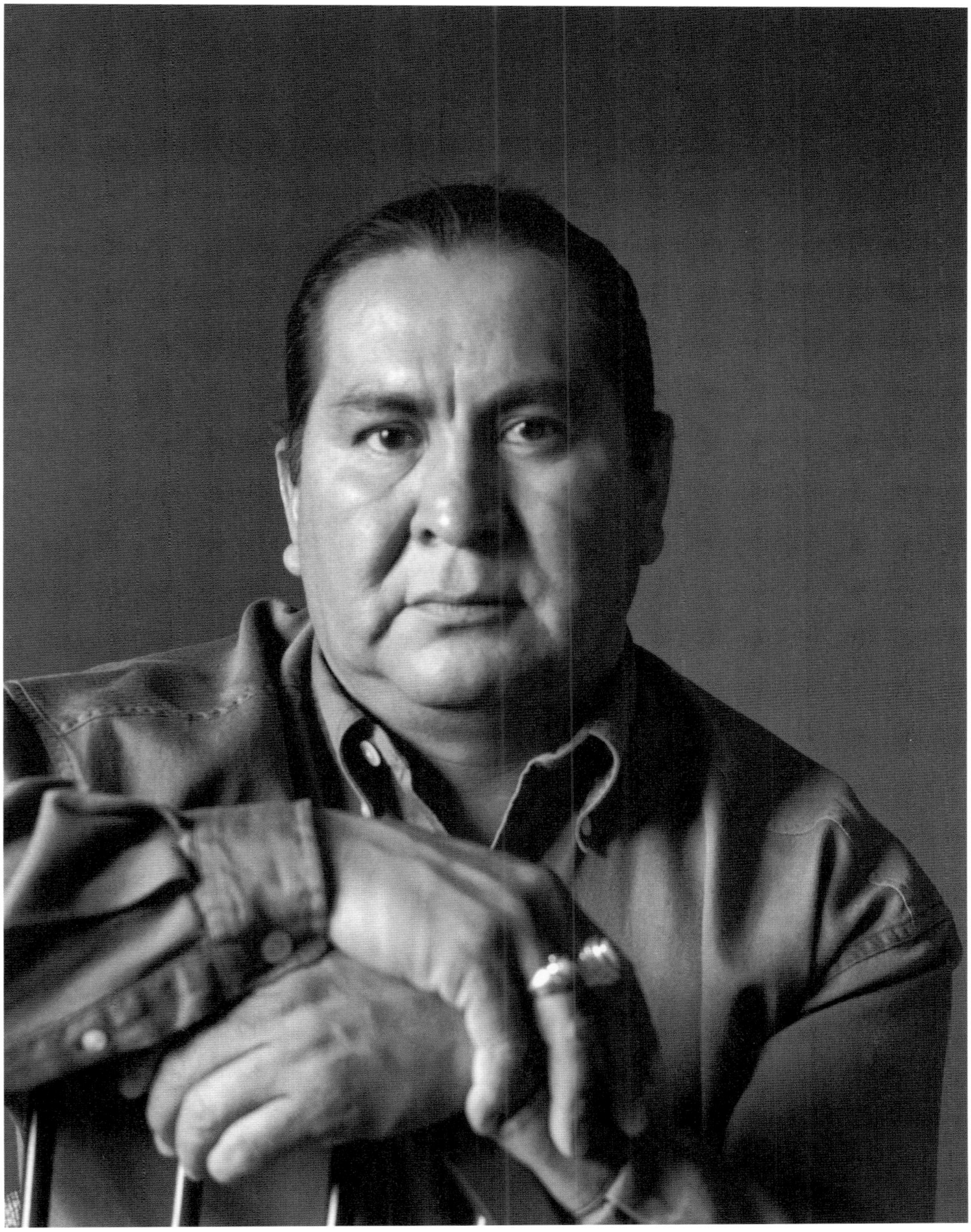

111

FLOYD R. SOLOMON

Painter and Printmaker

Laguna/Zuni

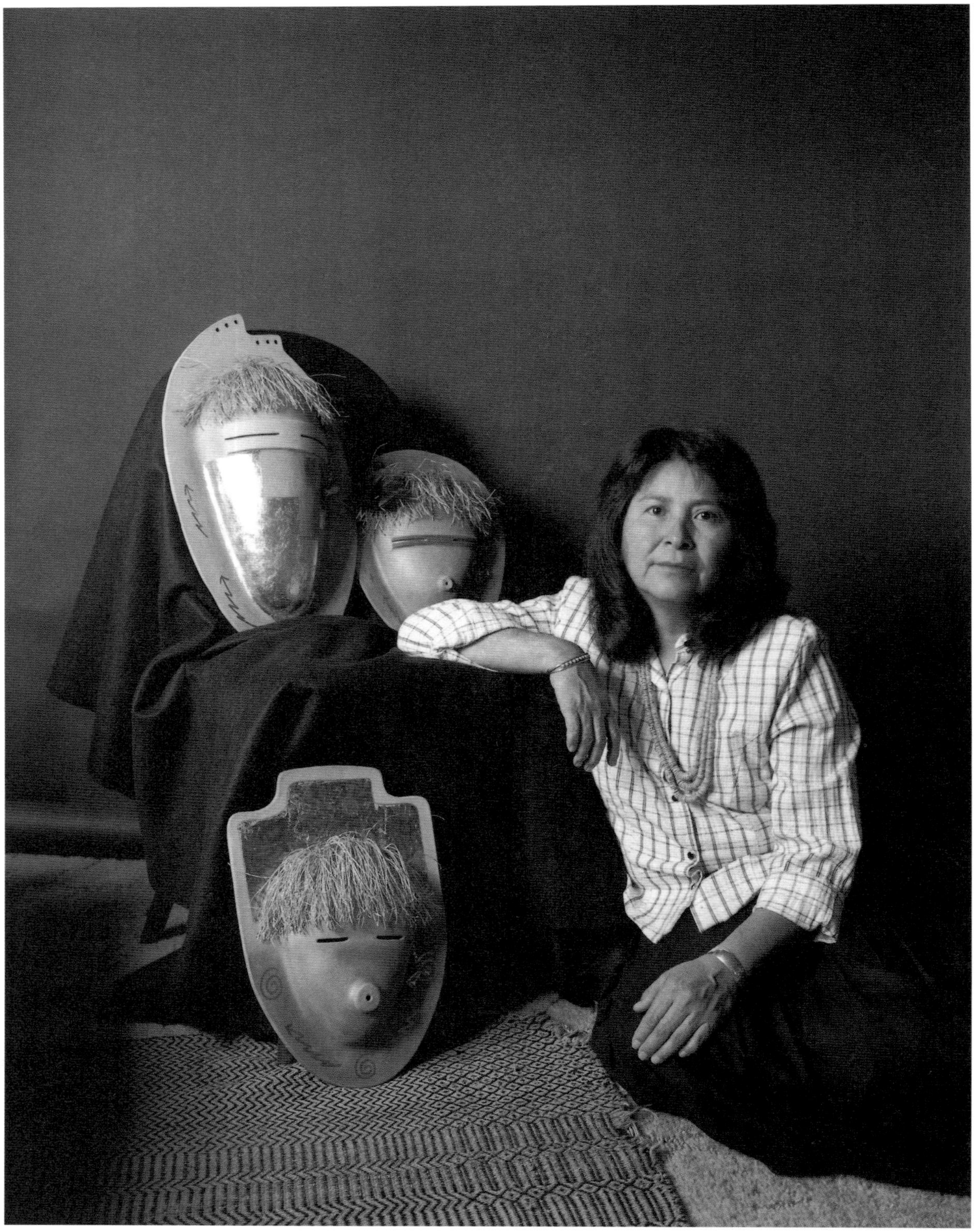

112

VERNA SOLOMON

Floyd R. Solomon's sister

Contemporary Masks and Pottery

Laguna/Zuni

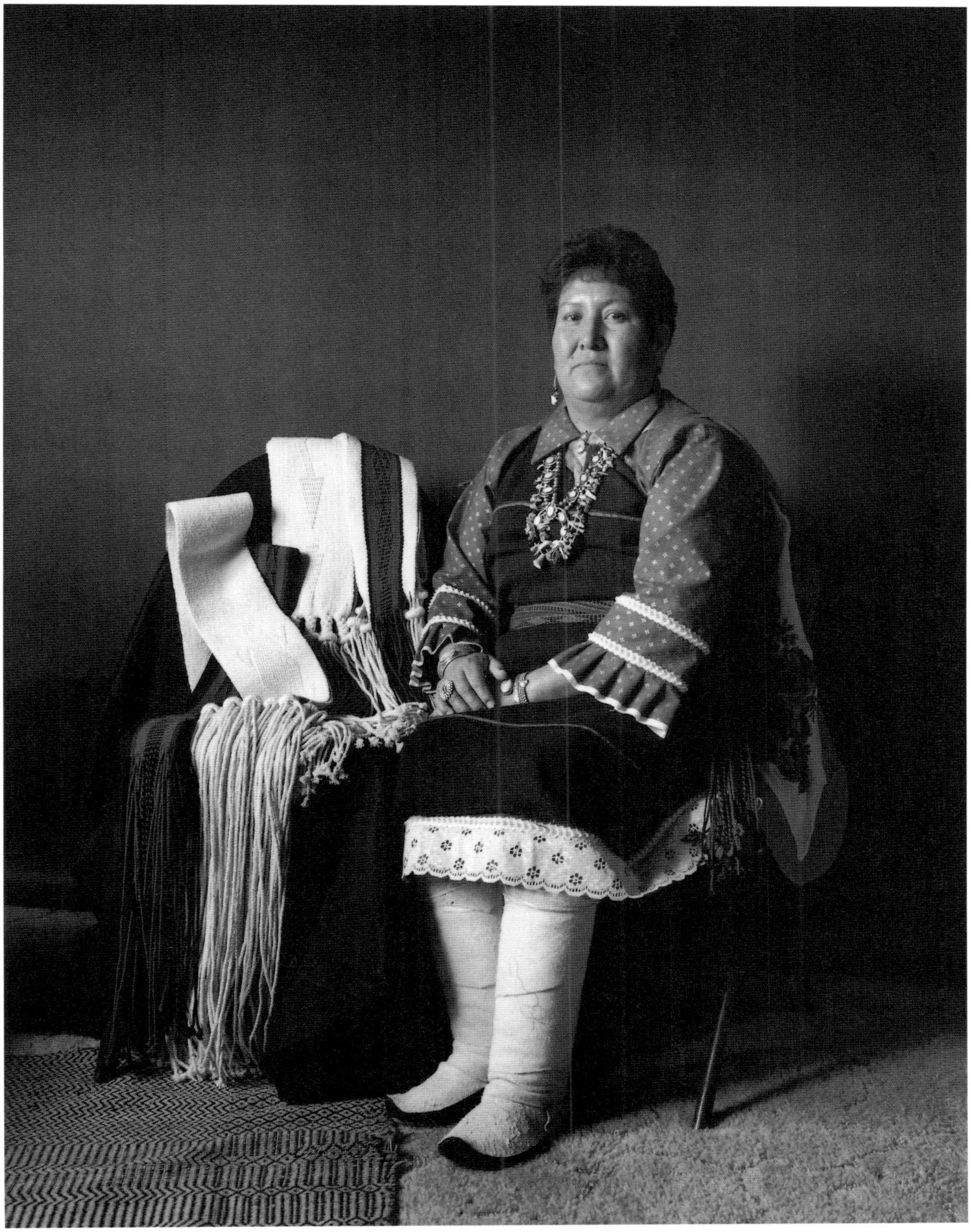

113

SUE DAILEY

Floyd R. Solomon's sister

Traditional Sash Weaver

Laguna/Zuni

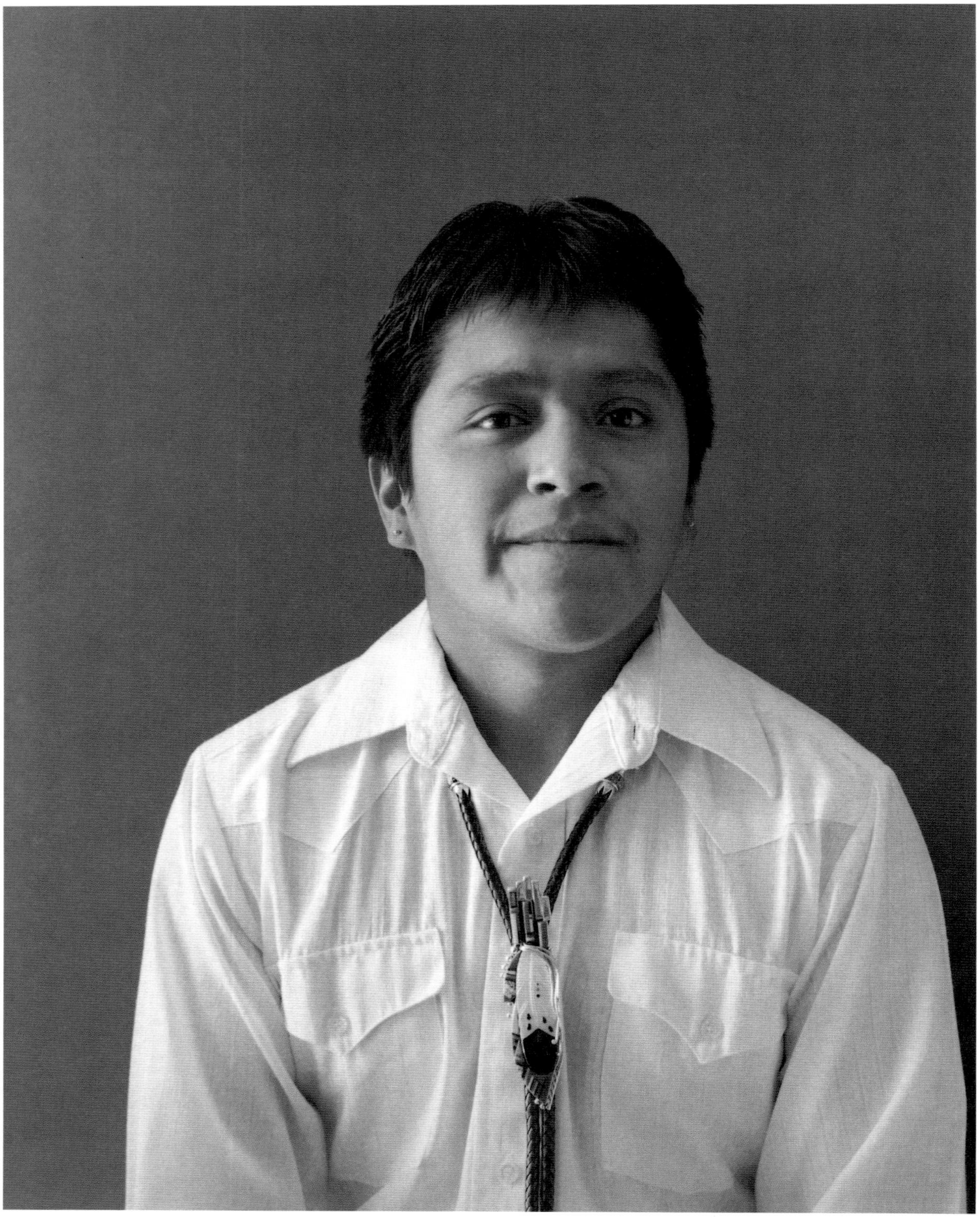

114

BRAD PABLANO

Contemporary Jeweler

Zuni Pueblo

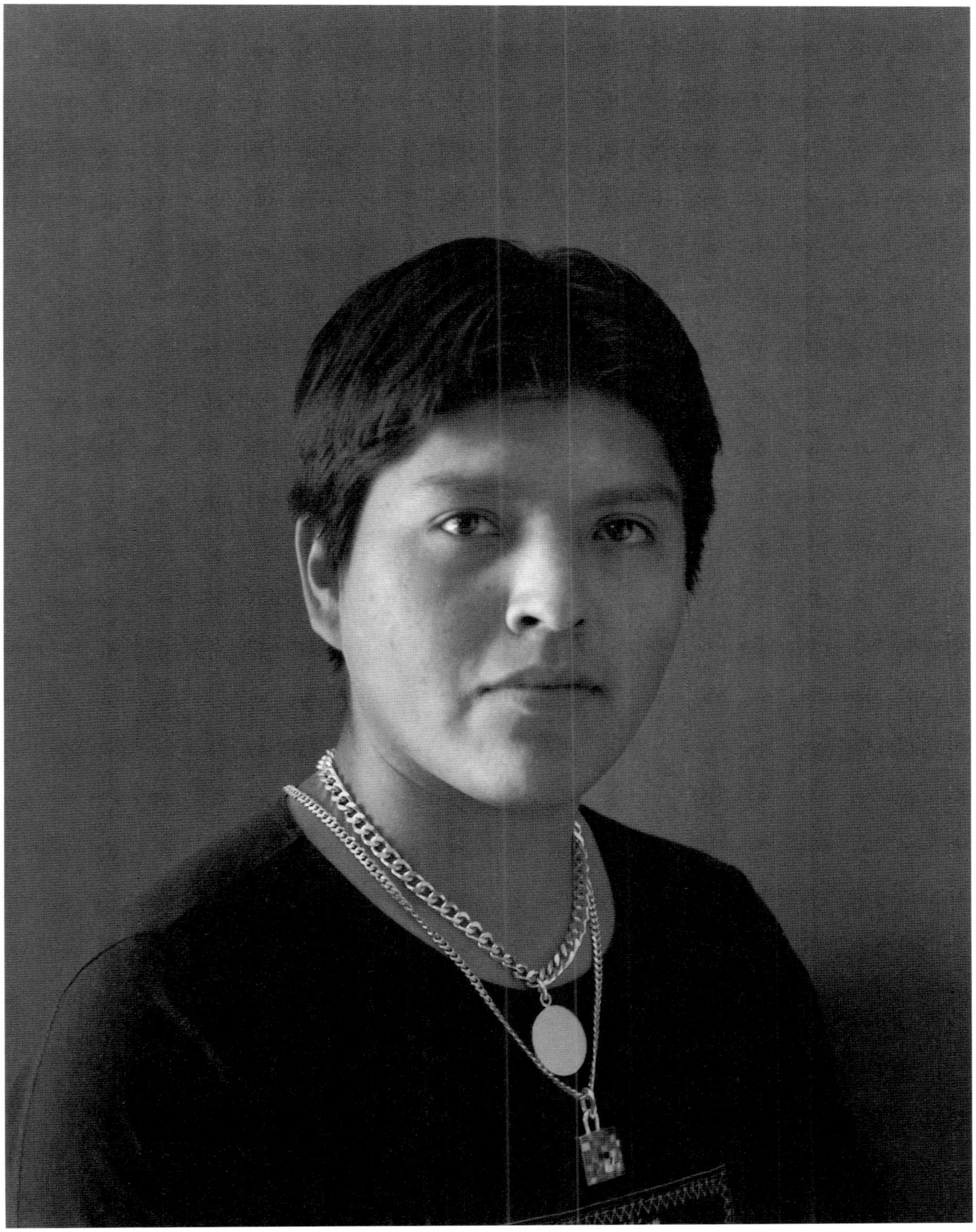

115

DYLAN PABLANO

Brad Pablano's brother

Contemporary Jeweler

Zuni Pueblo

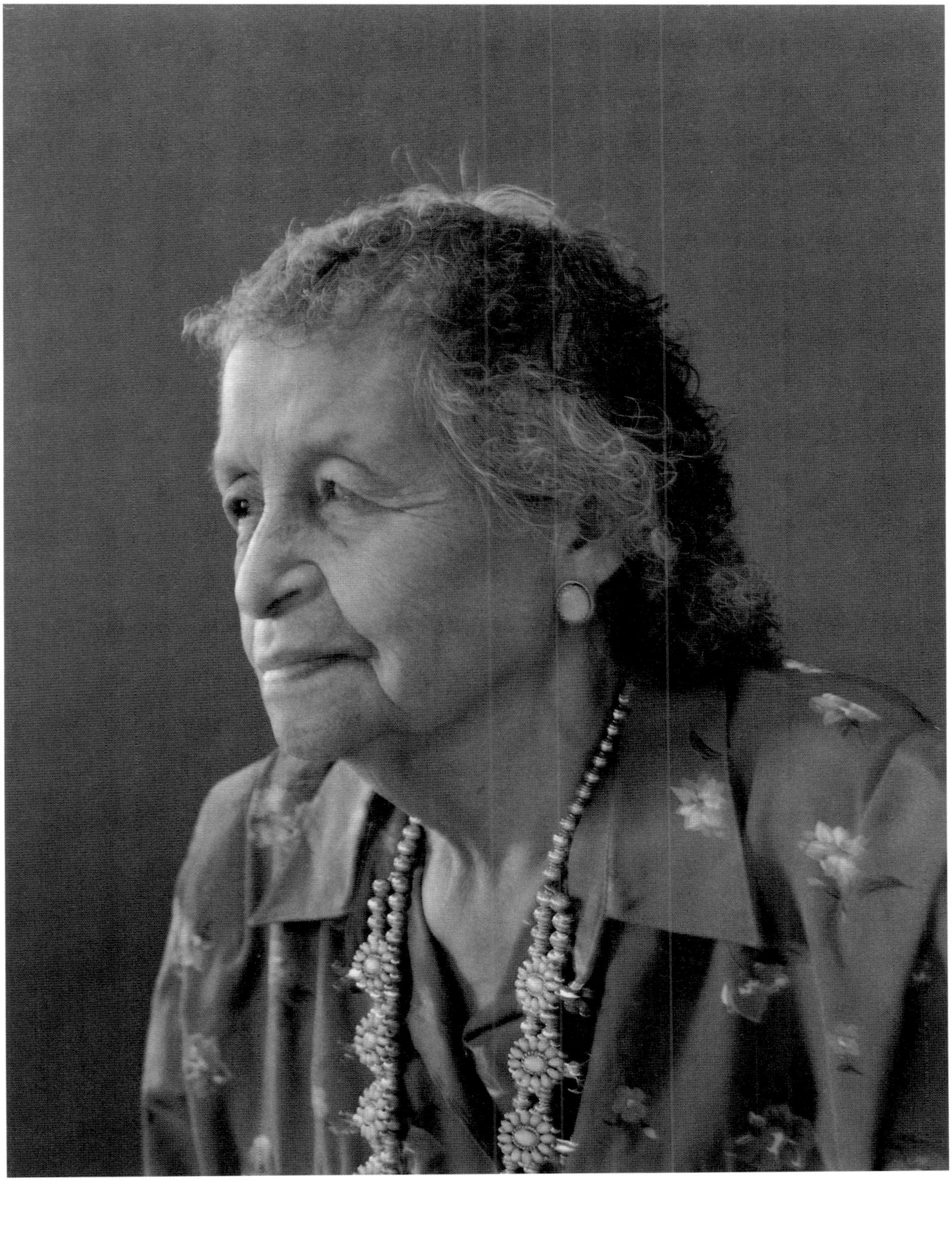

116

EDNA LEKI

Traditional Fetish Carver

Zuni Pueblo

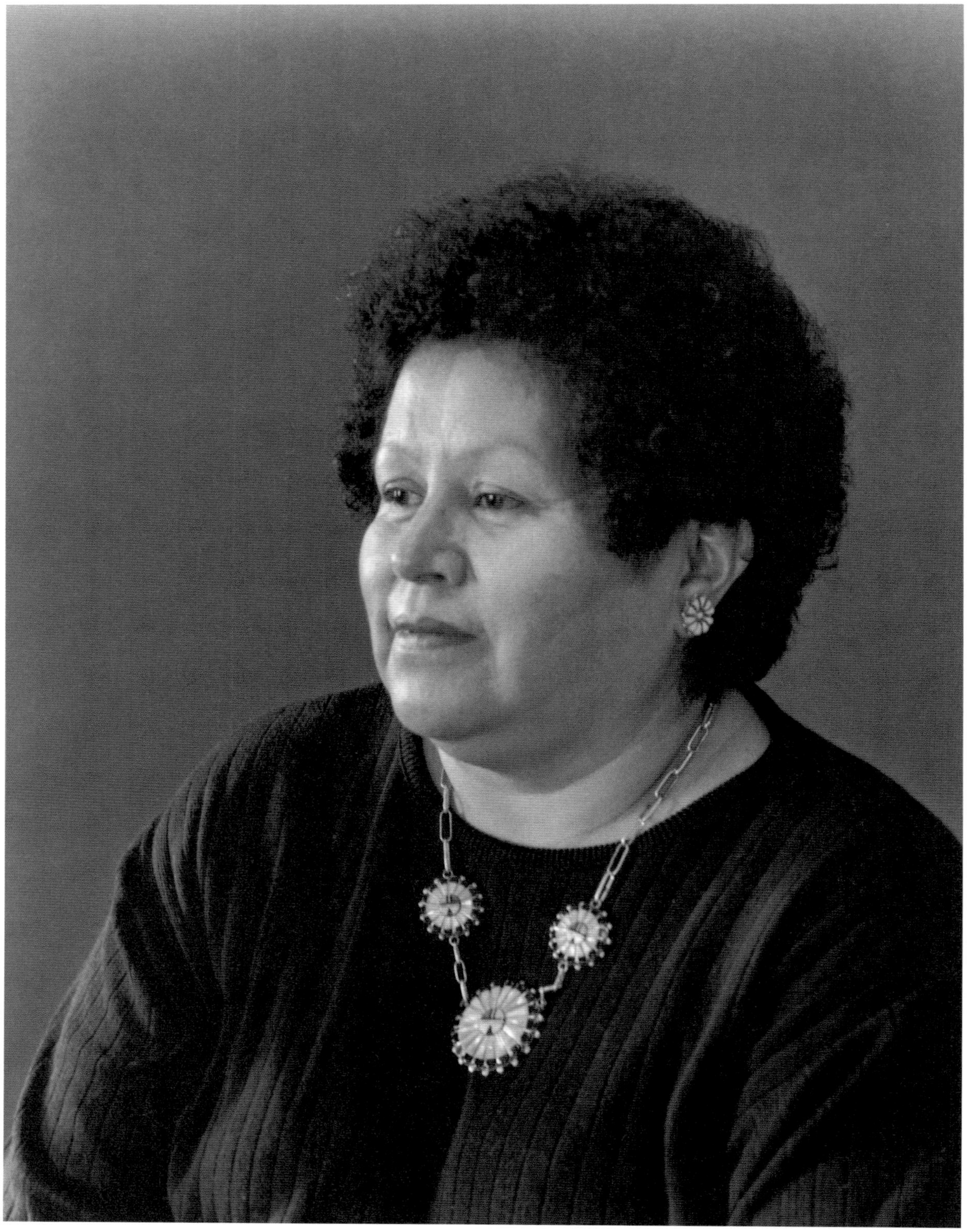

117

DINAH GASPER

Edna Leki's daughter

Traditional Fetish Carver

Zuni Pueblo

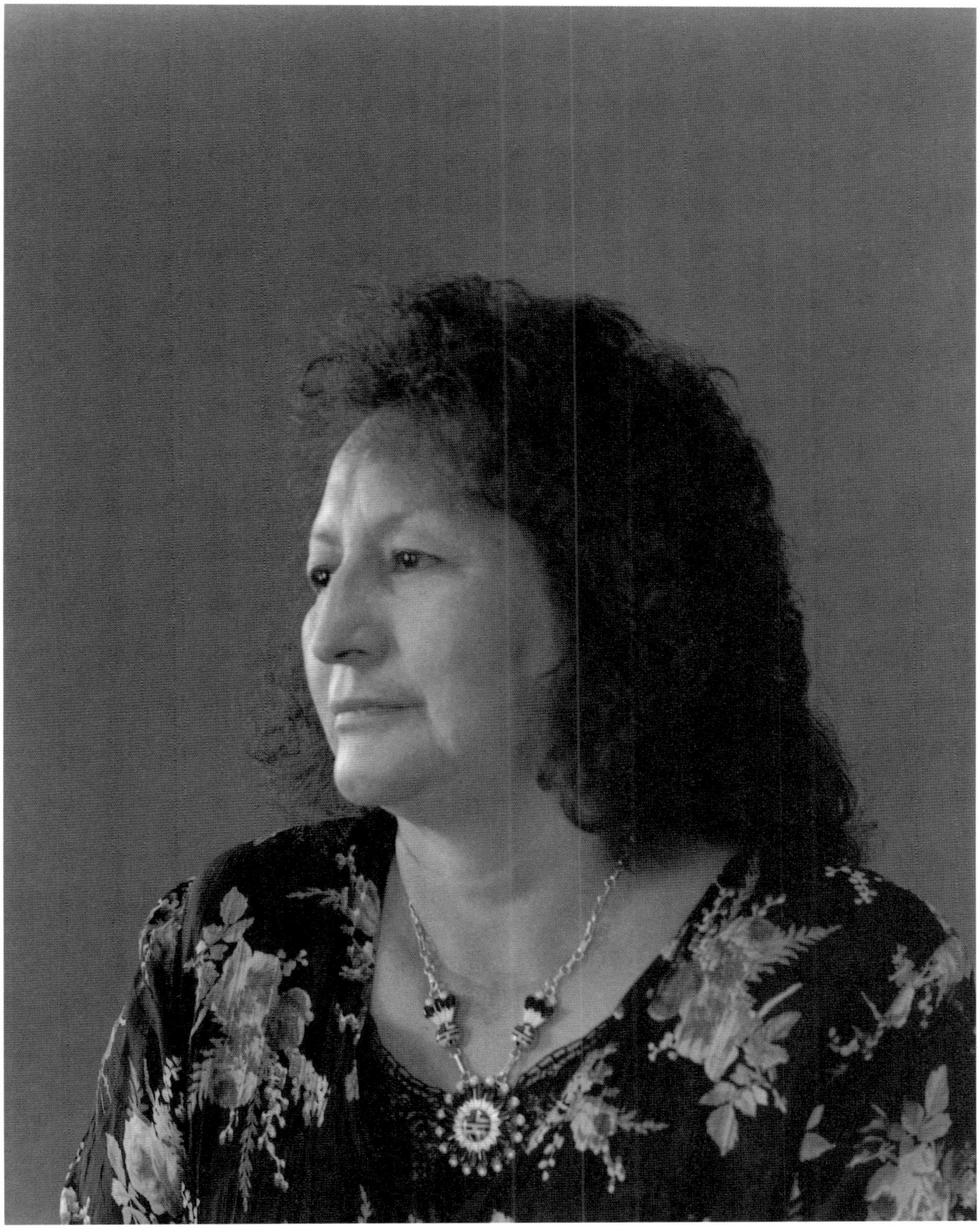

118

LENA BOONE

Edna Leki's daughter

Traditional Fetish Carver

Zuni Pueblo

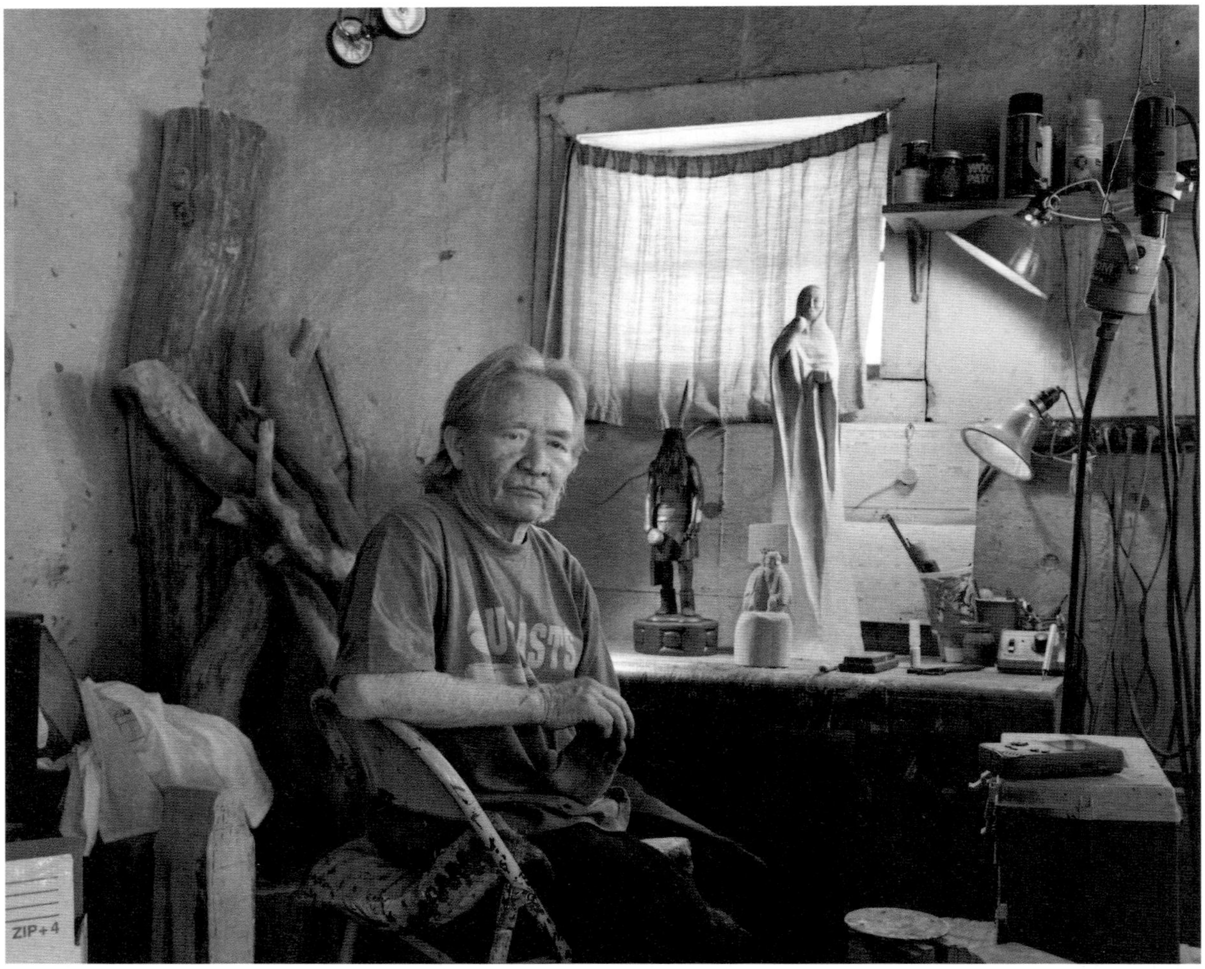

119

BRIAN HONYOUTI

in workshop

Traditional Kachina Carver

Hopi Third Mesa

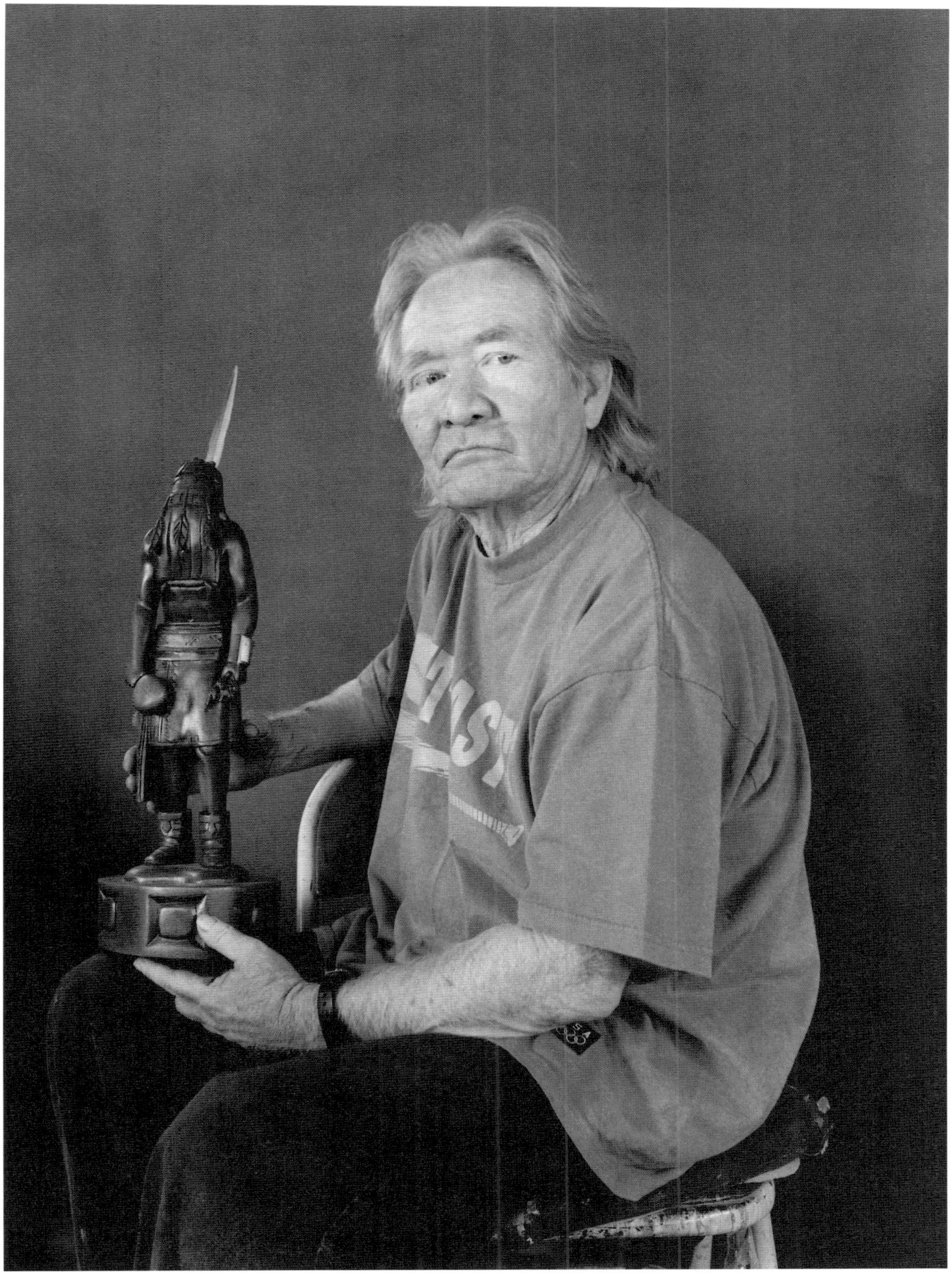

120

BRIAN HONYOUTI

Traditional Kachina Carver

Hopi Third Mesa

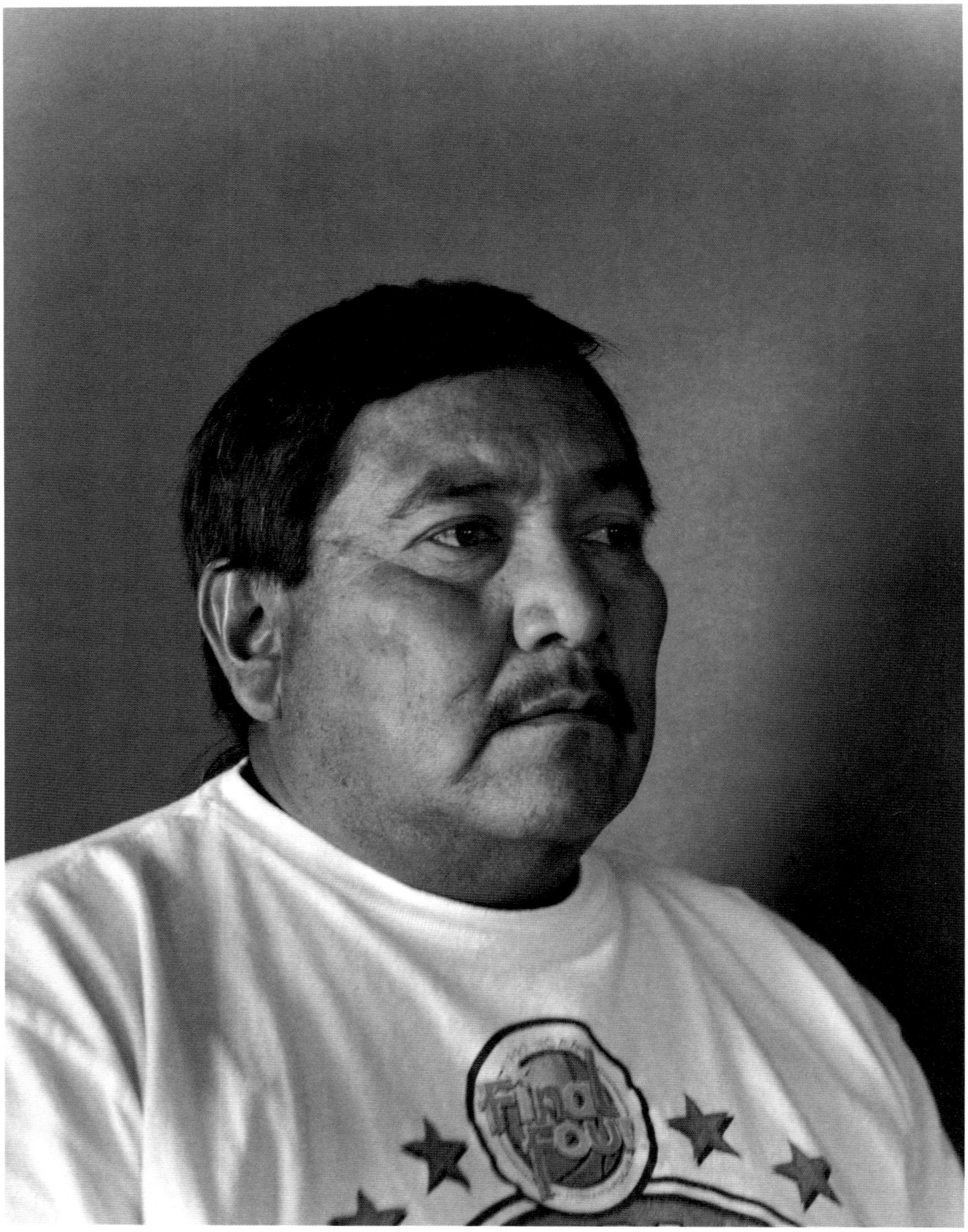

121

RICHARD HONYOUTI

Brian Honyouti's brother

Traditional Kachina Carver

Hopi Third Mesa

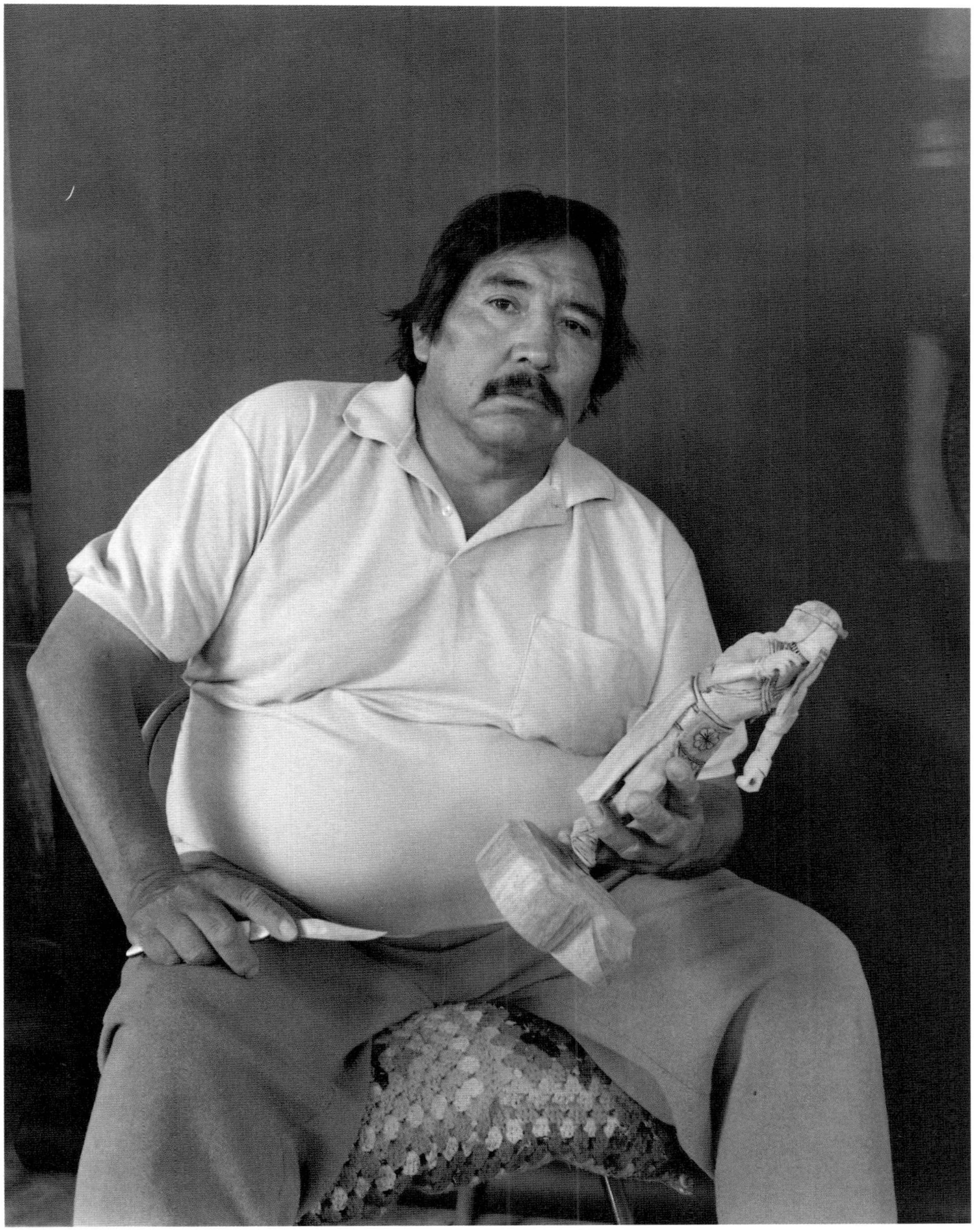

122

LAUREN HONYOUTI

Brian Honyouti's brother

Traditional Kachina Carver

Hopi Third Mesa

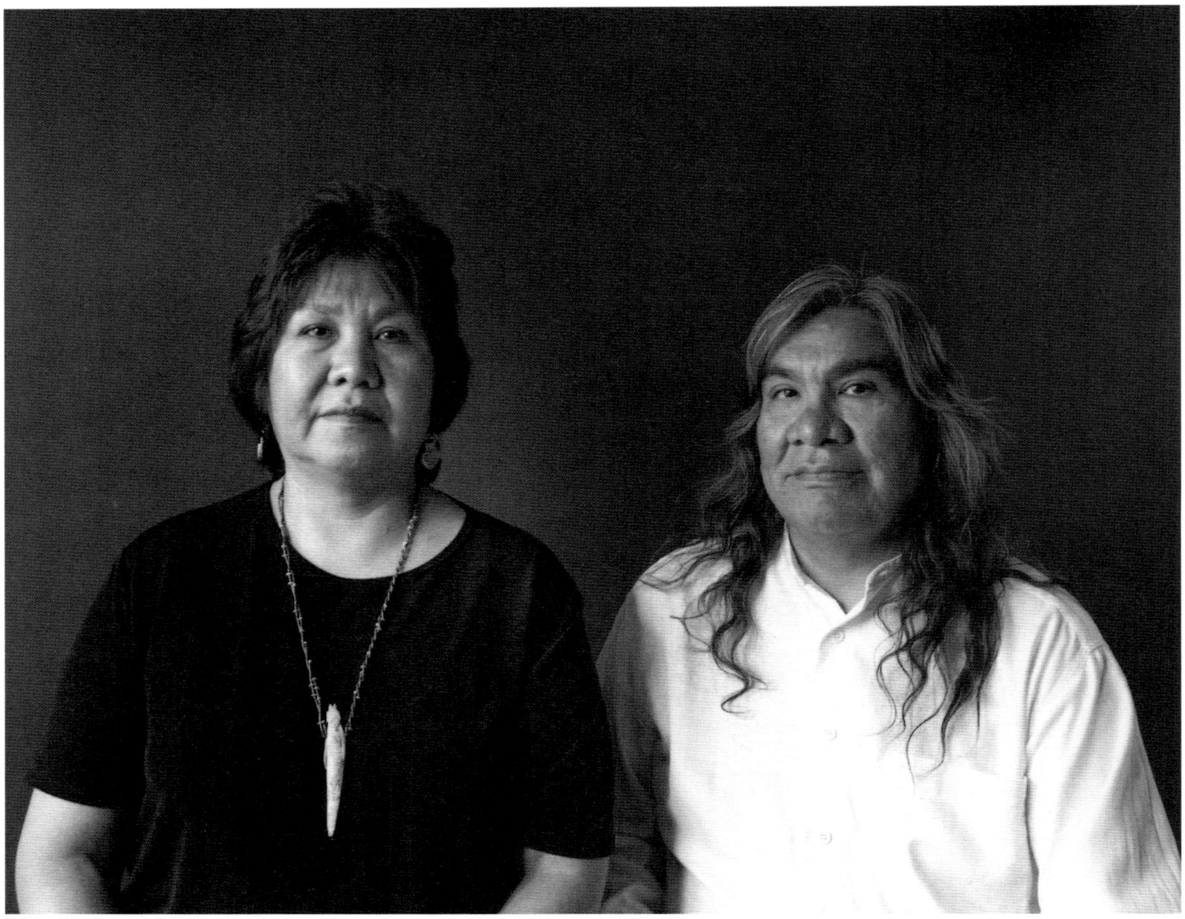

123

DAN V. LOMAHAFTEWA with sister LINDA LOMAHAFTEWA

Contemporary Artists

Hopi/Chocktaw

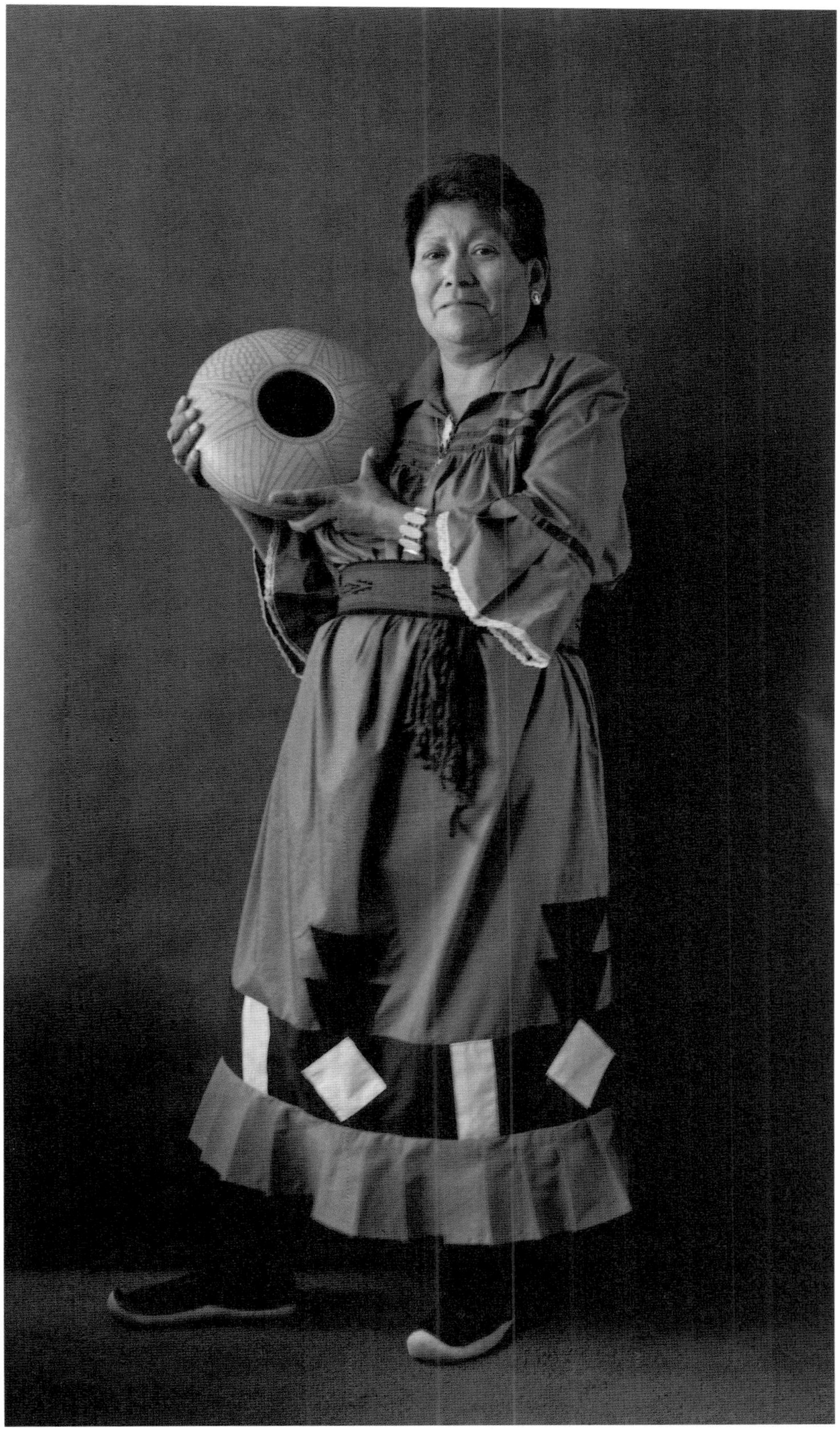

124

RONDINA HUMA

Contemporary Potter

Hopi First Mesa

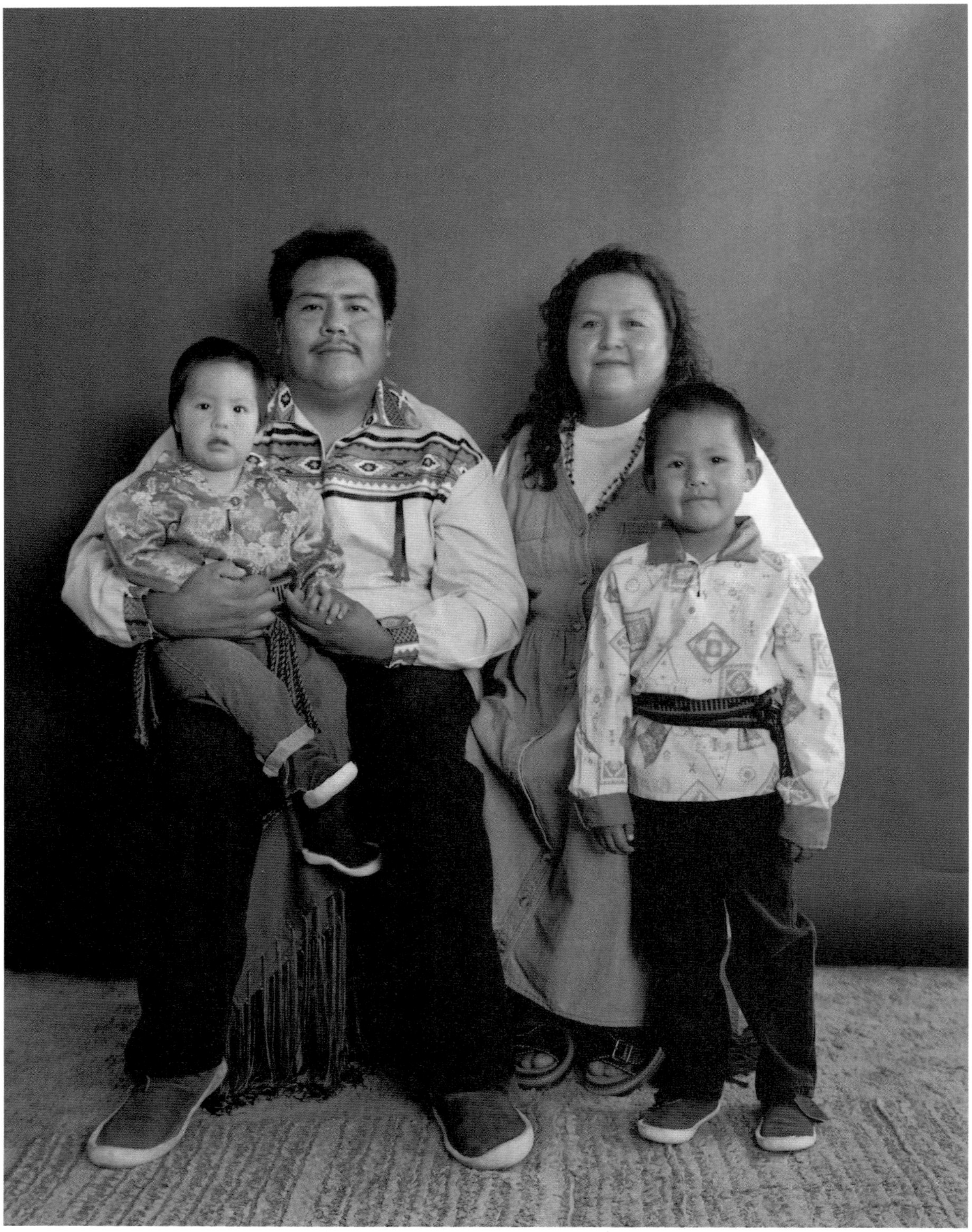

125

BRYSON HUMA, Traditional Kachina Carver,
with wife GLORIA MAHLE, Traditional Potter,
and children BRIAN and CHESTON HUMA
Hopi First Mesa

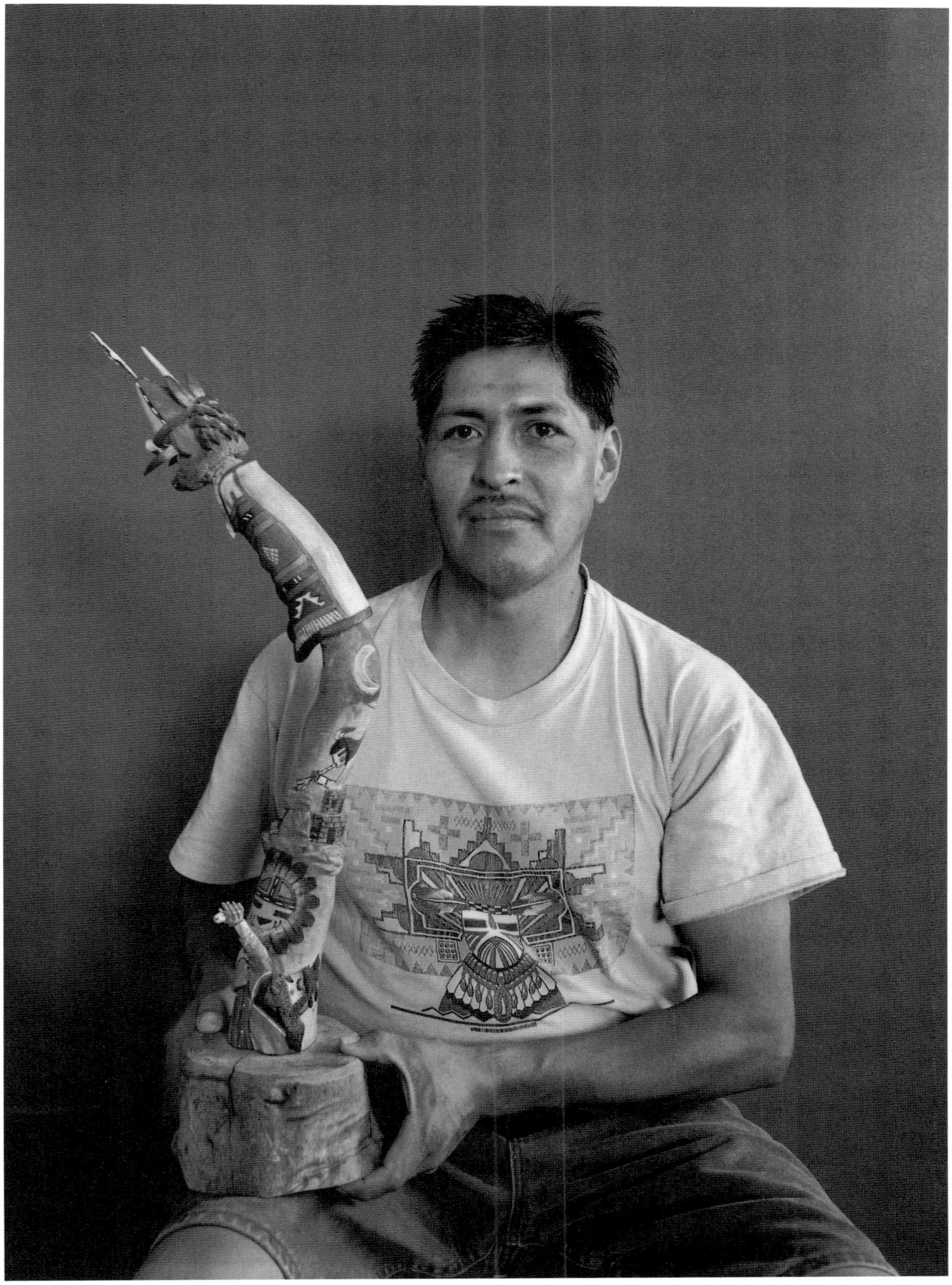

126

MARLON HUMA

Bryson Huma's uncle

Traditional Kachina Carver

Hopi First Mesa

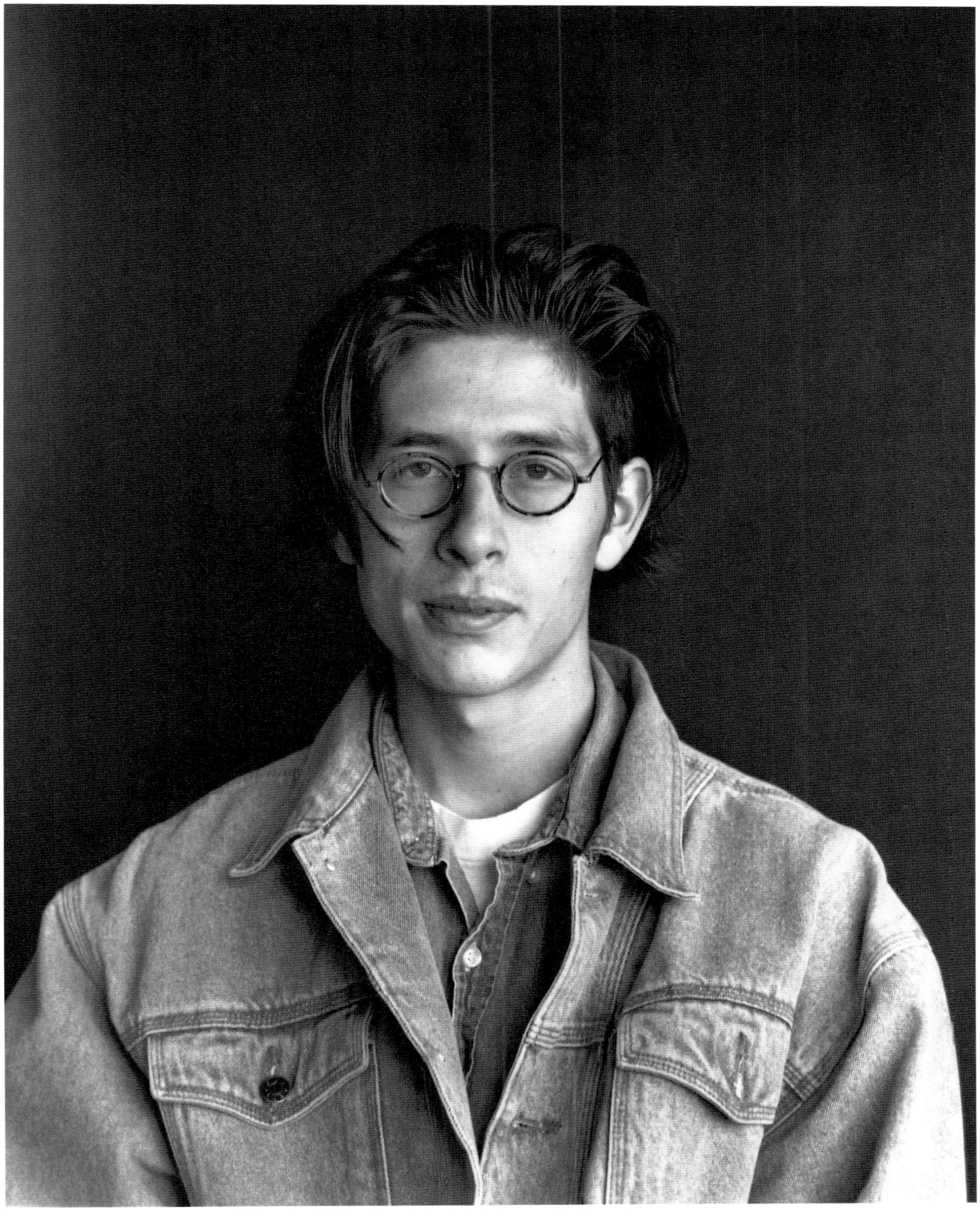

127

GREGORY LOMAYESVA
Contemporary Artist
Hopi Third Mesa

Portrait-making in the Pueblos

ALFRED L. BUSH
CURATOR, PRINCETON COLLECTIONS OF WESTERN AMERICANA

Toba Tucker, in these exceptionally sympathetic portraits of Pueblo artists, offers a gift that not only acquaints us with a compelling community of Pueblo people but at the same time reinvokes an astonishing feat of cultural survival—and the significant role in that accomplishment that these artists continue to play.

It would be easy to see the incorporation of the portrait into Pueblo society as evidence of the elasticity of even the most tenacious of traditional worlds. One could point out that the concept of the portrait should have fundamentally challenged the Pueblo world: that this celebration of the individual must have brought recognizable discomfort to this most communal of American societies. In a world constructed by tribal consensus and valued anonymity, this focus on the individual, such thinking runs, should have met resistance.

But the neat nexus of academic categorization coincides only imperfectly with the real world. The fact that the portrait so easily and quickly became part of the ordinary Pueblo household suggests that it is more accurate to see these photographs as one more instance in which Pueblo needs and European means converged. When the portrait did arrive the pueblos were prepared for it.

Reversing the Old World sequence, photographic portraits preceded painted and sculpted ones in the pueblos. Even the earliest of the Santa Fe and Taos painters—who imposed upon their Pueblo neighbors the romantic concept of the artist as an individual striving to create recognizably idiosyncratic creations—worked from the beginning not only from living models but also from photographs. Decades before members of the Northern Rio Grande pueblos came to rely on modeling fees in Taos and Santa Fe as a ready source of pocket change, the camera had brought them the portrait. It is tantalizing to speculate whether or not any of the work of Siegmund Seligman, who was operating a daguerreotype studio in Santa Fe as early as 1854, included portaits of Pueblo people. Although no examples of his work have survived, it would be decidedly atypical if he had not included Native subjects since photographers everywhere sensed a market for images of the "vanishing American." Pueblo portraits do survive by Nicholas Brown and his son William, whose Santa Fe studio opened in August of 1866. The following year, Alexander Gardner and William Bell were photographing among the pueblos as part of a railroad survey. In a hiatus of the survey's work, Bell set up a temporary portrait studio in Santa Fe's Exchange Hotel (on the site of the present La Fonda) where Indians were inevitably among his patrons.

Timothy H. O'Sullivan, at work for the Wheeler Survey in the early 1870s, posed several Pueblo people for his lens. In the same decade, John K. Hillers, as part of Powell's Colorado River expeditions and later as chief photographer of the Bureau of American Ethnology and the U.S. Geological Survey, was to turn out one of the more extensive bodies of images of the pueblos to survive from the nineteenth century. In 1879, Hillers maneuvered his giant photographic contraption up and down the Rio Grande Valley capturing the architecture of the pueblos and frequently their inhabitants as well.

In the 1880s, out of Santa Fe, Albuquerque, and Gallup, Ben Wittick produced another substantial body of work on the pueblos, including numerous field portraits. But it was his partner, R. W. Russell, who operated the Albuquerque studio during

Wittick's many field trips. He must be the one who produced most of the surviving studio portraits in which Pueblo families are posed against a painted backdrop of balustrade and garden. By 1884, Charles Lummis was developing cyanotypes of portraits in his darkroom at Isleta Pueblo as a means of endearing himself to his Native hosts. Matilda Coxe Stevenson introduced the camera as an anthropological tool among the pueblos in the mid-1880s. By the end of that decade, George Wharton James was distributing Pueblo portraits as well as ceremonial scenes, and once a year from 1885 on, the remotest patch of the United States bristled with tripods at the Hopi Snake Dance. This event became such an orgy of photographic creation that simply to reclaim their tiny dance plazas from the thicket of encroaching photographers, ceremonial photography was banned in 1915. The Hopi understood this prohibition did not extend to all photography. When itinerant photographers managed to get to any of the pueblos, there were always individuals and families willing to pose.

In Edward S. Curtis's attempt to reconstruct photographically "traditional" Native America, under the patronage of no less than J. P. Morgan and Theodore Roosevelt, he found his time among the pueblos in 1903–4 especially rewarding. His images are still as treasured by the Pueblo people as they are celebrated by the general public. Reacting to his romanticism, later photographers appeared more inclined to record what the pueblos themselves presented rather than a representation prescribed by the photographer. Laura Gilpin bridged both of these stances in her work in the pueblos from the 1930s. Lee Marmon, one of the earliest Pueblo photographers, who has been photographing at his home pueblo of Laguna since 1947, sought images of his neighbors that were very much of the moment. As straightforward, but more candid, is the impressive work of photographers such as Ulli Steltzer, who returned from sustained residences in Hopi in the early 1970s with a significant body of portraits. By the time Toba Tucker took her camera to the pueblos, photography was no longer the privileged activity of outsiders. Pueblo snapshots were as common as non-Indian ones. Photography had been taught at the Institute of American Indian Arts in Santa Fe since the 1970s. Larry McNeil, a native photographer on the institute's faculty, successfully encouraged the Santa Fe Indian Market to include photography by Indian photographers among its "traditional" arts in 1993. Seeking portraits from a community ever more sophisticated about photography and the art marketplace, Toba Tucker approached Pueblo artists with collaboration in mind. Sensitive to the Pueblo self-image, she is generously responsive to the community's agenda. That Pueblo artists have responded so openly to her camera is evidence of their recognition not just of a kindred creator but also of a fellow respecter of the communal. Toba's unassuming, almost anonymous vision is easily recognized by the Pueblo artist as a tool of community—as "traditional" art.

Early Pueblo photographic portraits were typically sealed up in frames of tin and painted glass to become celebratory family gatherings on the adobe walls of the sitters' homes (cheap wood engravings of Christian heros in similar but larger frames preceded them as syncretic religious shrines). Pueblo people embraced these family mementos with a single hesitation—their cost. But if we can infer from later practice, photographers often may have presented the Pueblo family with a portrait in exchange for the opportunity to sell further prints to a public endlessly fascinated by the American Indian. To the Natives, their portraits validated the ancient importance of family at the same time the new technology documented the multicultural fabric of their nineteenth-century lives.

Multiculturalism, of course, had not arrived with the Spanish. The Pueblos, even in their most ancient forms, shared the Southwest with other indigenous peoples, and whether this sharing was congenial or abrasive, the cross-cultural contacts were indelible. From these complex relationships the Pueblo world evolved into numerous distinct versions—each tribal manifestation seen as unique to its possessors. Like all vital and long-lived civilizations, the many-faceted Pueblo world, however structurally conservative, constantly changed. With the keen sense of desert survivalists, the Pueblos selected from these encounters what they saw as sustaining and made it their own. What was "traditional" at one moment might be unrecognizable to earlier versions of these worlds.

What legerdemain gives a Pueblo community the will to survive as a separate culture in the face of these endless acculturative assaults? What is the source of this confidence of being impregnable? More intriguingly, how does an individual Pueblo compartmentalize these multicultural onslaughts and remain faithful to his Pueblo identity? Their tenacious struggles for cultural survival, and the power of art not only to integrate worlds but also to enable a people to separate them, are the compelling subtexts of Toba Tucker's photographs in this volume. The artists she depicts are an anciently rooted vanguard for a people who choose to survive apart at the same time they partake of the larger world that surrounds them.

One of the first observations the Spanish made on contact was that besides their indigenous languages the Pueblos also "spoke Mexican"—meaning that one of the Pueblo trade languages was Nahuatl, the language of the Mexica (whom we often call Aztecs). The Indian allies from Mexico who followed the conquistadors surely interacted as much as the Spanish with their Pueblo neighbors. We forget that Tlaxcalan (however much concentrated in the barrio Analco on the far side of the Santa Fe River) was a major language in the newly founded Spanish outpost. The infinite intercalations of Comanche and Navajo, of Ute and Apache, of Tlaxcalan and

Mexica, of Spanish and French and Anglo, of Genizaro and Mestizo swept over the pueblos and, in a range of exchanges from a passing glance to intermarriage, left their mark. Even contacts between pueblos threatened the old ways, as was made clear by the complexities introduced by the Hopi inviting the Tewa to protect their First Mesa villages after the Pueblo Revolt of 1680.

No one better recognized the threat of these multicultural forces than the Pueblos themselves. Every colonizing danger urgently strengthened the characteristic Pueblo treasuring of the "traditional." Survival as Pueblos against the many forces that insisted on their cultural genocide was always the central issue. It is this concern for preserving what makes them uniquely Pueblo that continues to motivate the contemporary flourishing of "traditional" arts. Ceremonial life is the greatest of these. It celebrates the community by flaunting its "otherness" and defining the tradition by constantly reenacting it, and there have always been elements less than the full community that could contribute unusually to its strength. These are the local artisans who in perpetuating ancient crafts are the obvious preservers and promoters of things uniquely their own.

These artists perpetuate *as* individuals what is paradoxically communal: Their crafts demand they continually reassess what is truly indigenous. After the turn of the century, the new assimilative threat of tourism—spectacularly promoted by the Santa Fe railroad—presented a vast new patronage for these artists, and as the self-contained Pueblos found the venerable sources of their economy cut off, there was little alternative to participation in the larger world. One of the first paths that presented itself was selling crafts to tourists. It was the tourists, perpetuating their own differing traditions, who requested signatures on the bases of Indian pots. Though innocent of ulterior purpose, this cross-cultural act struck deeply at Pueblo identity. It was reinforced by the Taos and Santa Fe painters who set a tempting example by successfully promoting their work as signed individual creations. Thus this constantly reinforced path was thrust upon the potters first and then upon all Pueblo artists. Reputations as important as that of Maria Martinez of San Ildefonso would demonstrate that the signature *was* economically significant.

Though we have recently discovered that at least one indigenous American civilization—that of the Maya—produced artists of aristocratic standing who signed their works, this self-conscious concept of the special nature of the artist remained distant from Pueblo belief. The ancient Pueblos, despite trade contacts over millennia with the Maya area—for parrot and macaw feathers—conceived of craft as an anonymous activity. The signature so treasured by collectors of Pueblo art today was imposed by assimilation. The present role of the artist among the Pueblos, focused on signed pieces and production aimed principally at non-Indian consumers, is a thoroughly European–American enterprise.

Thus the paradox of the modern Pueblo artist: While signatures and self-promotion insist on singling Pueblo artists out from their community, it is their creations, deeply rooted in traditional life, that strengthen the identity of the pueblo as a whole. Each new pot emerging from a smoking earthen mound is the resurrection of shards found in the village's ancient fabric. Aware that the realities of the contemporary art market insist on individual celebration, these artists are comforted by the fact that this alien stance reinforces the most indigenous Pueblo focus: the community. Part of the creative process of every current Native artist is this troubling question for the modern Pueblo soul.

It is these paradoxical individuals that Toba Tucker offers us as a very contemporary Pueblo community. She has sought out the Pueblo artist with a care and admiration present in every photograph. She understands that each portrait is a collaborative project. Her work acknowledges that both artist (as photographer) and artists (as subjects) negotiate the result, and like all representational art, there is also a touch of the autobiographical to Toba's portraits. She clearly envies the sense of community she is photographing, as well as empathizes with the conflicted stance of the individual artists who comprise it. She makes these points in many ways. One of them is by clarifying the collaborative nature of her work. Another is by isolating the individual artist in front of blank scrims and then contrasting this isolation by offering other artists in the context of their studios, their art, their families, their pueblos. She and the Indian artists record in these images how this people manage to make even the individual enterprise of the artist a vital tool of community survival. She and her collaborators remind us of the immutable fact that these people are *Pueblos*—and that "pueblo" *is* community. She has gathered out of many ancient Pueblo communities a modern community of Pueblo artists. Communally they offer us these portraits. If the captains of the pueblos are its religious leaders, to Toba Tucker's eye these artists are the brave foot soldiers of Pueblo survival.

For aid and criticism in the writing of these pages I am particularly indebted to Richard Rudisill, Marni Sandweiss, and Lee Clark Mitchell. I also have relied especially on Richard Rudisill, *Photographers of the New Mexico Territory 1854–1912* (Santa Fe, NM: Museum of New Mexico, 1973); Luke Lyon, "History of the Prohibition of Photography in Southwestern Indian Ceremonies," in Anne Van Arsdall Poore, ed., *Reflections: Papers on Southwestern Culture and History in Honor of Charles H. Lange* (Santa Fe, NM: Ancient City Press, 1988); Alfred L. Bush and Lee Clark Mitchell, *The Photograph and the American Indian* (Princeton, NJ: Princton University Press, 1994); and Alfred L. Bush, "Photography of and by Indians," in Fred E. Hoxie, ed., *Encyclopedia of North American Indians* (Boston: Houghton Mifflin Co., 1996).